D1121475

Word of Honor

WITHDRAWN
UTSA LIBRARIES

WORD OF HONOR

Interpreting Noble Culture in Sixteenth-Century France

KRISTEN B. NEUSCHEL

Cornell University Press

Ithaca and London

Copyright © 1989 by Cornell University

All rights reserved. Except for brief quotations in a review, this book,
or parts thereof, must not be reproduced in any form without
permission in writing from the publisher. For information, address
Cornell University Press, 124 Roberts Place,
Ithaca, New York 14850.

First published 1989 by Cornell University Press.

International Standard Book Number 0-8014-2181-0
Library of Congress Catalog Card Number 88-47916
Printed in the United States of America
Librarians: Library of Congress cataloging information
appears on the last page of the book.

The paper in this book is acid-free and meets the guidelines for
permanence and durability of the Committee on Production Guidelines
for Book Longevity of the Council on Library Resources.

Library
University of Texas
at San Antonio

For Anna Condit Smith, and others
who have been with me

Contents

Preface

IN December 1562 two of the most powerful noblemen in France participated in what seems to us a bizarre ritual. One of them was a prisoner of war. The other, his captor, had honored him with the courtesy due a person of his rank. This courtesy extended to offering him the use of the only richly appointed bed in the château where he was confined. The honored prisoner declined the offer and insisted that his captor use the bed instead. In the end, sharing the bed became the only honorable alternative. So the prince de Condé and the duc de Guise, who had so recently faced each other across a battlefield, found themselves side by side in bed.

How shall we interpret such an incident? When I began this project several years ago, my goal was to test the clientage schema that historians had devised to explain the political life of the nobility in sixteenth-century France. Historians had posited the sixteenth century as a particularly important phase of the long-term development of royal power at the expense of the warrior nobility. "Clientage" described the increasing centralization of aristocratic life, with its focus on the crown, yet also allowed somewhat for nobles' persistent independence from thoroughgoing royal control. It was a model that needed, I believed, further investigation, since we must understand the motives for and patterns of nobles' political behavior if we are to understand the civil wars of the last half of the century, the related religious struggles and social tensions of the same era, and the eventual development of a more powerful monarchy in the seventeenth century.

I became convinced that the clientage model was flawed in part because evidence of nobles' actual behavior did not fully support it, and also because it did not seek to explain enough. Historians' determination to account for nobles' political life had short-circuited itself. We had not managed to enlarge our twentieth-century notions of what constitutes political behavior. In our rush to explain nobles' political behavior, we had missed much of what *was* political in the sixteenth century. Much evidence regarding nobles' lives and their public behavior was not adequately scrutinized. Some of that evidence looks almost ridiculous at first glance, such as the prince de Condé and the duc de Guise gesturing to each other over an empty bed. At the same time, much of it seems all too readily classifiable; the effusive courtesy that fills their letters to one another, for instance, can be set aside (even derided) as merely the style of these people's politics rather than its substance.

This book grounds the study of warrior nobles as political beings in an examination of certain facets of their culture. I conclude that French nobles in the mid–sixteenth century were not linked to each other by the exclusive ties of dependence and loyalty which the clientage model has depicted. Rather, I describe a tendency to build networks of relationships which were very broad. Every noble, however modest his stature, felt himself possessed of honor. This claim to honor was a claim to privilege and distinctiveness; it justified political autonomy, even rebellion against the crown. I identify material underpinnings for this behavior—for example, the continued decentralization of military power. I am also concerned, however, with its perceptual underpinnings. How could loyalty be episodic yet nevertheless sincere? How could seemingly trivial conflicts over precedence have real political importance? The answers to such questions must begin with an understanding of how the nobles' cognitive world was constructed by their experience with language. Like many common people of their day, these nobles lived with still largely oral modes of creating and exchanging knowledge. The perceptual skills fostered by oral communication include a weighting of concrete experience over abstract knowledge about oneself and the world. Thus nobles were very sensitive to small incidents that honored or shamed them. In general, the nobles literally constructed and perceived their motives and actions differently than we do ours. It is not surprising, therefore, that we find their behavior so difficult to interpret.

I have thus borrowed from ethnography and linguistics methods of inquiry that have been applied to popular culture in the same period in order to shift the investigation of warrior nobles' politics onto new ground. The result is not a definitive portrait of those nobles' culture, but an interpretation that accounts for more and opens further lines of inquiry. Perhaps the most important of these questions concerns the assumed—and largely unexamined—ground underlying earlier studies of clientage and royal power: the character of the state itself. Like other recent investigators of social and cultural history, I conclude that the state does not consist merely of a set of institutions ruling in the interests of the dominant classes. It is built also on accustomed forms of community life and psychological boundaries and supports sustained by each individual within it. So accustomed are we to the order imposed by the nation-state and to our own compliance with it that we cannot clearly see some of the most powerful connections linking institutional, social, and psychological life. Noble society in the sixteenth century eludes us if we presume the nation-state to be the only logical end of political life, the final source of order and rationality in society. In this book I strive to realize a goal suggested by the late Moses Finley when he wrote that history is a dialogue we have with ourselves in the present, assuming the voices of both the present and the past. It is only when we admit the near-inaccessibility, the ultimate elusiveness of the past that the dialogue can be useful.[1] I have tried to approach the French nobility with an assumption not of familiarity but of difference; I believe that the results of a dialogue on those terms are useful precisely because they, too, are unfamiliar.

Financial support for this project came from the American Council of Learned Societies, the Duke University Research Council, the Beneficial Foundation of Brown University, and the French government. Debts to individuals are harder to acknowledge. Over the course of this project, I became convinced that while writing per se may be a solitary creative enterprise, scholarship is the result of cooperation and sharing. The obligatory acknowledgments that preface any book do not adequately reflect the collaborative process that brought that book into being. This work is richer not merely

1. Moses I. Finley, "Desperately Foreign," in *Aspects of Antiquity* (New York, 1977), p. 15.

for the specific suggestions and assistance of a number of people but, much more important, for the ongoing engagement of these people in their own and in my intellectual enterprise. This kind of engagement provides not only specific direction from time to time but also continuous energy and inspiration. By thanking some of these people here, I am acknowledging debts that I hope to repay in kind, and not simply with words on a page. Since, as this book argues, we need to be attentive to the exaggerated power we presume printed words to have, I would not want to begin the book with such a presumption.

Nancy Lyman Roelker, Ann-Louise Shapiro, and Elinor Accampo have given advice and assistance of many kinds since the very beginnings of this project; my greatest debt is to them. William Reddy, Ronald Witt, Natalie Davis, and Orest Ranum read various versions of the manuscript, and each made useful suggestions. The arguments in Chapter 4 owe much to the collaboration of Rhys Isaac and Charles Zika; they are two of the best practitioners of intellectual community I have known. During the many stints of archival research necessary for this book, I received generous assistance from librarians and archivists, and from fellow searchers who shared their precious archive time with me. I thank especially Donald Bailey and David Sturdy among them. Finally, I thank Janet Ewald, Cynthia Herrup, Jean O'Barr, and Christina Greene for helping me to bring this project to a close—in large measure by sharing with me new questions that are now leading me on to new projects. My work is incomparably richer for the participation of all of these friends and colleagues.

I must also acknowledge two debts of a different sort. The first, to Dorothy Sapp, is a very large debt indeed—and one that, owing to her expertise in editing and word processing, I will not be able to repay in kind. Without her expertise—and her wisdom and humor—this book would not have come to be what it is. The second of these debts is to Mary Mathews-Brantley and Alan Williams, for helping me in their various ways to learn something about the joy of the task.

K. B. N.

Durham, North Carolina

Note on Citations
and Translations

THIS book argues that the actual appearance and precise wording of correspondence and other texts are essential to interpretation of their meaning. Hence lengthy citations from these sources always appear as in the original texts, that is, with all sixteenth-century spellings and grammar intact. Accent marks, which never appear in the texts, have been added sparingly in the interests of readability. The original texts are occasionally punctuated, but in a variety of ways: slashes, dots, and commas mark off phrases and sentences, sometimes in very arbitrary ways; some writers also indicate phrasing by starting a new line (though not a new paragraph, as we would do). I have not attempted to replicate these various unfamiliar devices precisely, but instead have generally replaced them with commas. I have also added punctuation where minimal readability requires it. I have aimed throughout to respect the original language of the documents, without making the false presumption that we are capable of reading the original as it was read at the time it was written or that we can truly reproduce sixteenth-century writing within the pages of a twentieth-century book. Unless I have noted otherwise, all translations of primary sources and secondary works are my own.

Abbreviations

AC Amiens:	Archives communales, Amiens
AC Laon:	Archives communales, Laon
AD Somme:	Archives départementales de la Somme (Amiens)
AN:	Archives Nationales, Paris
BN:	Bibliothèque Nationale, Paris

	Clair.:	Fonds Clairambault
	Colbert:	Cinq Cents Colbert
	Dupuy:	Fonds Dupuy
	MS fr.:	Manuscrits français

MC:	Musée Condé, Chantilly
Min C:	Minutier central des notaires de Paris

Word of Honor

– I –

Introduction:
The Problem of Clientage

I

HISTORIANS of early modern France have been at work rehabili-
tating the nobility, and with impressive results. The assumption that the warrior nobility had irrevocably descended into insol-
vency, powerlessness, and decadence by the sixteenth century has
been discarded. In its place has come evidence of the resilience of
nobles' landed income and seigneurial authority, as well as of their
social prestige and political power.[1] Against such a background of
new data and new interpretation, certain components of older interpretation stand out, as yet unscrutinized and unmodified. One such
component is the clientage model of noble political organization
in the sixteenth century. Warrior nobles, historians have argued,
were linked to one another by exclusive vertical ties of loyalty and

1. Reinterpretations of the economic and social status of the nobility include J.
Dewald, *The Formation of a Provincial Nobility: The Magistrates of the Parlement of
Rouen, 1499–1610* (Princeton, 1980); J. B. Wood, *The Nobility of the "Election" of
Bayeux, 1463–1666* (Princeton, 1980); J. Russell Major, "Noble Income, Inflation,
and the Wars of Religion," *American Historical Review* 86 (1981): 21–48; R. Forster,
The Nobility of Toulouse in the Eighteenth Century: A Social and Economic Study (Bal-
timore, 1960) and *The House of Saulx-Tavannes: Versailles and Burgundy, 1700–1830*
(Baltimore, 1971); Jean Meyer, *La Noblesse bretonne au XVIIIe siècle* (Paris, 1972).
Reinterpretations of the economic and political power of late-medieval nobility have
contributed to positive reevaluation of the nobility after 1500. See John Bell Henne-
men, "The Military Class and the French Monarchy in the Late Middle Ages,"
American Historical Review 83 (1978): 946–65; P. S. Lewis, ed., *The Recovery of France
in the Fifteenth Century* (New York, 1971).

dependence; the resulting clientage hierarchies were manipulated by a handful of court magnates who competed among themselves for control of royal largesse. In assembling a clientele, a courtier reinforced traditional vassalage ties and gained the allegiance of non-vassals by means of his control of royal offices, particularly provincial governorships and the power of appointment in those regions. Clientage relationships structured the rivalries among nobles during times of internal peace and determined nobles' allegiances during the civil wars that began in 1562.

This description of the structure of noble society in the sixteenth century has been shared by several generations of French historians. Ironically, it was first elaborated as part of an early rehabilitation of the warrior nobility. Lucien Romier, writing in the 1910s and 1920s, had no very great opinion of noble culture. Believing the nobility[2] to be economically desperate and hence a parasite on the state, he ridiculed it as "glutted" and "domesticated."[3] He was willing to scrutinize nobles as serious actors in the political life of the kingdom, however, while fellow historians ignored them to focus on the more attractive rising middle class and professional bureaucracy, and on confessional history as an explanation of the civil wars that dominated the second half of the century. Warrior nobles did wield real power, whether or not their purposes were progressive, Romier argued, and he sketched the pattern of clientage systems that helped to account for the power of leading nobles.[4]

More recent scholars have accepted the idea that such a clientage system existed, but have viewed it more favorably. J. Russell Major has argued, for example, that clientage systems were a creative response to the dissolution of vassalage ties and to greater dependence on the crown for income.[5] Major argues further that clientage relationships were not only a positive tool in the nobles' efforts to survive but also a crucial ingredient in successful royal government.

2. Throughout this book, the terms "noble" and "nobility" refer to *warrior* nobles, not to the larger group of people who were legally noble.

3. This description of the nobility is found in Lucien Romier, *Le Royaume de Catherine de Médicis*, 2 vols. (Paris, 1922), 1:209. Romier's other major works on this issue include *Les Origines politiques des guerres de religion*, 2 vols. (Paris, 1913–14), and *Catholiques et Huguenots à la cour de Charles IX* (Paris, 1924).

4. See *Origines politiques*, 1:i–ii, for Romier's justification of his approach.

5. J. Russell Major, "Crown and Aristocracy in Renaissance France," *American Historical Review* 69 (1964): 631–45.

The nobility was a still necessary intermediary between the crown and the provinces—and clientage systems enabled great nobles to preside over a remarkably effective government, in their own interests and in those of the crown. Thus recent scholarship has adopted the notion of clientage systems especially as part of a more positive assessment of the coherence of the French state. The traditional picture of a crown in the sixteenth century making strides toward absolutism despite the disruptive and chaotic behavior of many of its subjects is considerably modified by investigations such as Major's. The nobility was more fully integrated into the system of government than we had admitted. The kingdom was more decentralized and yet also more coherent than historians of Romier's generation had allowed.[6]

Since Major's restatement, the clientage issue has been further elaborated, but it has not been fundamentally altered or challenged. In various guises, it has been a standard component of analyses of French society and the state in the sixteenth century. J. H. M. Salmon makes use of the schema in a variety of ways in, for example, his well-known synthesis *Society in Crisis* (1975). Here he uses the term "clientage" to describe and explain what he believes to be various aspects of the changed relationship of nobility and crown which this era witnessed. He uses the term, in one sense, to contrast this relationship with the truly independent landed power of the nobility which he believes came to an end with the breakup of the last great appanages in the fifteenth century. "Clientage" is thus used to denote a new kind of relationship, particularly between great nobles and the crown, distinct from the territorial autonomy they had previously enjoyed. Salmon also applies the term, however, to describe the "problem" of the nobles' dependence on royal largesse, created by the wars in Italy which began under Charles VIII (d. 1498). The nobility became increasingly dependent on the monarchy for jobs, in essence, and for the increasingly costly means to carry them out, Salmon argues. But he also applies the term to the

6. Major's earlier work on the vitality of representative institutions in this period had emphasized the continued decentralization of the state and provided the context in which his later work on clientage was elaborated. See *Representative Institutions in Renaissance France* (Madison, 1960); *The Deputies to the Estates-General in Renaissance France* (Madison, 1960); "The French Renaissance Monarchy as Seen through the Estates-General," *Studies in the Renaissance* 9 (1962): 113–25.

nature of ties between nobles which this situation created—thus using the term to denote a kind of relationship characteristic of noble society in general.[7] In other recent studies, the existence of clientage networks continues to be assumed as a backdrop to court politics and to the complex religious and social upheavals of the second half of the century.[8]

The notion of clientage, then, like the concept of feudalism, has been used as a catch-all to describe a system of power relations as well as the social relations through which it found expression. It has proved a useful concept, in that it has provided scholars with a description of noble society which permitted them to take seriously the evident power of the nobility in the period. It has also enabled them to rescue the state from premature and anachronistic inclusion under the rubric of absolutism. Its shortcoming as an analytical category, however, lies precisely in its dual usefulness as a means both to describe noble political life and to characterize the state. It has allowed a conflation of two distinct—if interdependent—historical problems: the changing character of the aristocracy and the rise of the state.

This investigation is a critique of the concept of clientage as a description of warrior society and of relations between the nobility and the state in the sixteenth century. It focuses primarily on the relationships that linked Louis de Bourbon, first prince de Condé (1530–1569), with the warrior nobility of Picardy, where he was a major landholder and provincial governor. The notion of clientage, I argue, is a poor explanatory schema for describing nobles' political behavior and their relationships with the crown because it is firmly grounded in certain twentieth-century assumptions about the nature of political life; in this twentieth-century view, all political activity is seen solely in relation to the nation-state, and political life is considered in the abstract terms that have in fact been a historical product of that relationship. For warrior noblemen in the middle of the sixteenth century, "politics" was not distinct from living. And living as a noble in relation to other nobles was a very intimate busi-

---

7. J. H. M. Salmon, *Society in Crisis: France in the Sixteenth Century* (New York, 1975), pp. 95–101, 117, 234.

8. Mark Greengrass, *France in the Age of Henry IV* (London and New York, 1984); Mack P. Holt, *The Duke of Anjou and the Politique Struggle during the Wars of Religion* (Cambridge, 1986).

ness of physical familiarity and interdependence; it meant sharing food and weapons and shelter, it meant knowing one another face to face and relying on one another's physical daring and personal audacity. I am concerned with the nature of noble relationships as they were grounded in this lifeworld, as well as the conceptual frameworks with which the nobles understood them. I view the nobility not as an institution of the state but primarily as a culture. My task is to establish new terms with which to examine and understand the nobility, and, by extension, to view the nobility in relation to the state.

II

Previous studies of clientage relations among the nobility privileged the activities of great nobles, as they were the means by which noble society as a whole intersected with the state. Only in the most recent of this work have the motives and behavior of petty nobles, especially, begun to come to light. In his best-known work, *Les Origines politiques des guerres de religion* (1913–1914), Romier sketched the political behavior of the nobility which underlay court politics before 1559 as well as the civil wars after 1559. Romier argued that the rivalries among Henri II's principal courtiers and favorites were more or less focused in and defined by rivalry of the two greatest contenders for royal favor and control of royal largesse—Anne de Montmorency, connêtable de France, and François de Lorraine, duc de Guise. This major division at the court of Henri II carried over to inform the divisions after 1559 with only one real change. By 1561, the connêtable de Montmorency was almost completely alienated from two now prominent men he had formerly sponsored, his nephew Gaspard de Châtillon, amiral de Coligny, and the young prince de Condé, because of their adherence to the Reformed faith. Romier emphasized, however, that both Coligny and Condé had earlier suffered rebuffs at the hands of the duc de Guise and that their political behavior would continue to be characterized by antipathy to the Lorraine family and its followers.

Romier's description of these rivalries has been an important component of all later discussions of royal and noble politics during the middle of the century. However, when he moved away from the principal courtiers—their personalities, their interests, and the policies they championed—Romier's analysis became more vague. His analysis of the ties that bound lesser nobles to these courtiers was sketchy in its treatment of both the territorial dimension of the great nobles' power and the extent of the dependence of lesser nobles on these patrons at court. He did acknowledge, for example, that not all power was monopolized by the faction leaders; he also discussed a somewhat broader group of major noble families who had significant landholdings and hence provincial footholds and significant political clout. He imagined the attitudes of Guise's more prominent followers in 1560, for example, to have been a kind of contingent loyalty; he supposed that one of them might have said to Guise, "I'm with you, but you'd better manage my affairs properly!"[9] Self-interest, in some measure, qualified a noble's loyalty to the great courtiers. When Romier stated that three leading Angevin families were "clients of both the Guises and the Montmorencys simultaneously,"[10] he was acknowledging the importance of self-interest and, implicitly, the power of such families effectively to pursue that self-interest. But, oddly, he does not explore the implications of that acknowledgment, and it squares poorly with his own conclusions concerning the rigidity and exclusivity of the clientage system:

> With the exception of isolated *hobereaux*, all noblemen were linked to [one of] the three great families by vassalage, clientage or blood relationship. These three names (Guise, Montmorency, and Bourbon) constitute the history of the civil wars. They were the principal pieces on the chess board where Catherine de Médicis was trying to maneuver. Any policy or any action which caused one of these pieces to be moved, at court, induced a change in the relationship of this or that group of fiefs with the crown.[11]

The more distant his focus from the court, the less exact his analysis. Lesser nobles were dependent on families of local prominence for their advancement and survival. At one point, Romier described these relationships as ones of devotion to protectors; else-

9. Romier, *Origines politiques*, p. 328.
10. Romier, *Royaume de Catherine de Médicis*, 1:219.
11. Ibid., p. 233.

where he cited their reciprocal nature. Thus, with lesser nobles as with leading families, we are uncertain how much autonomy or, conversely, how much dependence characterized these relationships. Nor did he explain the connection of these local clientage networks to the three major court factions. He said only that this connection was "more or less direct."[12] In the end, we are left with a rather mechanical picture of the clientage system in the kingdom as a whole, and with plentiful hints that it functioned imperfectly.

Romier's ambivalence toward the nobility is revealed in the manipulative but also vulnerable role he envisions for Catherine de Médicis. She needed to "move" the nobility cleverly; but she also had to move *among* them. They were "figures" who needed to be adroitly handled, but also fellow players whose power had to be respected. Most frustrating are Romier's hints about the nature of this power. He suggests that it had its roots in vassalage and family ties, as well as in what he separately distinguishes as "clientage," but he offers no further clarification.[13]

J. Russell Major gave further consideration to many of the issues that remained implicit or incompletely considered in Romier's work. He explicitly depicts patron–client ties and the more traditional ties of vassalage as the principal components of the great nobles' power during the century. Major argues that these composite relationships among nobles were responses to new conditions that drew creatively on traditional feudal practices. He puts great weight on the fact that relationships between great nobles and their followers were often formalized by oaths reminiscent of feudal oaths, and he asserts that such relationships were grounded in expectations of reciprocal loyalty. He cites, as one example, an oath signed by a number of leading nobles who joined the prince de Condé in rebellion in 1562 to "hold ourselves in readiness as far as we are able in money, arms, horses." Patron–client relationships on a more routine basis were, he argues, likewise distinguished by loyalty and reciprocity. "Most clients rendered faithful service to their patrons and most patrons reciprocated by looking after their clients' interests."[14]

Consistent with this view of the nobility as necessary intermedi-

12. Ibid., p. 267.
13. Ibid., pp. 165–67 and 212–13; *Origines politiques*, 1:86–87.
14. Major, "Crown and Aristocracy in Renaissance France," p. 637.

aries in a still decentralized state, Major, unlike Romier, is able to discern initiative from below: clients' pursuit of their own interests. In provinces that still boasted estates, those bodies collectively represented clients' interests to the great noble governor, in return for votes of subsidies to him. In other provinces, Major argues, "landed nobility appears to have put direct pressure on its governors and patrons." The rebellion of a great noble was a lucrative enterprise for his supporters in the provinces; to some degree, Major suggests, the great noble was hostage to his clients' interests:

> The great noble who could not obtain enough concessions from the crown for his clients was faced with the choice of losing his influence over them or of revolting in the hope that the crown would purchase his submission. Thus, by rebelling, the Duke de Nevers increased his income from 40,003 *livres* . . . to 808,776, but at the same time his expenses jumped from 400,345 to 808,520 *livres*, strong circumstantial evidence that the real winners of the revolt were his followers.[15]

Routinely, a patron was expected to provide his client not only with offices and commands but also with legal and physical protection. As evidence of these expectations, Major cites individual examples of offers by prominent nobles of protection as well as rewards to followers.

He thus suggests that the reciprocity of noble relationships meant that, ultimately, nobles' loyalties remained qualified. For example, after describing an oath of loyalty which Henri de Rohan had made to the Queen Mother, Marie de Médicis, in 1620, Major adds, "A rebellion, of course, followed."[16] He thus implies that the oaths of loyalty to which he attaches so much importance cannot be taken at face value; on some level, nobles did not really "mean" them. But he does not delineate precisely how they should be interpreted. He cites many examples of service from below and protection from above, but very few of either disobedience or abandonment, so that the limits of patron–client loyalty do not emerge definitively. Is it possible to describe the limits of lesser nobles' loyalties? Above all, how

15. Ibid., p. 643.
16. Ibid., p. 636.

did they understand their position? Did they value loyalty but willingly embrace disloyalty if their interests were directly or drastically threatened? Did they feel duplicitous in doing so? Most nobles remained loyal, Major tells us. But even if most nobles commonly honored their professions of loyalty, the notion of loyalty will still not be a useful one to describe noble behavior if the larger context is not clear. "Loyalty" cannot be satisfactorily used to explain noble behavior if "disloyalty" is not understood. While the notion of loyalty may describe some of their behavior, it cannot ultimately explain their behavior. Major himself provides insights that lead us beyond his analysis. His description of the bargaining power of supposedly loyal clients suggests that self-interest could be a natural source of tension between greater and lesser nobles as well as a source of unity. Yet if loyalty is the norm, then we are left with no way to account for this behavior. In the face of Major's evidence, the term "loyalty," like Romier's "client," begins to lose meaning.

Major's analysis was groundbreaking in a number of respects, most notably, for my purposes, in his view that nobles' relationships were a reflection of the vitality of their power, and as such were deserving of detailed study. His work was complemented by and reinforced the many studies of individual provinces within the kingdom which, both before and after him, stressed the continued importance of localized interests and decentralizing forces within early modern France. Major's argument moves beyond Romier and connects with certain provincial studies also in the fact that he covers a longer period—approximately 1450–1650. Consequently, he is able to take a more flexible view of the top levels of the clientage system; he does not focus on one major rivalry and on the policies and issues of just a few years. In fact, we can see in Major's work an emphasis on the provincial governors as the collective leadership of the nobility—an emphasis that other scholars have since echoed and further pursued. As far as the limits of the give-and-take between lesser and greater nobles are concerned, Major's insights suggest that attention needs to be paid to the bargaining power of the supposedly dependent clients. His discussion opens the door to further and more systematic scrutiny of this issue.

Roland Mousnier's contributions to the history of the nobility in the sixteenth century have attempted to provide a more systematic framework for explaining and understanding nobles' relationships, but have not done so along the lines left open by Major.[17] His discussion, for the most part, eschews any concern for self-interest. Mousnier describes the ties that linked patron and client—"maître" and "fidèle," in his terms—as ties of affection and personal loyalty, not as ties dictated by material interest. He believes concern for material self-interest to have been alien to the very nature of the warrior nobility. The habits of largesse and liberality (which supposedly resulted in frequent indebtedness) were natural values for the elite of a society that operated according to notions of *quality*. Virtue led to riches, riches were a sign of virtue—they could not be undeserved. Mousnier asserts that the prevailing social hierarchy in the Ancien Régime was the result of a collective endowing of certain tasks within the society with esteem and hence with privilege. Since the social hierarchy was created and justified by collective adherence to the values that supported it—the notion that a qualitative distinction between persons flows from the esteem attached to their function—these ties linking lessers to greaters were virtually indissoluble. To understand those ties is to understand the way the society worked.[18]

Unfortunately, as a number of scholars have pointed out, Mousnier's analysis is flawed by his methodology.[19] Mousnier's arguments concerning the basis for the "glue" that held together the various groups in society are based on contemporary—that is, sixteenth- and seventeenth-century—political treatises, and not on analyses of the actual behavior of the historical actors. To presume, as he does, that contemporary theory can serve for historical analysis is to invalidate the very task of the historian of political and social life; Mousnier confuses certain contemporary ideals with contempo-

17. Mousnier's works include *Les Hiérarchies sociales de 1450 à nos jours* (Paris, 1969); *Les Institutions de la France sous la monarchie absolue*, 2 vols. (Paris, 1974); "Les Concepts d'"états,' de 'fidélité' et de 'monarchie absolue' en France de la fin du XVe siècle à la fin du XVIIIe," *Revue historique* 47 (1972): 289–312.

18. Mousnier, *Hiérarchies sociales*, pp. 6–ll.

19. See, for example, Armand Arriaza, "Mousnier, Barber, and the Society of Orders," *Past and Present*, no. 89 (November 1980), pp. 39–57; J. H. M. Salmon, "Storm over the Noblesse," *Journal of Modern History* 53 (June 1981): 242–57; and the trenchant criticisms of Sharon Kettering, *Patrons, Brokers, and Clients in Seventeenth-Century France* (Oxford, 1986), pp. 18–22, and William Beik, *Absolutism and Society in Seventeenth-Century France* (Cambridge, 1985), pp. 6–9.

rary material reality, and thus overlooks the complex relationship between them, which is the real stuff of political life. The inroads made by social history of premodern Europe and by women's history in particular have, in any case, undermined the notion that prevailing ideologies were held by or represented the values—either in whole or in part—of all the members of a society.[20] He fails, in short, to consider *power* as a factor in the construction of ideology. In view of these difficulties, Mousnier's failure to substantiate his claims concerning the bonds between nobles by also scrutinizing behavior is particularly problematic. He argues that the ties of "fidélité" were personal ties freely entered into, and were virtually absolute. The "fidèle" identifies himself and his interests totally with those of his "maître"; he puts himself entirely at the disposal of his protector: "in sum, he espouses all of the causes, all of the desires and all of the interests of his master."[21] The professions of loyalty— or the attestations of the desirability of loyalty—which Mousnier offers as illustration usually concern bureaucratic functionaries, not warriors.[22] Mousnier's belief in contemporaries' acceptance of qualitative distinctions and in the tightness of the bond linking "inferiors" to their "superiors" throughout the society thus demands verification if it is to carry weight.

Building on the work of both Major and Mousnier is that of Robert Harding on the provincial governors of the sixteenth and early seventeenth centuries. By analyzing the functions of the governors and the reasons for their effectiveness, Harding makes a significant contribution to the issues of the cohesion of the state and the prominence of the nobility within that state during the sixteenth century. He scrutinizes relationships between the governors and the mass of nobles by assessing the loyalties elicited for the state by the dispensing of patronage through the governors' hands. His discussion goes further than that of either Major or Mousnier in both detailing the substance and suggesting the possible limits of hierarchical patron–client ties between nobles.

20. The works that raise these issues are by now much too numerous to permit even a representative list. An interested reader might begin with Joan Kelly, *Women, History, and Theory* (Chicago, 1985), and Natalie Z. Davis, *Society and Culture in Early Modern France* (Stanford, 1975).

21. Mousnier, "Concepts d'"états,'" p. 304.

22. Mousnier, *Institutions de la France*, vol. 1, chap. 3.

First of all, Harding's schema makes allowance for complexity and flexibility at the top. He notes, for example, that prominent nobles often served as ad hoc commanders or short-term administrators in addition to their functions as established governors; the relations of such temporary commanders to local populations (both noble and nonnoble) would have differed from the more common relationship of a provincial governor with local roots. In addition, Harding tackles what Romier leaves implicit by asserting that, although a handful of the greatest nobles controlled patronage at its source, the political life of the kingdom did not begin and end with their concerns alone. He argues that the "power elite" of the governors—which included the greatest families, of course—were the effective *conduits* of this patronage, and must be considered as a group if the patronage links that held the kingdom together are to be understood.[23]

Harding also digs more deeply into the ties of lesser noblemen to this elite than does either Major or Mousnier. While he follows Mousnier in stressing hierarchical loyalties, he finds their underpinnings more material than affective. He isolates in particular the governors' use of appointments to the gendarmerie and to other military posts and to positions in their households as concrete mechanisms that linked provincials to them. Lesser nobles, he asserts, began their careers in governors' households within the provinces, and then moved into places in the gendarmerie or perhaps to even more prestigious commands, all in the name of the king. The households of the various governors, Harding affirms, were the mechanism by which "landed power was mobilized for the purposes of royal government." However, he also makes allowances for flexibility and initiative from below in the midst of this hierarchical system. In tracing the role of governors as intermediaries between provincials and the crown, for example, he mentions the fact that multiple brokerage—that is, the enlisting of help from several members of the elite at once by someone of modest rank—was possible.[24] In his fullest explicit discussion of possible flexibility within the hierarchical system he states:

23. Robert R. Harding, *Anatomy of a Power Elite: The Provincial Governors of Early Modern France* (New Haven, 1978), pp. 44, 34.
    24. Ibid., pp. 22–23, 44, 33.

A considerable social stigma was attached to *infidélité*; it was this, not the law that punished breaches of the tacit contracts, but it was not necessarily *infidèle* to move to a new clientele or to combine old loyalties with new ones. The greater the social and economic distance between patron and *fidèle*, the more likely it was to be an exclusive relationship. Ordinary household servants and gendarmes rarely knew more than one master but subordinate governors and royal officers were more likely to have multiple patrons.[25]

With these statements Harding has opened a number of doors toward better understanding of the system of nobles' behavior. He has introduced the possibility of multiple ties and the notion that "unfaithfulness" had varying allowable limits. Behavior changed according to the circumstances accompanying each relationship. In particular he implies that behavior changed with rank; power, not merely abstract principles, made certain behavior allowable and other behavior intolerable.

These assertions, while allowing for flexibility in Harding's system, raise the question of how well that system accounts for nobles' behavior. We would like to know more about what *fidélité* was considered to be, and under what circumstances a nobleman could change his attachments without suffering negative consequences. Harding's argument on the concept of fidelity as a motor for nobles' behavior and as the explanation for hierarchical relationships is undermined, in other words, by the fact that neither fidelity nor infidelity is fully explained. Fidelity cannot be the explanation for nobles' behavior if infidelity was also acceptable.

Indeed, the very flexibility of the system he describes casts doubt on the truly systematic nature of it. He attempts to describe the great variety within the clientage system as he sees it. He depicts different "cadres" of clients of great nobles: "military," "domestic" and "political," corresponding to a commander's troops, his household, and his clients in the province at large. "Clientage," he concludes, "was a complex and multifaceted social institution." Elsewhere he admits that "*fidélité* was an open and relatively loose system."[26]

25. Ibid., p. 36.
26. Ibid., pp. 21, 36.

But further interpretive problems arise when he does explore the concept of fidélité in greater detail. He says:

> Fidélité was based on the mutual expectations of patrons and clients rather than on one-for-one exchange at the same point in time as in a business transaction. Clients performed services for patrons who were morally bound to reciprocate, but the time and exact nature of the reciprocation were not specified in advance. Obligations were indefinite because the goods and services exchanged were putatively philanthropic. To appearances, the affective dimension of the relationship prevailed over the materialistic side. Years or decades of service, often at the client's great expense, might be necessary before the hoped-for reciprocation was forthcoming, and in the interim there were only effusions of total loyalty and boundless love. Yet the materialistic expectations surfaced when exasperation peaked, and this happened often enough to create a whole genre of surviving correspondence to governors from disenchanted clients.[27]

He thus defines fidelity as a set of mutual expectations that—we must presume, since he does not say so explicitly—justify infidelity when they are not honored. Yet Harding does not pursue this argument. Rather, he seems to regard the expectations themselves as destined to inevitable or at least frequent disappointment, because nobles expressed them in wholly idealistic terms. He leaves unresolved the question of whether the nobles knew that their language of obligation cloaked a hidden reality of actual interaction. The relationship between ideals and reality is still unclear.

A final difficulty lies in the terms Harding chooses to describe the distinction between expectation and reality. Expectations (ideals) are couched in terms of affection and reality in terms of material gain. There is a suspiciously modern ring to the dichotomy Harding posits here. Whether such ways of thinking about human motivation existed in precisely these terms in the sixteenth century remains to be seen. What is easier to establish is that the dichotomy of affection versus gain is routinely loaded, in our own culture, with its oppositional nature, as well as with the expectation that gain is the real motive behind human behavior in political life. The construct

27. Ibid., pp. 36–37.

that human society is separated into a private (pure) arena of affection and a public (corrupt) world of competition was compellingly described in the nineteenth century as a "natural" dichotomy of gender roles. Two interpretive questions are thus raised: first, whether the affection/gain dichotomy is the most useful way to describe nobles' motivation and to account for their relationships; and second, on another level, whether Harding's entire schema of the coexistence of ideal versus real behavior may not be flawed because it is a reflection of modern habits of dichotomizing motivation. The entire structure of his argument, in other words, may be suspect because of the terms he has chosen to depict nobles' behavior. The precision of Harding's analysis of ties between nobles thus may be limited in what it can reveal about nobles' motivations and of the ties between them because of the assumptions on which his scrutiny is founded.

These patterns of dichotomizing nobles' political behavior generally—ideal versus reality, faithfulness versus gain—may be particularly persistent in historians' analyses because of their familiarity in the present. In one sense, Harding's work echoes Romier's in that he is willing to allow self-interest as a motive for nobles' relationships and as an explanation of their political behavior generally. A principal difference between Harding's views and those of Romier is Harding's conclusion that nobles' self-interest was not such a bad thing. For Harding—building on much intervening work on the character of royal government in the period—the self-interest of leading nobles was demonstrably linked to the coherence of that government. Yet Harding may also quite clearly be regarded as an heir to Mousnier in his reliance on the notion of fidélité.[28] The true significance of these polar categories is the persistence with which they have survived as explanations of nobles' behavior. By taking up each pole and richly extending analysis of it, Harding has revealed the limits of these means of accounting for nobles' behavior in the sixteenth century—limits dictated by the constraints of the construct itself. By advancing affection and gain simultaneously and yet in opposition, Harding must inevitably suggest that affection was an ideal (the exchange between nobles was "putatively philanthropic"), and an increasingly inappropriate one, in view of its

28. See the assessment by Salmon, "Storm over the Noblesse," p. 249.

results. Further, the more Harding ties the self-interest of the nobility to the interests of the emerging state, the more such vows of affection must appear marginal and useless to political life. New and very persuasive evidence of nobles' economic successes in the sixteenth century has further tested the usefulness of this dichotomy by adding weight to an assumption of the rationality of nobles' self-interest.[29] Yet despite these challenges, the terms of the discussion have proved very difficult to shift or to recast, and continue to characterize historians' discussions of nobles' relationships.[30]

I seek to replace some of the limiting assumptions on which earlier analyses of nobles' political behavior have been founded. Although I consider the issues of the flexibility and multiplicity of nobles' relationships, among others, I take an approach that is largely distinct from those of the historians considered here. I am concerned primarily not with institutions but with the manner in which the nobility actually behaved. The unique feature of the nobility as a political institution is the nobles' claim to political power by virtue of their personal identity. Any attempt to understand them as political actors must simultaneously consider them as persons—not merely or even primarily as individual personalities but collectively, as social beings united by distinct values, expectations, and self-regard. The picture of the relationships between nobles which emerges from a scrutiny of their behavior is sufficiently at odds with the conventional clientage model—even as elaborated by Harding—to suggest that we are misled if we consider those relationships only as they were connected to the state; such a focus, I argue, has distorted or altogether missed the larger context that impinged on nobles' behavior. I locate the motives for nobles' political behavior within a warrior culture that was still materially and psychologically independent of the state.

Lesser nobles, supposedly tied to their superiors by bonds of loyalty and material dependence, simply did not behave obediently. The pattern of behavior of the nobles who at one time or another joined the first prince de Condé in rebellion in the 1560s reveals as

29. Major gives a useful summary of recent studies of noble economic status in "Noble Income," expecially pp. 40–48.
30. For example, Mack P. Holt, "Patterns of 'Clientèle' and Economic Opportunity at Court during the Wars of Religion: The Household of François, Duke of Anjou," *French Historical Studies* 13 (1984): 305–22.

much autonomy as dependence. Private violence was widespread; even very humble nobles came and went from fighting with Condé as it suited them to do so. And not only did they support Condé's strategies only fitfully, but they also fought on their own, in more localized arenas, where their lives and their property could be—and had to be—best protected.

This pattern of violence parallels the pattern of routine competition among nobles during the 1550s and during the more peaceable years of the 1560s. The daily interaction of nobles, primarily as revealed by their letters, does not sustain a model of strictly hierarchical or exclusive relationships. Indeed, their correspondence reveals a tendency to build networks of relationships which were very broad. Lesser nobles often solicited help from the supposed rivals Guise and Montmorency at the same time, and later professed indebtedness to each of them. Further, recognition was extended to and support was sought from virtually every fellow noble with whom any nobleman came into contact—members of other local families, as Romier suggested, relatives by blood and marriage, and noblemen of all ranks encountered in military service. Some ties were more resilient and fruitful than others, naturally. If we choose a single province and focus on a man who was both a landholder and a governor there, it is possible to test the importance of such factors as vassalage and household service in sustaining nobles' relationships. Evidence viewed from this perspective shows that even relationships nurtured by such means were not exclusive ones, and that loyalty—at least as we have so far conceived it—is not a useful means to characterize or even idealize nobles' behavior.

The independence to which noblemen were accustomed was made possible by and was in part a reflection of widely dispersed means of violence. To defend himself on his own estates, a nobleman had to have ready access to the means to fight—in some cases, means adequate to withstand a royal force sent against him. My analysis, in other words, bears out what Major's work has suggested: the crown did not yet have a monopoly on violence. But we have to go further—it did not yet monopolize authority or legitimacy, either.

It is we who picture the state as the central or crowning figure in a diagram of power relations, a reference point from which distance can be measured and power thereby calculated. But those noblemen did not regard themselves primarily in terms of the state. Power, initiative, authority, legitimacy: these things could and did spring from nobles themselves, not only from the king. It is clear from the evidence of letters and memoirs that even minor nobles felt themselves to be distinctive and possessed of "honor." This self-image encouraged independence from the control of greater nobles. Among all nobles, it legitimated the right to private violence. The persistence of private violence documented here seems to reflect what other scholars have noted: the care and calculation with which nobles managed their property, both in general and for the specific purpose of making war.[31] But qualitative as well as quantitative resources were a motor for their behavior; and qualitative distinction empowered all nobles, not merely the few, as Mousnier has suggested.

Further, participation in a system of honor created a sensitivity to symbolic power as both a motor for and a goal of public life. Some of the events of great significance to nobles were seemingly trivial moments of personal insult or self-aggrandizement. The importance attached to such incidents was, in turn, simply one expression of a general tendency to weight moments of action—personal arguments, triumph in battle, and other incidents of honor or shame—as the building blocks of political life. Power could be defined and relationships structured by means of ephemeral events of this kind. Nobles were "rational" in their pursuit of gain. But we must work to understand what "gain" meant to them and what means to pursue gain felt useful to them. Nobles' rationality in these matters bears little resemblance to current notions of economic rationality and must be carefully delineated in its own terms. As one historian has noted, material life is not an objective state of affairs, but rather a set of conditions informed by perceptions; material "reality" is perceived and structured by the concepts used to describe it.[32]

Merely to point to the power great nobles could wield or to the fact that royal largesse was dispensed does not establish the nature of greater nobles' relationships with more modest noblemen or the nature of relationships among modest noblemen themselves. The

31. Denis Crouzet, "Recherches sur la crise de l'aristocratie en France au XVIe siècle: Les Dettes de la maison de Nevers," *Histoire, économie, société* I (1984): 41–43.

32. Stuart Clark, "French Historians and Early Modern Popular Culture," *Past and Present*, no. 100 (1983), p. 81.

fact of the flow of patronage from the court is easily documented by letters, receipts, and royal and noble accounts. Owing to the existence of other material and ideological sources of power, however, dependence on those resources was not absolute. Hence lesser noblemen did not direct unqualified loyalty upward, toward patrons at court. Nor was loyalty, such as it was, exclusive. Most noblemen did not depend on a single patron for their share of royal largesse. They cultivated relationships with a vast community of more and less prominent fellows, including the greats, Guise and Montmorency, and the crown itself. Any of a noble's ties might on occasion prove fruitful to him. The "system" worked from the top down in a similar fashion; patronage was dispersed by means of the same complex relationships. Much of our difficulty in clearly envisioning nobles' relationships stems from the difficulty of envisioning nobles themselves as particular sorts of human beings inhabiting a particular sort of material and perceptual world in which plural and competing "loyalties" make sense. As we analyze their world of political action, we need to understand something of their accustomed ways of regarding themselves, of interacting with others, and of conceiving the world in which they acted.

In reaching these conclusions, I have followed lines of inquiry first broached, in French historiography, by Lucien Febvre. Febvre was one of the first historians to examine structural limitations on the formation of thought as a constituent of culture.[33] He identified material as well as linguistic elements among these structures. People of the sixteenth century were different from us, not simply because they had different ideas about certain things but because they constructed their world in wholly different terms. Notions of theirs which look familiar to us are nevertheless not and cannot be the same notions we hold. In his most famous example, Febvre argues that while the term "atheism" existed then as now, it expressed a notion that was understood by means of a radically different symbolic and linguistic environment in the sixteenth century— one that, saturated with and inseparable from religious imagery, rendered unattainable the concept of atheism in our sense of the

---

33. Useful discussions of Febvre's work from this perspective are ibid. and Patrick H. Hutton, "The History of Mentalities: The New Map of Cultural History," *History and Theory* 20 (1981): 237–59.

word.[34] Thus, Febvre concluded, ideas vary from one culture to the next because the entire perceptual framework within which ideas are constituted varies.

Many works have since built on Febvre's efforts and on those of his colleague Marc Bloch to depict the *mentalité*, the conceptual and perceptual worlds, of medieval and early modern individuals. The larger body of this work has followed their emphasis on the material constituents of culture (more central to Bloch's work than to Febvre's); this work has lately included new investigations of warrior families and regional noble society in the early modern centuries.[35] However, by drawing on ideas and methods from ethnography, semiotics, and sociolinguistics, historians have also recently gained new tools with which to develop Febvre's insights about the operations of language in structuring thought. We now can more fruitfully examine how linguistic resources influence the availability of conceptual categories and how speech events create and enforce meanings within a culture. These insights have led in turn to new investigations concerning the relationship between material and symbolic shapers of mentalité. Thus the world of politics in a given culture, we now can discern, is defined by wealth, social structure, and institutional access, and by ways of imagining, representing, and legitimizing political power. The very concept "politics" is itself fully variable, and is dependent for its meaning on other categories that exist alongside it.[36]

The combination of material and symbolic factors creates a sys-

34. Lucien Febvre, *Le Problème de l'incroyance au XVIe siècle: La Religion de Rabelais* (Paris, 1942; repr. 1968). An excellent translation is now available: *The Problem of Unbelief in the Sixteenth Century: The Religion of Rabelais,* trans. Beatrice Gottlieb (Cambridge, Mass., 1982), chap. 9.

35. Jean-Marie Constant, *Nobles et paysans en Beauce aux XVIe et XVIIe siècles* (Lille, 1981); Robert Muchembled, "Famille, amour et marriage: Mentalités et comportements des nobles artésiens à l'époque de Philippe II," *Revue d'histoire moderne et contemporaine* 22 (1975): 247–55. Useful discussions of the study of mentalités by Febvre, Bloch, and their successors are André Burguière, "The Fate of the History of *Mentalités* in the *Annales,*" *Comparative Studies in Society and History* 24 (1982): 424–37, and Georg G. Iggers, *New Directions in European Historiography* (Middletown, Conn., 1984), chap. 2. Clark, "French Historians and Early Modern Popular Culture," surveys much of the work on the problem of mentalité since Febvre, and points out the limits of its concern with material culture.

36. Regarding the interdependence of meanings, see Malcolm Crick, *Explorations in Language and Meaning: Toward a Semantic Anthropology* (London, 1976), Introduction.

tem of perception and experience—about politics, say—which is by definition, in *all* cultures, an inherently conservative cultural system in the literal sense of the word. Novel thoughts or new conditions do not readily cause a redefinition of the explanatory schemes or of cognitive categories. Cultures change slowly, gradually, by means of the accretion of many acts of interpretation which incorporate new events or ideas into the cultural schema, and slightly shift the content of discourse each time. Febvre was insistent on this conservative characteristic of mentalité. Human systems of meaning are by definition coherent ones. Tensions and contradictions exist, but only within the terms that are available in that culture; that is, only in the terms in which tension or contradiction can be imagined.[37] We thus should expect the cognitive systems of sixteenth-century subjects to be persistent and resilient. And we should expect change to occur not in the way it occurs in our culture but only in the way it could occur in the culture at hand. The process of change is itself culturally bound. Febvre argued specifically that sixteenth-century subjects did not expect logical harmony within their system of thought; they were not pressed to "resolve" seeming contradictions. Thus we cannot expect the "atheist" Rabelais to have seen the significance of alleged "unbelief" and to press on with it. Not surprisingly, he did not.[38]

I investigate warrior culture in the sixteenth century from the perspective of some of these premises regarding cultural construction and change. Central to my discussion is the evidence of nobles' uses of language which survives in letters, memoirs, and reports of their speech. I have made use of recent work by sociolinguists in interpreting nobles' language of patronage—the professions of deference, obedience, and friendship which are found in all of their letters. These were verbal formulas that were used to convey a much wider range of meaning about the relationships they were describing than they now seem to convey to us, whose uses of language are quite different. Hence our impression of the rigidity of

37. Marshall Sahlins, *Islands of History* (Chicago, 1985), especially chap. 1.
38. See *Problem of Unbelief,* pp. 355–70, 451–54, and Conclusion. Febvre's analyses of linguistic evidence anticipated the later work of Michel Foucault on the anarchical interpenetration of words and things in the sixteenth century (*Les Mots et les choses,* Paris, 1966) as well as the work of ethnolinguists and anthropologists on the structure of oral communication.

clientage hierarchies and the dichotomy of idealized versus actual relationships can be traced in part to a linguistic barrier. Though most nobles were literate in the strict sense of the word, they nevertheless lived in a world of largely oral experience of language. In the words of one scholar, the nobles had not yet "interiorized" the capacities of literacy.[39] By permitting the reorganization of lived experience at a distance from it, literacy fosters abstract analytic capabilities. Particularly as revolutionized by printing, literacy also privileges visual apprehension of information. Thus schematized diagrams of power relations, for example, represent a form of knowing that is familiar to us but that was not known to noblemen of the sixteenth century. On the contrary, the nobles' experience of power privileged lived moments of action over abstract analysis.

Many recent studies have raised these issues with regard to nonelite groups in early modern society. Natalie Davis and Robert Scribner, for example, have scrutinized the role of oral communication as a transmitter and an interpreter of Reformation ideas.[40] Carlo Ginzburg and David Sabean have attempted to penetrate the cognitive world of the oral cultures of Italian and German peasant communities.[41] Sabean has reached some conclusions that are of particular interest to historians of the nobility. He asserts that the relationship between individual and community in the oral village culture he examines differed from the one we know. Without the speculative and analytic distance from the self and from others which literacy provides, villagers did not cultivate the distinct interior space where a private emotional life could occur—the private life that to us actually constitutes personhood. Anger, for example, tended to be an objective state of hostility toward a person with whom one was in conflict. One was angry at a fellow villager over some social fact that was known to all because it was acted out. A villager alienated from his fellows because he was the object of a lawsuit could signify his alienation by refusing to participate in

39. Walter J. Ong, *Orality and Literacy: The Technologizing of the Word* (London and New York, 1982), chaps. 3 and 4.

40. Natalie Z. Davis, "Printing and the People," in *Society and Culture in Early Modern France* (Stanford, 1975), pp. 189–226; Robert W. Scribner, "Oral Culture and the Diffusion of Reformation Ideas," *History of European Ideas* 5 (1984): 237–56.

41. Carlo Ginzburg, *The Cheese and the Worms* (London, 1980); David Warren Sabean, *Power in the Blood* (Cambridge, 1984).

community rituals, such as the taking of communion. Resolution of anger was similarly externalized and objectified. One would remain angry as long as, say, a lawsuit was in progress, but when the case was legally resolved, it would be emotionally resolved as well.[42] The villager would express and simultaneously experience emotional resolution by *acting* differently.

My scrutiny of noblemen points in similar directions. Noblemen made their hostilities and alliances known to others and to themselves by acting them out. Hence political configurations—particularly feuds between nobles—were quite volatile because physical belligerence was always available as a kind of action. But though they might lead to war, they might be as easily defused. Because alliances and oppositions depended on action, they were fluid at the same time that they were volatile. This kind of action represents a somewhat different relation to motivation in the nobles' world than the kind that obtains in ours. The anthropologist Marshall Sahlins depicts this issue when he poses a question about a familiar situation: Is a friend a friend because he helps you, or does he help you because he is your friend? In some societies, Sahlins argues, practice adheres more closely to the first of these two possibilities; in others, to the second.[43] By comparison with our own, French warrior society was closer to the first; it weighted incidental performance over continuous states of being. In a very real sense, then, the possibility of *being* a client was a behavioral and psychological possibility that postdates sixteenth-century warrior society. The chapters to follow will further explicate some of the terms in which politics was conceived and lived by these men. What will emerge from those chapters will be less a precise diagram of noble society than a series of glimpses of that society in action. This will be the deliberate and desired result of the methods of inquiry that have been put to use here; the connection between the form and content of knowledge will be replicated in argument.

Patronage and clientage schemas have of course had a wide application beyond the study of sixteenth-century France. "Patronage" and "clientage" have become touchstones of most descriptions of late medieval and early modern political life: they represent histo-

42. Sabean, *Power in the Blood*, chap. 1.
43. Sahlins, *Islands of History*, pp. 27–28.

rians' efforts to describe the elusive blend of private power and public function which obtained in these states. The goal of succeeding efforts to reevaluate, nuance, or challenge these schemas should not be only to dispute the definition of the terms, or to say "clientage" *really* was in fact *X* and not *Y*.[44] Rather, it should be also to probe further the components of the analysis—the evidence as well as the presumptions—which led to the "clientage" label in the first place. Historians who have investigated nobles' finances, for example, have challenged a presumption that goes back to Romier and beyond: that the nobility was in virtual decay in the sixteenth century. A recent, very persuasive study of the functioning of absolutist government in seventeenth-century Languedoc has taken a similar approach, and on an ambitious scale. It reconsiders the entire landscape of social and political power in the seventeenth century; not surprisingly, it cuts a new path through historiographical debates and links them in new ways.[45]

My aim here is to reopen the terms of the discussion about warrior society in sixteenth-century France, which until now has been largely constrained by the terms of the clientage debate. Scrutiny of the warrior elite will then be open to the methodological and theoretical questions that so far have been used more fully to study popular culture in the same period. The result will be a better understanding of nobles' political behavior than the clientage schema has provided; we will more effectively explain nobles' behavior, and more of their behavior will become visible to us. Equally important, this investigation, like many of the recent studies of popular culture, will help to reevaluate the terms of the discussion about the state itself.

The clientage theory of the early modern state has reflected a modern presumption that society is wholly equivalent to and dependent on the state. The significance and consequences of the historical growth of the state are obscured when no analytical distance is gained. Study of popular culture has been indispensable in our efforts to achieve a more distanced perspective. In many such studies, for example, the state does not appear as a benign agent of internal

---

44. See the skillful nuancing of the concepts of patronage and clientage in Dale Kent, *The Rise of the Medici: Faction in Florence, 1426–35* (Oxford, 1978), and Sharon Kettering, *Patrons, Brokers, and Clients.*

45. Beik, *Absolutism and Society.*

"peace" or "rationalization"; rather, it "makes peace" and "rationalizes" by undermining and controlling open-ended and community-based systems of conflict resolution. Obviously, the nobility was and would remain a privileged elite within early modern society. It had always been part of the state in the sense that it had been part of the apparatus of power. But integration into a *centralized* state that monopolized allegiance and defined the bounds of political life required nothing less than a cultural transformation of the warrior nobility. I describe the nobility before that transformation was achieved and suggest what some of the terms of that transformation were. Hence I reflect on the character of the nation-state as it was to take shape in the seventeenth century. Perhaps the most salient characteristic of that state has been its ability to cover its own tracks.

III

This book focuses primarily on the nobility of a single province—Picardy—and on one provincial governor whose decision to rebel against the crown throws his ties to provincial noblemen into bold relief. Although it concerns Picard noblemen for the most part, this is not a regional study as such. In my efforts to understand nobles' behavior and attitudes, I have used evidence from beyond the bounds of the province when such evidence seems appropriate. While nobles' correspondence yields information about individual relationships, for example, the nature of the apparent relationship between two individuals expressed in their letters to each other cannot be fully evaluated without a larger understanding of the terms in which all relationships were couched. In order to view these terms, I have scrutinized a large sample of nobles' correspondence. In addition, important evidence from outside Picardy has been used when the source in question was particularly rare or precious. One such source consists of household account books. Some very general accounts have survived to document the Picard household of Condé's brother, Antoine de Bourbon. These accounts not only list the officially salaried noblemen of Antoine's household but also record some of their activities in the service of the Bourbons. Thus they can be used to identify links between Picard families and the Bourbons, and to reveal something of the nature of those associations. Far more detailed household records of other great noble families have survived occasionally. They can include almost daily records of expenditures, food consumption, purchases of clothing, and maintenance of horses, coaches, and buildings; the material culture of noble life and the kinds of bonds it nurtured among noblemen—through the sharing of food and shelter, for example—can be glimpsed here far more clearly than in any other kind of document. Hence I have made use of such documents, even though they originate outside of Picardy, in a collateral branch of the Bourbon family whose lands were in Anjou. Perhaps rarer still, given contemporary habits of making use of writing, are lengthy narrative accounts of ordinary behavior which appear at times in letters, reports, and memoirs. As Chapter 4 will argue, such accounts provide glimpses of how noblemen routinely interpreted each other's words and actions; thus I have often made use of such documents as they have turned up, whatever their geographical origins.

Flexibility concerning boundaries is often necessary when one confronts the limited bodies of evidence about premodern Europe. Moreover, Picardy was a province of unusually flexible boundaries. It had been one of the few provinces never to have been consolidated into a single feudal principality, such as the neighboring duchy of Normandy and the counties of Champagne and Flanders. Administrative jurisdictions of various sorts crisscrossed the province, dividing it up, in a certain sense creating it, in different ways for different purposes. Among these jurisdictions, the most important to the nobility's military and political activity was the provincial *gouvernement*, one of eleven such major units of provincial defense and administration in the kingdom. Great noblemen served as governors of these areas, assisted by other local nobles who served as their "lieutenants."[46] The gouvernement of Picardy in the sixteenth century consisted of a wedge of territory centered on the Somme River and the vital towns along it, from Abbeville to St-Quentin. The most important Bourbon seigneuries in the region in the sixteenth century, the châtellenie of La Fère and its dependencies, lay

---

46. Robert Harding's study traces the development of the *gouvernements* and the functions of the governors and lieutenants: *Anatomy of a Power Elite*, Introduction and chap. 1.

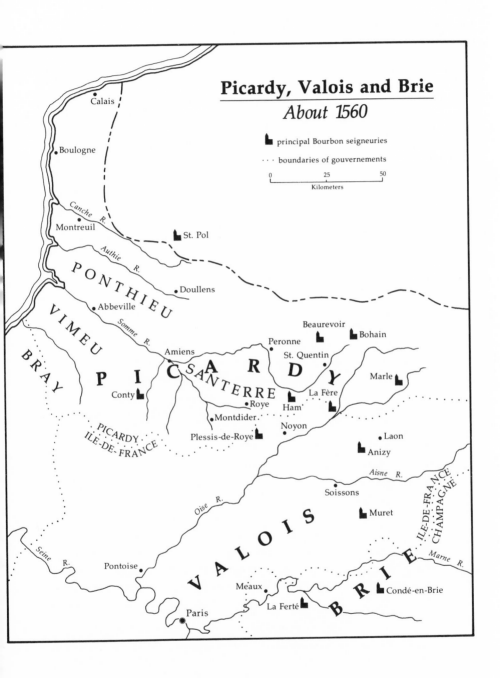

Picardy, Valois and Brie
About 1560

■ principal Bourbon seigneuries

· · · boundaries of gouvernements

0   25   50
Kilometers

Calais

Boulogne

Canche R.

Montreuil

St. Pol

Authie R.

PONTHIEU

Doullens

Abbeville

Somme R.

VIMEU

BRAY

PICARDY

SANTERRE

Conty

Amiens

Peronne

Beaurevoir

Bohain

St. Quentin

Marle

La Fère

Roye

Ham

Montdider

Noyon

Plessis-de-Roye

PICARDY
ILE-DE-FRANCE

Laon

Anizy

Aisne R.

Soissons

ILE-DE-FRANCE
CHAMPAGNE

Oise R.

Muret

VALOIS

Seine R.

Pontoise

BRIE

Marne R.

Meaux

Condé-en-Brie

La Ferté

Paris

27

on the fringes of the gouvernement. Other Bourbon estates, a bit farther east and south, lay wholly within the governorship of Ile-de-France. Contemporary references to locations "in Picardy" or of persons "Picard" suggest that Picardy could be thought of in very vague terms: in fact, virtually anything lying north of Paris, from Senlis to Calais.[47] A few of the Bourbon estates in the northeastern part of the kingdom did lie outside of what could even very loosely be called Picardy. These estates, most of them Condé's, were located near the Marne in Brie. Contemporaries commonly identified locations by referring to smaller and more precise geographical areas rather than to administrative units: the Amienois or the Laonois, Vimeu or Santerre. Neither the plurality of such divisions nor the complexity of administrative divisions seems to have felt unnatural or confusing to them. Their experience of jurisdiction was grounded in the seigneurie, which was a complex of rights and not simply or necessarily a coherent territory. They were accustomed to managing a variety of their own and others' claims to authority. These claims, stemming from persons (including the king and such corporate entities as towns), did not need the territorial "logic" that is induced by the abstract perception of uniform space made possible by modern familiarity with maps.

However loosely defined the borders of Picardy, it is nevertheless important to consider some of the features of the political geography of the region in any investigation of nobles who held lands there. The region was a prosperous one, and this prosperity was of course reflected in the characteristics of noble society. Like Flanders, Picardy had been marked by early dense settlement and precocious urban growth. The towns in both regions had competed vigorously with one another and with the local nobility for jurisdiction over the countryside. While the strength of the Flemish towns had made them the victors over all but their count, the somewhat less vigorous towns of Picardy had remained competitors with a broader spectrum of nobles. The presence of the king had helped to ensure that no single claimant would succeed in taking control of the entire province; Picardy was the only region beyond the royal foothold in

---

47. E. Lambert, "Les Limites de la Picardie," *Société archéologique, historique et scientifique de Noyon: Comptes rendus et mémoires* 34 (1972): 53–65; on the flexibility of boundaries over time, see also Pierre Feuchère, "Dans le nord de la France: La Permanence des cadres territoriaux?" *Annales: E.S.C.* 9 (1954): 94–100.

the Ile-de-France where the kings of France had exercised continuous authority through the early Capetian period. The Carolingian-Capetian patrimony had included lands in the heart of the province, and the early Capetians had tried earnestly to protect their control of them. Beginning definitively with Philip Augustus, the crown was able to extend its authority in order to tap the region's wealth.[48]

The rich agriculture, prosperous local manufacture, and lively internal trade of the province, together with the intrusion of royal authority, had sustained numerous rival power bases during the Middle Ages; the comtes de St-Pol, Vermandois, Soissons, the sires de Coucy, rivaled each other and a number of lesser lights. This dispersed authority continued in the sixteenth century. A group of about ten leading families controlled the major provincial commands in the name of the king. These families represented what may be distinguished as the provincial elite—the families in each province immediately below ducal and princely families in wealth and stature. The men of these families governed the important towns of the region and monopolized the local commands of companies of the royal gendarmerie.[49] They were active in the defense of the province during the Imperial Wars of the 1540s and 1550s, and collectively governed the province in times of peace.

Included in this group in the mid–sixteenth century were René, baron de Mailly, scion of the main branch of the Mailly family, whose barony lay between Amiens and Arras; François and his brother Louis d'Ailly, sires de Picquigny and *vidames* to the bishop of nearby Amiens; Louis de Lannoy, sire de Morvilliers; François de Hangest, sire de Genlis; Louis de Halluin, sire de Piennes; Louis d'Ongnies, sire and later comte de Chaulnes; François de Gouffier, sire de Crèvecoeur-le-grand, between Amiens and Beauvais; Jean

48. Robert Fossier, *La Terre et les hommes en Picardie*, 2 vols. (Paris and Louvain, 1968), vol. 1.

49. The gendarmerie or *compagnies d'ordonnance* (the latter term refers to the royal ordinance that had established them) had been created in 1445 and were the heavy cavalry component of the royal standing armies. These units included more lightly armed archers, but the heavily armed cavalrymen known as *hommes d'armes* (armed with lances and, later, firearms) were usually noblemen. See Philippe Contamine, *Guerre, état et société à la fin du moyen âge: Etude sur les armées des rois de France, 1337–1494* (Paris and The Hague, 1972), pp. 278–90, and the summary of sixteenth-century developments in John David Nordhaus, "*Arma et Litterae*: The Education of the *Noblesse de Race* in Sixteenth-Century France" (Ph.D. dissertation, Columbia University, 1974).

d'Estrées, an aged warrior with lands scattered throughout the region. The two most important families among this group, in terms of commands exercised, were the Monchy-Senarpont and the Humières families. Jean de Monchy, sire de Senarpont in the Vimeu, commanded at Corbie and Boulogne and captained a company of the gendarmerie in the 1550s, and became lieutenant of the gouvernement of Picardy in 1560. He also kept residences in Amiens and Abbeville and exercised significant informal authority there. Two generations of the Humières family governed the three most important fortress towns in the province: Péronne, Montdidier, and Roye. These towns were situated along a line that cut through the heart of the Santerre, the fertile upland region east of Amiens. For centuries they had been coveted prizes in themselves, as they would be in the Imperial and Religious wars, and keys to the strategic dominance of the entire region.

Noblemen from a large number of somewhat more modest families also held important military commands in various lesser towns, or in the companies of the royal gendarmerie under the captaincy of a member of a leading family. While provincial wealth sustained this local power, it also—together with the province's strategic value as a border zone— continued to make sixteenth-century Picardy a region where the king was most anxious that his authority be felt. Leading nobles, with their important role in provincial government, not surprisingly found that their interests quite often coincided with the monarchy's desire for internal order. As the history of the civil wars demonstrates, however, they had the power readily to defy royal authority if they chose. In the light of these conditions, the independence of action which more modest nobles displayed during the civil wars becomes particularly striking; the persistence of localized fighting and independent initiative beyond the control of the monarch's authority, in this province where that authority was relatively strongly felt, suggests that the model of nobles' freedom from centralized control must also be applicable to other regions, even less accustomed to cooperation with royal government.

Another issue that arises in any investigation of the political behavior of the French nobility in the sixteenth century is that of religious conviction and conflict. The civil wars that began in 1562 and dragged on until the late 1590s are conventionally called the "Wars of Religion." There is no doubt that the adjective "religious" appropriately describes the origins and significance of these conflicts in some measure, as well as of the sporadic violence that preceded them and disrupted the periods of peace between them. Money and weapons were sent to Huguenots from Geneva. The networks of Reformed churches that had been established by 1562 became practical, strategic centers of resistance after that time.[50] The belief in the exclusive veracity of Catholic or Reformed doctrine and the fear of pollution or extermination by adherents of the other both spurred and legitimated violence by both sides.[51] Religious life and the wider life of each community or social group were always, everywhere and in all circumstances, interconnected. Scholars of the period of the Reformation in England, Germany, and elsewhere, as well as scholars of France, have explored many dimensions of this interconnection: the role of religious ritual as a source of community identity; the relationship between economic hardship and anticlericalism; the coincidence of religious ideology and social organization in spawning protests and violence.

The interconnection of religious life with social and political life has not been so successfully investigated where the nobility are concerned. Most discussions about the religious life of the nobility locate it in the realm not of community life but of private conscience.[52] Some Huguenot noblemen—very few—are described as genuinely pious. The majority used religion as a cloak for personal ambition—for more power and more riches, to be gained by armed rebellion if necessary. Embrace of the Reformed religion was an expression of political disaffection by particularly desperate or ambitious noblemen, according to this view. These conclusions reflect some of the same limitations as the analyses of nobles' political behavior solely in terms of the state. Both rest on twentieth-century assumptions about the relationship of inner life and public life, of thought and action. The ideal, in both cases, has been "disinterested" loyalty: constant service without duplicity, sincere faith without ambition. We would do well to adjust and amend these

---

50. Robert M. Kingdon, *Geneva and the Coming of the Wars of Religion in France* (Geneva, 1956).

51. Natalie Z. Davis, "The Rites of Violence," in *Society and Culture*, pp. 152–88.

52. See, for example, Salmon, *Society in Crisis*, pp. 127–31; June Shimizu, *Conflict of Loyalties: Politics and Religion in the Career of Gaspard de Coligny, Admiral of France, 1519–1572* (Geneva, 1970).

notions about nobles' public lives generally and, by implication, about their religious lives specifically.

Other, generally more recent investigations of the patterns of nobles' conversion to Protestantism have uncovered the social ties that led to conversion. Conversions followed well-established kinship relations and preexisting ties between local noble families. In leading families, at least, women often converted first, and then enjoined their brothers, husbands, and sons to follow their example. But an awareness of these patterns is more a knowledge of modes of transmission than an understanding of nobles' religiosity per se, as we can see in the fact that analyses of the *meaning* of conversion still wrestle with the issue of sincerity.[53]

Religious loyalty undoubtedly supplemented other grounds of common interest in determining the relationships that nobles formed and the resilience of those attachments. If the nobles were not linked to one another by exclusive hierarchical ties, however, then religious loyalties cannot have been transmitted neatly down a chain of command, from greater to lesser nobles. The prince de Condé was certainly the highest-ranking Huguenot leader in the kingdom (barring one underage nephew), and rebellion for religious security was made more feasible by the cloak of his royal name than it otherwise would have been.[54] But the fact that Condé converted does not mean that a clientele dependent on him converted after him; such patterns of dependency did not exist. Moreover, the pattern of religious affiliation was affected by a variety of factors that further complicated the ways in which religious interests overlapped

---

53. Some of this research is summarized in Jean-Marie Constant, "La Pénétration des idées de la Réforme protestante dans la noblesse provinciale française à travers quelques exemples," in *Les Réformes: Enracinement socio-culturel*, XXVe colloque international d'études humanistes, Tours (Paris, 1985). Nancy L. Roelker goes further than most analysts of nobles' religiosity in getting at the nature and significance of noblewomen's religious experiences: "The Appeal of Calvinism to French Noblewomen in the Sixteenth Century," *Journal of Interdisciplinary History* 2 (1972): 391–419. See also the discussion of the relation of nobles' expectations of violence and death to expectations of justice and grace in traditional Catholicism in Francois Billacois, *Le Duel dans la société française des XVIe–XVIIe siècles* (Paris, 1981). Manfred Orléa suggests that religious experience expressed aspects of noble mentalité: *La Noblesse aux Etats généraux de 1576 et de 1588* (Paris, 1980).

54. Condé and his nephew, the future Henri IV, were the highest-ranking nobles *in France*; of course, Henri's mother, Jeanne d'Albret, was a queen in her own right in Navarre as well as a princess of the royal blood of France.

with other bonds between nobles—such as those created by household service or by proximity of landholdings. Conversions to Protestantism, for example, can in some cases be traced to exposure to the Gospel while many noblemen were confined at garrison duty or as prisoners of war in the northeast during the Imperial Wars in the late 1550s. We have much to learn about the sheer numbers of conversions among the nobles, about the patterns and the meanings of those conversions, and above all about the nature and meanings of their religious experience—all of which call for full study in their own right. My analysis of coincidental social and political life will suggest some avenues along which such analyses might proceed.

In any case, shared religious convictions did not ensure concert of interests. The pattern of violence after 1562 reflected the plurality of ties each noble cultivated: Picard Huguenot noblemen came and went from Condé's arena of fighting, arranged private truces with the king, and settled squabbles with their neighbors. Indeed, Protestant noblemen could quite easily—and frequently did—clash with each other over matters of local influence within the province. Perhaps the most dramatic evidence of the lack of unity of interest among Condé and the mass of Huguenot nobility rebelling "under" him is the fact that the Prince himself looked beyond provincial associates for support in his struggles against the crown. Condé relied on large numbers of nonnoble warriors who may or may not have been steadfast Huguenots but who were certainly available for hire. The Prince was himself available to justify the rebellion of any Huguenot inclined to take up arms; but how useful his name, his military targets, his deals with the crown were for lesser nobility depended on their individual needs and circumstances. Similarly, Condé benefited from the support he did receive from other nobles, but he cultivated other support simultaneously. The overlapping but distinct arenas of nobles' concern—from strictly local power to the goal of influence over the king—stand out clearly even in an analysis of the wars as religious wars.

The period I consider is approximately the first decade of religious war—the period ended by the death of the prince de Condé in March 1569. This date was obviously a watershed for Huguenot resistance, and, as we shall see, the onset of the third war, in which Condé died, also marked a change in the crown's reaction to the rebellion. I also consider the preceding decade of war against a foreign enemy: Spain and the Empire. This was the last decade of a war for control of northern Italy and the frontier with the Low Countries which had been started by Charles VIII (d. 1498) and which was ended by treaty in 1559. This decade conveniently coincides with the first years of Condé's adult life; he was married for the first time in 1551, at the age of twenty-one, and his youthful military career can be traced, with greater or lesser difficulty, through the remainder of the 1550s.

This is not a narrative history of those two decades, however. I eschew a consistently chronological approach in favor of more topical consideration of nobles' behavior. What the nobles were *doing*, in the broadest sense, cannot be deciphered in any other way. This is therefore also not a narrative account of Condé's career. The major landmarks of Condé's adult life and the familiar events of these two decades are provided here as a backdrop, to orient the reader, to the largely thematic analysis that follows.

Because Condé enjoyed great stature during the 1560s and because he chose to wage war against the crown, the outlines of his life are fairly well known.[55] He first comes to center stage after the death of Henri II in 1559, when his status as Prince of the Blood took on special political weight in view of the uncertain capacities of the young king, François II. From 1559 to 1562, Condé shared the attentions of religious dissidents with his elder brother Antoine; the two also shared claims to greater control of royal policy and of the flow of royal largesse. Their interests were not fully aligned, however. In 1560 Condé became embroiled in the infamous Amboise affair, a plot by a group of disgruntled noblemen to wrest control of the young king from members of the Guise family. Their attempt to seize the king at the château of Amboise was labeled treasonous and some of them were executed. Condé only narrowly escaped execution himself. Antoine had been able to rely on his greater clout as First Prince of the Blood to further his claims to power at less threat to himself. The brothers' interests were driven further apart early in 1562 by Antoine's definitive rejection of the

---

55. Reliable works treating the events of Condé's life include Henri d'Orléans, duc d'Aumale, *Histoire des princes de Condé pendant les XVIe et XVIIe siècles*, 7 vols. (Paris, 1863–96), vol. 1 (1863); Eugène Saulnier, *Le Rôle politique du cardinal de Bourbon* (Paris, 1912); Lucien Romier, *Catholiques et Huguenots à la cour de Charles IX* (Paris, 1924).

Reformed faith. In that year Condé fully assumed the role with which he is best associated: protector and supporter of the Huguenot struggle. His authority in that role was enhanced by Antoine's death later that year, leaving the Prince to share primacy as Prince of the Blood only with Antoine's young son.

Condé had been born in 1530, the twelfth of thirteen children, and was the youngest son of the family. The Prince's sudden involvement in royal policy and court intrigue after 1559 was thus due also to the fact that several older siblings had died. Between Condé and Antoine in age were François and Jean, who had died in 1544 and 1557 respectively, and two other sons, both named Louis, who had both died young. Their remaining brother, Charles, became the cardinal de Bourbon. Condé was, in short, the youngest of a bevy of sons; his relative invisibility before 1559 is understandable.

Indeed, the drift of his entire family to center stage by the 1560s was by no means inevitable. By 1560 or so, the thinned ranks of his family, combined with the prospect of a succession of underaged kings, made the Bourbon royal blood seem endangered and rather precious.[56] Earlier, kinship with the Valois kings would not have added much to Condé's status. His distant cousin the connétable de Bourbon (also descended from the youngest son of St. Louis, by whom they all claimed their place in line for the throne) had severely compromised his kin by his alleged treason (that is, his alliance with the emperor) against François I in 1525. By that time Condé's father, Charles de Bourbon, duc de Vendôme (d. 1537), had already distinguished himself as a warrior and served for a number of years as governor of Picardy; he wisely pursued a career of earnest and unstinting service on behalf of the crown thereafter. His sons could begin their careers unhampered by any extraordinary jealousy or prejudices against them, but not necessarily better off for being Princes of the Blood.[57]

The eldest son, Antoine, inherited Charles's title of duc de Vendôme and made a very fortunate marriage to the heiress of the kingdom of Navarre: Jeanne d'Albret. The largest single portion of his inheritance, however, lay in Picardy. Antoine followed his father

---

56. See the discussion of the increasing "preciousness" of royal blood by Richard A. Jackson, "Peers of France and Princes of the Blood," *French Historical Studies* 7 (1971): 26–46.
57. Saulnier, *Cardinal de Bourbon*, pp. 2–3.

almost directly as governor of the province. Charles served from
1519 to his death in 1537 and Antoine served from later that year
until 1555, when he assumed the governorship of Guyenne after the
death of his father-in-law, the king of Navarre. When Condé was
married in 1551, a number of the family's holdings in Picardy were
settled on him, and the marriage brought him further lands. His
wife, Eléonore de Roye, was of an old Picard family and eventually
became her parents' principal heir to estates that more than doubled
Condé's holdings in the province. Like his elder brother and their
father, Condé became governor of the province. He was appointed
in 1561 and retained the post until his death.

The fighting that Condé directed has distinguished the three civil
wars begun before 1569.[58] In the spring of 1562, after losing a series
of armed (though not yet violent) confrontations with the duc de
Guise and other rivals, he withdrew from the court to the town of
Meaux, and then engineered the seizure of Orléans. He hoped to use
the city as a base from which to seize other centrally located urban
centers, which could become his bargaining tools with the crown.
Several thousand noblemen—including virtual peers from throughout the kingdom as well as modest provincial noblemen—joined
Condé there. Following the seizure of several other towns, negotiations and royal attempts to relieve the captured towns proceeded
together. It was not until December that a true pitched battle took
place—at Dreux, west of Paris. Two of the principal antagonists,
Condé and Montmorency, were captured. The earnest negotiations
that followed resulted in an edict of peace in March 1563.

The outbreak of hostilities in September 1567, marking the beginning of what is now termed the second civil war, stemmed from an
attempt, led by Condé, to seize the person of the king. Again the
major strategic objective of the main Huguenot force under Condé
was to control territory and resources in the center of the kingdom,
and thus bring the king to the bargaining table. A major battle was
fought at St-Denis in November, but hostilities dragged on until
another edict was produced in March 1568. This time the official
truce had little effect. At the end of that summer, Condé, Coligny,

---

58. Summaries of the phases of the official wars can be found in Georges Livet,
Les Guerres de religion (Paris, 1962), and in Jean de Pablo, *L'Armée huguenote entre
1562 et 1573, Contribution à l'étude de l'histoire des institutions militaires huguenotes* 2
(Archiv für Reformationsgeschichte, 49, repr.): 192–216.

and their entourages, probably to escape an attempt to capture or kill them, fled their estates in the east for the greater safety of western France, and the "third" civil war was under way. Condé died after the battle of Jarnac, near Angoulême, in March 1569.

These are the highlights of the political history of the 1560s. The chapters that follow do not dispute this record of events, though they do dispute the contention that these events reflect the competition between distinct clientage hierarchies—chiefly that of the Bourbons versus that of the Guise family. More generally, I reinterpret the factors that constituted nobles' political life and reassess what constituted significant political "events." I do so by scrutinizing nobles' ordinary lives and the material circumstances that shaped them, and by analyzing nobles' habits of mind. One of my goals is to provide an analysis of noble culture which renders nobles' "particularism" and "disloyalty" more explainable—indeed, which renders them less in need of explanation. A further goal is to require of future studies more in the way of explanation of how and on what terms this culture did become transformed into the partner and subordinate of the state which it was not, as yet, in the sixteenth century.

– 2 –

The Pattern of Violence:
Picard Nobles at War, 1562–1569

I

TRACING military activity is a useful way to approach nobles' behavior, because violence leaves a relatively visible record. Fighting, particularly in rebellion against the crown, was an overt act that did not escape the notice of contemporary observers eager to bestow praise and blame. Indeed, in many cases a single mention of a noble's participation in battle is virtually the only evidence remaining of both his actions and the interests represented by those actions. The actual pattern of violence in the civil wars of the 1560s corresponds only imperfectly with the official chronology of wars delimited by Condé's strategy. The cleavage between the interests of this great noble and the interests of his many sometime followers is dramatically seen as we observe them pursuing their various objectives by independent means.

A rather unusual document from the civil war period which survives in the British Library helps to identify individual members of Condé's entourage in 1562. This "Liste des gentilhommes de l'armée protestante" names rebel noblemen who joined Condé at Orléans in the spring of that year.[1] The list is incomplete, as it names only the more prominent nobles, and not all of them: as comparisons with narrative accounts of the first civil war establish,

---

1. The list is reproduced in *Correspondance de Théodore de Bèze*, ed. H. Meylan, A. Dufour, et al., 9 vols. (Geneva, 1960–), 4:266–71.

the names of several quite powerful noblemen who joined Condé
are omitted. Nevertheless, even when it is compared with the relatively informative narrative accounts, the "Liste" stands out as an
unusual and valuable source for anyone interested in tracing nobles'
participation in the wars.

Sixty of the seventy-three individuals on the list can be positively
identified. A first impression of these names seems to confirm the
expectations of Romier or Major concerning support for Condé
among the nobles: almost one-third of these sixty individuals were
from Picardy and contiguous regions of Valois and Brie, the sites of
Condé's governorship and of his own landholdings. The remaining
two-thirds of the names can be roughly separated into two other
territorial groups: one from such western and southwestern regions
as Angoumois, Poitou, and Saintonge, which corresponded to the
territorial strength of the leading Huguenot princes La Rochefoucauld and Soubise; and a final group from Ile-de-France and Normandy, where the Châtillon family was strong. Yet this convenient
portrait is destroyed when the details of each noble's participation
are established—insofar as they can be established on the basis of
surviving sources.

One of the most prominent Picard names to appear on the list is
that of Louis de Lannoy, sire de Morvilliers. Morvilliers was approximately ten years Condé's senior and was a warrior of established reputation. His grandfather Raoul de Lannoy had considerably raised the fortunes of his somewhat obscure branch of the great
Flemish Lannoy family through service to the beleaguered crown in
the fifteenth century. The family lands included a number of seigneuries clustered near their principal residence at Folleville, a fortified
château south of Amiens which Raoul had extensively remodeled.
The family also held scattered lands north of Amiens and several to
the south, near Beauvais. Like his father before him, Morvilliers
was captain (military commander) of Amiens. In this capacity he
had been responsible for the defense of the town during crucial
phases of the fighting against Imperial forces during the 1550s, including the aftermath of the French defeat at St-Quentin, when
Amiens had been the only sizable fortress guarding the approach to
Paris. To this post Morvilliers later added the command of a royal
compagnie d'ordonnance and the governorships of Boulogne and
Dunkirk after those territories were retaken from the English in

1558.[2] These were positions of great importance, for these towns, with Calais, were for years afterward felt to be menaced by the possibility of invasion from England. Morvilliers resided often in the Boulonnais after he assumed the post of governor, and, as surviving correspondence indicates, reported on conditions there directly to the king.[3]

After joining Condé at Orléans in the spring of 1562, Morvilliers was dispatched by the Prince to direct the defense of Rouen. At that moment, Rouen was controlled by the Protestant faction of its citizenry; it was being threatened from within by civil turmoil and from without by Catholic forces. According to the contemporary historian Jacques-Auguste De Thou, Morvilliers was chosen to govern Rouen for the Huguenots because he was a highly respected and experienced commander. De Thou records that Morvilliers was successful both in quieting civil unrest and in outwitting Catholic troops in several engagements around the town.[4]

Yet in the midst of this seemingly successful and certainly crucial defense of Rouen, Morvilliers abruptly quit his command and left the town on August 18, only a few months after the general fighting had begun. Supposedly disgusted by the Huguenots' plans to secure English aid for their cause, he left Rouen for Dieppe. There he tried to enlist the help of two local commanders in preventing an anticipated landing of English troops, but he succeeded only in causing the two men to be thrown into prison by the suspicious Dieppois. This "new mortification," according to De Thou, persuaded Mor-

---

2. Victor de Beauvillé, *Recueil de documents inédits concernant la Picardie*, 4 vols. (Paris, 1860–1887), 4:265–66, 284–86, 316–18, 321–34, 628–30; Georges Durand, "Les Lannoys, Folleville, et l'art italien dans le nord de la France," *Bulletin monumentale* 70 (1906): 329–404; P. Roger, *Noblesse et chevalerie du comté de Flandre, d'Artois et de Picardie* (Amiens, 1843), pp. 199–201. Concerning Morvilliers's appointment as captain of Amiens (1550) and as a captain of a compagnie d'ordonnance (1561), see Fleury-Vindry, *Dictionnaire de l'état-major française au XVIe siècle*, pt. 1, *Gendarmerie* (Bergerac, 1901), pp. 261–62. Some correspondence has survived to document his duties in Amiens: BN, MS fr. 20529, fol. 54, Morvilliers to duc de Guise, 14 October 1557, Amiens.

3. See, for example, BN, MS fr. 15542, fol. 66, Morvilliers, "advis au roy," ?16 September 1563, Boulogne; BN, MS fr. 23193, fol. 253, Morvilliers to L'Aubespine, 30 March 1567, Boulogne.

4. Jacques-Auguste De Thou, *Histoire universelle*, 16 vols. (London, 1734), 4:191–239.

villiers to abandon his involvement entirely. He left Normandy and retired to his château of Folleville in Picardy, where he remained unmolested throughout the remainder of the first civil war.

A second prominent Picard named on the "Liste" was François de Hangest, sire de Genlis. His landholdings included seigneuries in the prosperous Santerre region as well as the seigneurie of Genlis, near Noyon. The various offices and honors held by members of his family included the bishopric of Noyon. Genlis himself had held a number of minor commands during the Imperial Wars and had been rewarded with the captaincy of a compagnie d'ordonnance in 1558, following his participation in the retaking of Calais.[5] In 1562 Genlis behaved much like Morvilliers: he abandoned the rebel force late in the year, before the conflict was resolved. According to De Thou, Genlis became angered when royal peace proposals were rejected in favor of continued fighting. Other sources suggest that he was troubled by accusations that his brother had too readily surrendered the town of Bourges to royal forces that summer. In any case, one night in early December, as the other leading nobles were planning an attack on the nearby royal army, Genlis slipped out of the rebel camp. He paused to explain to his next in command (whom he could not persuade to accompany him) that he was withdrawing because the truce proposals had been rejected, but that he was not "renouncing either the Reformed religion or the *parti* of the Protestants."[6] He then returned to Picardy by way of the royal encampment, where he may also have explained his behavior. The rebel leaders he had abandoned, fearful that Genlis had betrayed them, called off the attack they had planned.

Both Morvilliers and Genlis, then, behaved more as sometime allies of Condé than as his loyal followers. The behavior of other prominent nobles identified by the "Liste" echoes this pattern. After Genlis, the next Picard name to appear on the list is that of Louis de Halluin, sire de Piennes. Piennes remained with the rebel force for a few months only; taking advantage of a royal offer of amnesty, he

---

5. Concerning the Hangest family and its landholdings, see Bonnault d'Houët, "Genlis ou Jenlis: Histoire d'un fief picard," *Bulletin de la société des antiquaires de Picardie* 12 (1904): 36–53. For Genlis's commands and appointments see Fleury-Vindry, *L'Etat-major*, p. 242.

6. De Thou, *Histoire*, 4:471–72.

retired to Picardy in late 1562, and was rewarded with the command of a royal compagnie d'ordonnance.[7] The next Picard on the list, identified as "the young Senarpont," was a son of one of the most prominent and respected of Picard noblemen. His father, Jean de Monchy, sire de Senarpont, in the Vimeu, had been captain of a royal ordinance company since 1552 and had served as lieutenant of the gouvernement of Picardy since 1560. Both Catholic and Huguenot contemporaries provide clear evidence that Senarpont was a steadfast adherent of the Reformed faith, and he had demonstrated support for Condé on other occasions; in 1561, for example, when Condé made his triumphal return after being cleared of complicity in the Amboise conspiracy, Senarpont helped to escort him to court. Yet despite such gestures, Senarpont never afterward joined the Prince in revolt, even though his religious sympathies brought attacks on his authority within Picardy.[8] While we know virtually nothing of the son's activities beyond the fact that he appeared alongside Condé in 1562, we do know that his father carefully charted an independent course (or led what may have been careful family strategy) during the wars.

Another name on the "Liste" is Rubempré, most probably referring to André de Bourbon, sire de Rubempré. Rubempré belonged to a bastard line that was descended from Condé's great-grandfather and that had been established in Picardy together with Condé's own branch of the family. He had served under the command of one of Condé's brothers in a royal compagnie d'ordonnance in the 1550s.[9] Nevertheless, Rubempré also abandoned the Huguenot force long before the end of the first war; indeed, his withdrawal from the rebellion is documented by his presence in October 1562 at a religious procession led by the cardinal de Bourbon and the bishop of Amiens in Amiens.[10] Interestingly, in Rubempré's family can be

7. Ibid., p. 465. Piennes's appointment as captain of a royal compagnie d'ordonnance is dated from April 1563 by Fleury-Vindry (*L'Etat-major*, p. 238). However, a letter from the Queen Mother to Piennes, dated 20 October 1562, shows that he had already been awarded the command: BN, MS fr. 3187, fol. 30, Catherine de Médicis to Louis de Halluin, sire de Piennes, 20 October 1562, "camp devant Rouen."

8. De Thou, *Histoire*, 4:50–51.

9. There were four officers under the captain of a company of the gendarmerie: a *lieutenant*, an *enseigne*, a *guidon*, and a *maréchal des logis*. Rubempré was guidon and, later, enseigne under Jean, comte d'Enghien: Fleury-Vindry, *L'Etat-major*, pp. 75–76.

10. François Rumet, *Chronique du pays et comté de Ponthieu*, ed. Ernest Prarond (Paris, 1902), p. 69.

found another display of independent behavior, paralleling the case of Senarpont. The husband of Rubempré's sister was Jean, sire d'Estrées, an esteemed warrior and staunch Huguenot. He held lands in Bray and Soissonais, as well as other important seigneuries in the Boulonnais. Yet, like the elder Senarpont, he never took up arms against the crown with his Picard coreligionists.[11]

One might expect that noblemen of the stature of Morvilliers, Genlis, and Senarpont would behave more as allies than as followers of Condé. They represented the provincial elite—the families of greatest stature and power within the province. Each of these men had had many years of experience in positions of independent command in the decades preceding the civil wars. They had commanded companies of troops and governed major towns. As a matter of course, they had operated within networks of personal ties that were much more vast than the ties expressed by their association with Condé. Genlis, for example, had fought almost continually with the duc de Guise in the campaigns of the 1550s. Surviving correspondence between the two men suggests long-standing familiarity between them, even transcending the businesslike relationship that all prominent warriors would have cultivated with the Duke.[12]

The elite of provincial noblemen—represented by Senarpont and Morvilliers—were not alone in their ability to act independently of the leadership of a great noble. Noblemen of lesser stature also displayed a certain independence in their conduct during the wars. The actions of two noblemen from the area of Provins during the second civil war (1567–68) are instructive. In 1567, following its defeat at the battle of St-Denis in November, the rebel force under Condé drifted eastward through Brie and into Champagne, planning eventually to rendezvous with German mercenaries on the eastern borders of the kingdom. According to the local chronicler Claude Haton, the Huguenot leadership decided to invest and secure the strategic town of Provins, in Brie, but were dissuaded from carrying out their plan by a local Huguenot notable, the sire de St-Simon. St-Simon, Haton tells us, explained that the town had taken care to maintain neutrality since the civil wars had begun, and

11. *Notices brayonnes: Les Estrées au pays de Bray* (Neuchâtel-en-Bray, 1885).
12. See the letters from Genlis to Guise: BN, MS fr. 20515, fol. 43, 27 June 1552, Guise; BN, MS fr. 20544, fol. 130, 11 June 1553, Genlis; BN, MS fr. 20544, fol. 15, 30 October 1555, Genlis; BN, MS fr. 20545, fol. 103, 14 December 1555, Châtelet.

pleaded that it now be left ungarrisoned and unpillaged by the Huguenot forces. This description of St-Simon's intervention carries weight because Haton was a staunchly Catholic and royalist observer, always ready to decry the actions of local Huguenots. Indeed, he was otherwise severely critical both of St-Simon's insistence on maintaining the Reformed faith on his own lands and of his participation in the revolts against the king. In any case, St-Simon's defense of local interests was successful: the Huguenot force bypassed Provins.[13]

A second local notable, Claude de La Croix, baron de Plancy, could not deter the Huguenot force from sacking Sézanne, another town in the region. Condé had sent representatives to the town to negotiate a payment in return for a promise not to molest it. Yet despite these negotiations, the entire army later entered the town, sacked and burned it, and then further humiliated the inhabitants by demanding still new "ransoms" of wealthy citizens. At this point the baron de Plancy, apparently incensed by this breach of faith, abandoned the Huguenot army and withdrew to his nearby estates.[14] This display of independence is particularly striking in view of other surviving evidence that shows Plancy to have been closely associated with Condé both before and after the incident at Sézanne. A land grant dated August 1567, before the second war began, describes Plancy as "living in the entourage of [literally, in the "suite" of] the Prince."[15] And several years after the war, Plancy reappears in association with Condé: he is named as Condé's procurator for the purpose of settling certain of the Prince's debts to Parisian tradesmen.[16]

Other instances of independent action are seen in the case of Antoine de Gourlay, sire de Jumelles, whose title came from a small

---

13. Claude Haton, *Mémoires*, ed. Félix Bourquelot, 2 vols. (Paris, 1857), 1:464.

14. This reconstruction is suggested by G. de Plancy in *Le Marquisat de Plancy et ses seigneurs* (Arcis-sur-Aube, 1895), pp. 84–85. The fact of Plancy's withdrawal from the Huguenot force is reported by Haton: "Il quitta le prince et sa cohorte huguenotique avec leur party et s'alla rassoir en sa maison audict Plancy" (cited in ibid., p. 85).

15. AN, Y 108, fol. 219r–v, Etienne de Marchis, sire de Marchis-pres-Dreux: donation à Claude de La Croix, baron de Plancy, 20 August 1567.

16. AN, Y 116, fols. 168–170v, 10 December 1574. The act concerns the management of Condé's children's inheritance by their uncle Charles, cardinal de Bourbon. Plancy is mentioned as having previously acted on behalf of Condé in 1569.

seigneurie dependent on one of Condé's holdings in the Amienois. Jumelles fought with Condé's army, at least temporarily, in 1562, and appeared later, in 1580, to help defend the family's château of La Fère in Picardy for Condé's son. During the third civil war, however, Jumelles fought with the combined force of rebels from France and the Low Countries along the eastern border of the kingdom, rather than with Condé's force in western France. Moreover, between the wars, Jumelles lived and exercised his Reformed faith on his own, in the midst of a largely hostile population in the Amienois. In 1570 his name was reported to the *échevins* (aldermen) of Amiens after a minor fracas along one of the roads leading into town. Some passers-by had taunted him and threatened him as he returned from worship at a fellow Huguenot's estate outside the town.[17] Jumelles's party and the passers-by were all armed. Jumelles demanded the right to avenge the insult he felt he had suffered at the hands of these citizens of Amiens. The aldermen of the town consequently worked to pacify both Jumelles and their own restive citizenry. Neither association with Condé's cause nor proximity to one of Condé's estates protected him; so long as he attempted to reside on his own estates, Jumelles was largely beyond the sphere of Condé's influence.

He did choose to frequent his own estates. The disturbance near Amiens demonstrates this fact, and so, strikingly, does another incident in 1569. In March of that year, Jumelles returned from fighting in the east under the command of the Prince of Orange. A royal official in the town of Roye listed the names of Jumelles and three other noblemen and those of about a dozen townsmen from Roye in a report identifying those who had rebelled in the latest war. All of the townsmen reportedly had taken refuge in Condé's nearby château of Plessis-de-Roye. Jumelles and each of the other noblemen simply went home—Jumelles to a nearby estate of his wife's.[18]

Like the more prominent Morvilliers and Genlis, then, such lesser nobles as Plancy and Jumelles apparently followed personal strategies that led them to join Condé at certain times and to defend

17. AC Amiens, BB39, fol. 172r–v, 13 November 1570.
18. BN, MS fr. 4717, fols. 81–82, "Rolle et estat des noms, surnoms, qualités et demeurances des gentilhommes et aultres qui ont porté les armes contre le Roy notre sire . . . estant du ressort de la jurisdiction et gouvernance de Roye," 27 March 1569, ?Roye.

themselves independently at others. Plancy's abandonment of Condé's army during the second civil war did not signify a renunciation of his association with the Prince. Rather, it reflected Plancy's determination—and his freedom—to support Condé on his own terms. The cases of Plancy and Jumelles also suggest the necessity of such autonomy. Fighting alongside Condé did not protect (indeed, it directly threatened) Plancy's local power base, nor did it solve Jumelles's routine needs for self-defense. Similarly, the sire de St-Simon tried to influence the Huguenot army's tactics in order to meet his own goals of protecting the region surrounding his estates. Thus surviving fragments of evidence, pieced together, reveal a pattern of independent action by a variety of rebel nobles with regard to the fighting led by Condé; they also point toward some of the causes of that independence.

Other evidence of this kind further illuminates the conditions and consequences of these nobles' independence. The sire de Morvilliers, for example, participated in both the second and third wars. Though documentation concerning his role, particularly in the second conflict, is quite sketchy, it is certain that he was not present at the attempted seizure of the royal family at Meaux on September 26, 1567, which triggered the second war. As late as September 30 he was still in Boulogne, where he wrote an anxious letter to the Queen Mother concerning unrest in the region under his charge. This letter is significant not only because it documents Morvilliers's whereabouts at the outbreak of the war but also because it reveals his concern for his personal predicament.

> Madame, le service de vos majestés me donne une telle jalousie que je ne puis que me contrister grandement en une saison sy deplorée que celle que je vois presentement, car combien que depuis peu de jours il ayt pleu au Roy faire publier que tous ses subiets eussent à se contenir en repos et asseurance suivant ses edicts de la pacification, neanmoins soubs le bruict qui a couru de ce qu'n aulcunes villes de la Picardie on a apperceu que ceulx de la religion y ont esté tellement intimidés qu'ils en sont sortis à grandes troupes mesmes en abandonnant tous leurs biens. J'ay esté fort esbahy que plusieurs gentilhommes et aultres de ce pays se sont incontinent retirés devers moy en ceste ville avecq une telle desfiance qu'ils disoient estre prests de s'absencer et de se retirer arriere de ses quartiers à l'exemple des aultres. Mais considerant l'im-

portance que c'eust esté en ceste frontiere et sachant bien aussy l'intention de vos majestés n'estre aultre que de faire vivre chacun en paix et tranquilité, je les ay asseurés et retenus tous aupres de moy sans les laisser plus effrayer ny courir deça et dela, ce de quoy il ma semblé ne debvoir faillir de vous advertir incontinent par homme expres, tant pour ce que je scay bien quil y en a tousiours qui ne faillent poinct en tel temps de donner des advertissements à tors et à travers comme aussy pour entendre de vos majestés en quelle sorte je me debveray conduire parmy tels deportemens et avoir les moiens pour ce faire selon mon desir au gré et contentement et pour l'etablissement du service de vos dictes maiestés en ce lieu de frontiere, ainsy que j'ay donné charge à ce porteur de vous le desduire plus particulierement sy ainsy le vous plaist entendre pour y remedier, et actendant je y besogneray comme il fault.[19]

Madame, the service of your majesties incites such jealousy in me that I can but be greatly saddened at such a deplorable time as the present, because even though it pleased the King just a few days ago to decree that all his subjects should maintain themselves in peace and trust following his edicts of pacification, nevertheless following the rumors that have passed through some of the towns of Picardy some of the [Reformed] religion have been so intimidated that they have left in great numbers, abandoning all of their property. I have been greatly surprised that many gentlemen and others of this region have suddenly gathered around me in this town and they have such mistrust that they say they are ready to leave here and to gather [ready to fight] with others elsewhere. But knowing the significance this would have on this frontier and knowing well that the intention of your majesties is only to allow everyone to live in peace and tranquillity, I reassured them and kept them here with me and have not allowed them to alarm or rampage around the countryside, of which it seemed I ought not to fail to inform you immediately by this bearer [sent] expressly, as much because I know well that there are always those who do not fail to spread evil rumors as to hear from your majesties how I ought to manage amidst such misconduct and to have the means to do so according to my desire and will and for the establishment of the

19. BN, MS fr. 15543, fol. 16, Morvilliers to Catherine, 30 September 1567, Boulogne.

service of your said majesties in this frontier region, as I have told this bearer more fully to explain to you if it pleases you to listen to him so as to remedy the problem and, waiting, I will take care of things as necessary.

Clearly, Morvilliers is not ruling out the possibility of joining the rebellion against the crown. He has implicitly justified any action he may later take by invoking the fact that Huguenots in the area have been intimidated to the point of fleeing their homes, despite royal edicts prohibiting such persecution. This argument—self-defense in the face of ineffectual royal protection—was among those officially advanced by Condé and the rebel Huguenot leadership to justify their taking up of arms at various junctures. In the last section of the letter particularly, however, Morvilliers seems also to be eager to maintain the security of the Boulonnais during the period of unrest: he asks for advice and assistance in this task. His letter thus simultaneously justifies different outcomes—either of which, depending on the circumstances, will serve his interests. What is most important for our present purposes is that Morvilliers explains his predicament and justifies his actions to the crown directly and individually. This need and desire to defend himself independently to the crown reflects the same kind of independent stature which enabled Morvilliers to abandon the rebel force in 1562 when it suited him to do so—and, one might add, to join the rebel offensive in 1567 only when it suited him to do so.

Genlis's conduct in the second war is somewhat better documented than that of Morvilliers and exhibits a more explicit independence. Genlis was probably present with Condé's forces at the battle of St-Denis in November. But for the most part, his activity in the second war was confined to the Soissonais region, where he spearheaded an attempt to seize Soissons, Coucy, and Noyon. This strategy may or may not have been deliberately coordinated with the maneuvers of the main rebel force under Condé. The main force moved eastward through Brie and Champagne after the battle of St-Denis, then drifted slowly westward again after a rendezvous with German mercenaries in Lorraine. When the peace negotiations, which had been carried on since January, finally resulted in a treaty in March, this force was encamped in the Ile-de-France. The sources reveal that Genlis and the noble forces that fought with him negoti-

ated independently with the crown in early 1568 to bring an end to
the conflict in their region. Moreover, Genlis himself came to an
individual accommodation with the crown as early as February—
more than a month before other nobles who had fought with him in
the Soissonais agreed to terms.[20]

One such nobleman was Jean d'Aprement, sire de Vendy.
Vendy's name appears on the 1562 "Liste," though no details concerning his participation in that war appear to have survived. Theo-
dore de Bèze records that in the 1567–68 conflict Vendy was dele-
gated by Genlis to command Soissons after the town had been
seized.[21] Happily, a letter that Vendy sent to the king from Soissons
has survived. It is dated April 6, 1568:

> Sire, j'ay receu les lettres qu'il a pleu à vostre maiesté m'escrire, aus-
> quelles n'ay voullu faillir vous faire response qui est que j'ai tousiours
> faict pour le soullagement du pauvre peuple tout ce qui m'a esté possi-
> ble de sorte que je n'aye jamais pris un seul grain de bled sur eux mais
> seulement sur les ecclesiastiques, mais voyant que nous commancions
> à en avoir faute j'en ay pris trente ung muyd en la maison de monsieur
> d'Estré de quoy je suis obligé . . . quant aux vins nous en avons pris
> sur les villages mais non pas tant que nous n'en soyons demourés
> courts de quelque quantité, et neust esté les dernieres forces qui sont
> venues pardeça tout le pays estoit encore tres bien. Quant au comman-
> demant qu'il plaist à vostre majesté me faire de remettre ceste place
> entre les mains de monsieur de La Chappele je l'ay faict à la mesme
> heure, ensemble l'artillerie et munitions de guerre.[22]

> Sire, I have received your letters, to which I must answer that I have
> always done everything I could to ease the burden on the people
> hereabouts, the proof of which is that I did not take a single morsel of

20. De Thou mentions Genlis's presence among the Huguenot notables before
the battle occurred: *Histoire*, 5:360, 372–73. The campaigns in the Soissonais and
Noyonais are mentioned in a number of surviving letters from commanders in the
region to the king and to other nobles. See in particular BN, MS fr. 3628, fols. 20r-
v and 90–91, ? to Louis de Gonzague, duc de Nevers, 3 and 16 December 1567,
Paris. See also Bonnault d'Houët, "Genlis," pp. 40ff.

21. Théodore de Bèze, *Histoire ecclésiastique des églises reformées au royaume de
France*, ed. G. Baum and E. Cunitz, 3 vols. (Paris, 1883–89), 2:432.

22. BN, MS fr. 15545, fol. 121, sire de Vendy to Charles IX, 6 April 1568,
Soissons.

grain from them but instead took it only from churchmen. But then, seeing that we were beginning to run short, I did take 31 measures [muids] from the house of M. d'Estrée, for which I owe him. . . . As for wine, we did take some from the villages, but not so much that we were not still short of supply ourselves. And in any case, we were not the last troops to have traveled through the area, and it was in good condition when we left. As for your order to surrender Soissons to the sire de la Chapelle, I did so the moment I received it, along with the artillery and munitions that are here.

At the time this letter was written in April, Vendy's commander, Genlis, had long since made his separate peace with royal forces and had retired to his estates. Vendy had remained in Soissons through March, as negotiations for a general truce proceeded; then he had finally relinquished control of the town to the royal representative, the sire de la Chapelle. Yet, even though he had remained in arms until the general peace concluded by Condé's agents, Vendy can be regarded as an independent agent in the fighting. Rather like Morvilliers, he was addressed directly by the crown, and he replied directly.

The actual limits of Vendy's independence are further clarified by a second surviving letter by a royalist Picard, the sire de Chaulnes. Dated February 17 of the same year, this letter is a report to the duc d'Anjou, brother of the king and titular commander of royal forces, on conditions in the region. Chaulnes relates the decision made by many of the rebels to cease fighting, since Genlis has done so, and the decision of others to withdraw to Soissons. "These others," he says, "refuse to . . . take advantage of [this situation], wanting instead to hold out for the general peace which can be had from the King, and which the Prince [de Condé] is resolved upon." He continues:

Le sire de Vendy gouverneur de Soissons a envoyé devers ledict sieur prince et m'a promis ce pandant que luy ne ses gens n'entreprendront rien en tout le gouvernement de Picardie, et s'il y entreprend le dict sire de Genly m'a juré et affirmé que luy et ses gens ils leur coustera la vye ou ils l'empeschereont et romperons tous les passaiges de la riviere d'Oise qu'ils ne pourront passer que par Chaulny, Noyon et ceste ville de La Fère, et je les garderay bien de passer par ceste ville quil ne my couste la vye celluy qui est à Noyon pour le Roy ne fera moins et ledict sire de Genly m'ayant asseuré d'en faire autant à Chaulny.[23]

The sire de Vendy, governor of Soissons, has sent a message to the Prince, [but] he has nevertheless promised me that neither he nor his men will undertake any further action anywhere in Picardy. And the sire de Genlis has sworn and affirmed to me that if [Vendy] does undertake anything, it will cost them their lives; or, at least, he [Genlis] and his men will keep them from doing much, and we will cut all the passages over the river Oise, so that they would be able to cross the river only at Chauny, Noyon, or here, at La Fère. I will be guarding La Fère with my life, and the royal commander at Noyon will do no less, and the sire de Genlis has assured me that he will do the same at Chauny.

Clearly Vendy's position was weaker than Genlis's. This letter depicts Genlis's status as equal to that of the royal power in the area. Genlis is able to strike a bargain with the royal representative, Chaulnes. Moreover, it is plain that there is no higher authority operating in the region than the combined force of these men; together, Chaulnes and Genlis are the guarantors of the region's security. Indeed, Vendy was potentially threatened by his former ally, since Genlis, having abandoned the fight himself, seemingly would not permit him to continue the struggle. The significance of this letter, then, is that it suggests the vulnerability that could accompany the independence of a noble such as Vendy. Vendy could take refuge within the security of a general peace, yet he was not fully "protected" by this association with Condé's general strategy. He was still held accountable by the crown for his actions and he was still vulnerable to any action the local commanders, Chaulnes and Genlis, might take. Nevertheless, he had considerable room for maneuver. He assumes, and is assumed by others to have, the authority to act on his own. And his choices are not necessarily more predictable than Genlis's; Chaulnes and Genlis have to guard against the possibility that Vendy and his men may suddenly change tactics.

Vendy did in fact emerge from this conflict unmolested. Not all rebel nobles were so fortunate. De Thou provides an example in the

23. BN, MS fr. 15545, fol. 97, Louis d'Ongnies, sire de Chaulnes, to the duc d'Anjou, 27 February 1568, La Fère.

case of a gentleman named St-Etienne, who left the rebel force at Orléans in November 1562 and returned to his home in Champagne. According to De Thou, St-Etienne's local opponents suspected him of withdrawing only to carry on the fight at home. Soon after his arrival in Champagne, he was attacked at his home by a group of warriors attached to the duc de Nevers's Catholic force in the region.[24]

One minor noble who learned with finality the limits of Condé's protection was the sire de Cocqueville. In 1568 Cocqueville raised troops in the Amienois and Ponthieu for the Huguenot cause by the authority of Condé and Coligny. The recruits under Cocqueville later fell to pillaging and sacking towns and monasteries north and west of Amiens. Within a month, Cocqueville and three captains under his command were arrested and executed by a royal force sent to quash their campaign. What must be stressed here is that Coligny and Condé had, at least tacitly, authorized Cocqueville's gathering of troops in Picardy, but later disavowed his actions. Thus isolated, Cocqueville became easy prey.[25]

24. De Thou, *Histoire*, 5:272–73.

25. Cocqueville's campaign is recorded in the memoirs of François Rumet, a resident and one-time mayor of Abbeville: François Rumet, *Chronique du pays et comté de Ponthieu*, ed. Ernest Prarond (Paris, 1902), pp. 69–70. Rumet characterizes Cocqueville's troops as "huguenotes . . . ramassés de toutes nations" and at least 1,800 strong.

Haton describes the campaign in the greatest detail in *Mémoires*, 2:535–37. He claims that Cocqueville raised troops by the express authority of Coligny, who wanted to assemble a force to invade the Netherlands. Condé, "qui tacitement advouait cette entreprise . . . les fit séjourner [en Picardie]," while waiting for a royal answer to Huguenot complaints of Catholic behavior. When the crown did not seem pressed to reassure the Huguenots, Coligny wrote to Cocqueville, instructing him to remain in Picardy (until the domestic situation was resolved, Haton implies, in case Cocqueville's troops might be needed within the kingdom, rather than in Flanders). At this point, Cocqueville's troops began their rampage through the areas of Ponthieu and Vimeu.

Haton's reconstruction is not contradicted by any other source, though his rendition of Coligny's and Condé's involvement cannot be verified. What is clear is that Cocqueville's forces were not merely small, marauding bands: a special royal force, commanded by the prominent maréchal de Gonnor, was required finally to quash them. Also, the written accounts that have survived are distinctive for the *fear* with which they recount the campaign. Cocqueville's was a substantial body of troops, far exceeding in numbers the local Huguenots who joined it. One can infer, then, that Cocqueville's troops were assembled with time and planning. Such preparation would not have been possible without the assent of the Huguenot leaders. On the participation of local Huguenots in the campaign, see A. de Calonne, *Histoire de la ville d'Amiens*, 2 vols. (Paris and Amiens, 1899–1900), 2:45.

It is probable that the Huguenot leadership had been willing to tolerate, even to encourage, a certain amount of violent behavior on the part of such associates as Cocqueville. The months of supposed peace that separated the second and third civil wars in 1568 were hardly peaceful. Hundreds of surviving letters attest to the fact that, throughout France, it was a period of unrest and of recrimination by both Catholics and Huguenots. Cocqueville's troops—troops that Condé could easily justify to the crown as necessary for self-protection—were certainly not the only ones to remain armed during these months. Yet the limits of what the Huguenot leadership would sanction in its supporters' behavior seem to have been quickly reached in Cocqueville's case. The only sources that depict Cocqueville's actions are, typically, ones hostile not only to the Huguenot cause but also any disruption of provincial order. Consequently, Cocqueville's campaign in Picardy is condemned, fearfully, as a pointless rampage. In any case, Cocqueville's version of fighting could not be reconciled with the strategies of the powerful nobles under whose direction he had initially acted, and he was unable to defend himself once their approbation was withdrawn.

Further insight into the potential vulnerability of Condé's noble supporters is provided by Antoine de Croy, prince de Porcien. Porcien's case would seem, superficially, to be vastly different from that of Cocqueville, as Porcien was one of the more prominent nobles in the Huguenot entourage. He was descended from a family of great Burgundian advisers of the fifteenth century and was married to Condé's niece; a number of letters survive to attest to the involvement of the prince and princesse de Condé in the lives of Porcien and his young bride.[26] Further, he had been associated with the Huguenot leadership since taking part in the various conferences during the reign of François II at which the leaders had debated resistance to the Guise ascendancy at court.[27] In April 1562 Porcien attempted to seize Provins while the Huguenot force was establish-

26. Porcien was married to Catherine de Clèves, daughter of the duc de Nevers, Condé's brother-in-law. Condé had been closely associated with his sister Marguerite, duchesse de Nevers, and with her children since his youth. See below, chap. 3. Some distinctly familiar letters from Eléonore de Roye to Porcien and his wife survive from the 1560s: BN, MS fr. 3196, fols. 14, 21, 47, Eléonore de Roye to Porcien, 25 May 1563, St-Germain-en-Laye; 6 June 1563, Bois de Vincennes; 15 April 1564, Troyes.

27. J. Delaborde, "Antoine de Croy, prince de Porcien," *Bulletin de la société de l'histoire du protestantisme français* 18 (1869): 124–37.

ing itself in Orléans. It appears that in succeeding months he raised troops in the Ardennes region, near some of his lands. Later he helped to escort into France the German mercenaries whom the Huguenot leadership had hired. In December of that year, Porcien participated in the battle of Dreux with the main rebel force.[28] His activity becomes particularly interesting as the first war draws to a close in the spring of 1563. An unusual number of letters has survived from the years after the first war which document Porcien's activities and his relationships with other nobles. These letters reveal Porcien's vulnerability in his pursuit of independent violence and the repercussions of his behavior for Condé.

The first group of letters, from the spring and summer of 1563, reveal that Porcien had been assigned the task of escorting the German mercenaries out of the kingdom, now that the conflict had ended. Condé and the crown were arguing as to how the money to pay the *reiters* would be collected, but both were agreed that none would be given to the Germans until they had actually left French territory. Escorting the reiters, then, was clearly a thankless task. The letters reveal that Porcien had to cope with pressure from court as well as with the restiveness and belligerence of the reiters, who probably felt that it was only by continuously harassing the crown that they could hope ever to be paid. In a letter dated April 18, Condé dispatched Porcien to supervise the Germans' withdrawal; he and the Queen Mother had just learned that the reiters were stalled and were devastating the area around Fontainebleau. The Queen had commanded Condé to exert better control over his allies' departure.[29]

A second letter, dated May 12, reveals a more anxious Condé, fearful that his truce with the crown was being menaced by the continued restlessness of the reiters. Condé informs Porcien that the Queen is quite angry over news that the Germans are tarrying within France; in fact, Catherine will be sending her own dispatch to Porcien to express her dismay. This kind of continued disturbance could easily "reignite the war," Condé continues. Then he repeats to Porcien, in full and effusive detail, his instructions for encouraging

28. Haton, *Mémoires*, 1:27; De Thou, *Histoire*, 4:273, 462–63, 479.
29. BN, Colbert 24, fol. 223, Louis de Bourbon, prince de Condé, to Antoine de Croy, prince de Porcien, 18 April 1563, Chenonceau.

their former allies to quit the kingdom. Porcien is to remind them that they will be paid as soon as they have left France, and to assure them that Condé will always "use his good offices for them not only now but all his life, both in general and on individual occasions." He closes the letter with a rather anxious "hoping you will forget none of your duty. . . ."[30]

Yet another letter, three weeks later, is still more expansive in its instructions to Porcien. Condé describes at great length precisely how Porcien is to reassure the reiters' commander, Marshal von Hesse. It is clear that the atmosphere at court was becoming increasingly strained, at least in part because of this outstanding problem of the reiters. This strain is evinced by the unusual length and the agitated tone of Condé's instructions. However, the letter also provides more direct evidence of Condé's concern. The Prince asks Porcien to come to court just as soon as the reiters have been escorted across the border, bringing with him "good and honorable *compagnie*," in view of the "troubles" that were beginning to brew there.[31] This series of letters, in short, suggests the potential dependence of Condé on his associate Porcien. Condé's leverage at court depended in large measure on Catherine's ability to trust him; the good faith with which he executed the terms of the peace treaty, including the removal of the German forces, was at this point a crucial indicator of his trustworthiness. And Condé was clearly dependent on Porcien for the careful management of the reiters problem. Further, like other prominent nobles, Porcien enjoyed a certain independent status vis-à-vis the crown. Catherine communicated with Porcien directly concerning the reiters problem. Her letters to him are evidence of the crown's reliance on nobles of consequence for the management of such problems and of the rewards such service to the crown might bring the noble in question. In a letter dated May 31, for example, Catherine reminds Porcien that if he successfully completes this task, he will be rendering no small service to the King, "with whom I can assure you I will lend a hand so that he will be grateful to you when the occasion presents itself."[32]

---

30. Ibid., fol. 225, Condé to Porcien, 12 May 1563, St-Germain-en-Laye.
31. Ibid., fol. 229, Condé to Porcien, 4 June 1563, Bois de Vincennes.
32. Ibid., fol. 227, Catherine de Médicis to Porcien, 31 May 1563, Bois de Vincennes.

In short, she promises him an eventual reward for the task he is doing.

Of course, the same situation—the reiters problem—could quite easily become a source of pressure on Porcien. Porcien himself reveals the potential difficulties of his position in a letter to the Queen Mother, also dated May 31.[33] First, he refers to concrete problems he faces: the reiters have not, in fact, stopped foraging in the countryside for provisions, despite what other correspondents may have told the Queen. He has been unable to curtail their foraging because nothing has been provided for them—again contrary to what the Queen has been told by other officers. Porcien's next remark is the most revealing of the letter: he begs the Queen not to be angered by these occurrences. He insists that the retreat is proceeding more smoothly now than it was earlier, these incidents of foraging notwithstanding. He is clearly distressed by the possibility that the crown may hold him responsible for the disturbances the mercenaries are causing.

The relationship of Condé and Porcien, during these months of settlement following the first war, displayed characteristics of an association between two mutually dependent—if not mutually trusting—allies. Porcien acted as an independent agent in his handling of the reiters. His direct correspondence with the crown during these months is reminiscent of Morvilliers's correspondence from the Boulonnais. Yet, despite Condé's dependence on him, Porcien was easily threatened by his isolation from court and by the volatile nature of his task. Porcien's fears of isolation are further documented by additional surviving letters from these years following the first war. Several letters to Porcien from May and June 1563— particularly those written by Coligny and his brother Andelot—are remarkable for the copious reassurances they contain.[34] Another letter written in June is noteworthy because it was sent by a lesser nobleman whom Porcien had clearly solicited for reassurance and support. The aged gentleman replied to Porcien at great length,

33. BN, MS fr. 4682, fol. 54, Porcien to Catherine de Médicis, 31 May 1563, Montirauder.

34. See BN, MS fr. 3196, fol. 11, Gaspard de Châtillon, amiral de Coligny, to Porcien, 12 May 1563, n.p.; ibid., fol. 18, François de Châtillon, sire d'Andelot, to Porcien, 31 May 1563, Châtillon; ibid., fol. 19r–v, Coligny to Porcien, 6 June 1563, Châtillon.

referring to his long years of association with Porcien's father and to his esteem for Porcien himself; however, he excuses himself from active service to Porcien by invoking his ill health.[35] Potential isolation and vulnerability accompanied independence even for very prominent noblemen; Porcien was seeking moral and material support wherever it might be found.

Indeed, Condé's and Porcien's personal strategies became increasingly divergent as the months passed. In a group of letters written at the end of May, Porcien secretly warned the leaders at court that he had learned of "many enterprises" that threatened the Huguenots' security.[36] Catholic partisans, he believed, would soon attempt to murder the prominent Huguenots at court. Porcien warns Condé to "remain on his guard," to gather around him his most trusted associates, and to avoid exposing himself to danger by participating in an anticipated campaign against the English. Porcien's instructions to his personal messenger to the Prince include a plea that the Prince believe these warnings. Letters to Andelot and Coligny, accompanying his letter to Condé, repeat this plea; Porcien begs the two to persuade Condé of the truth of his information. Records of Condé's reactions to these warnings have not survived, though he did participate in the fighting against the English. In the succeeding months, he seems to have continued his strategy of containing his political activity within the nonviolent bounds of court life. By 1565 he had cultivated a less belligerent relationship with the major Catholic figure at court, the cardinal de Lorraine, and he had increased his personal fortune considerably by means of a second marriage.

Porcien, on the other hand, seems to have avoided the court and to have experimented with freelance insurgence. In the spring of 1564 the connétable de Montmorency informed Porcien, in a very authoritarian letter, that the Queen had heard that he and his brother had been assembling arms; he warned Porcien that they must immediately issue a denial.[37] Evidence of Porcien's restiveness two years

35. BN, MS fr. 3196, fol. 24, ? to Porcien, 16 June 1563, Paris.
36. BN, MS fr. 4682, fol. 54v, Porcien to Condé, 31 May 1563, Montirauder, copy; ibid., fol. 55, Porcien to Gaspard de Châtillon, amiral de Coligny, n.d., Montirauder, copy; ibid., fol. 55v, Porcien to Eléonore de Roye, princesse de Condé, n.d., Montirauder, copy; ibid., fol. 53, "Instructions à monsr. de Feuguères pour faire entendre à monsr. le prince de Condé," n.d., n.p., copy.
37. BN, MS fr. 3212, fol. 81, Anne, connétable de Montmorency, to Porcien, 31 March 1564, Troyes.

later, in May 1566, is provided by another censorious letter, this time from Jeanne d'Albret. Jeanne, married to Antoine de Bourbon, was Porcien's aunt by marriage. She was queen of the independent Pyrenean kingdom of Navarre and ruled over extensive seigneuries in southwestern France as well. She had openly embraced the Reformed faith in 1560. Since that time, she had struggled against her husband for the control of their son and heir (the future Henri IV), and had begun the difficult task of establishing the Reformed religion in her lands. Like any other great noble, she was concerned at all times to maintain a workable relationship with the crown. This had been a particularly difficult task for Jeanne in past years, as she was estranged from her husband, who was First Prince of the Blood and essential to the crown's strategies in dealing with the Huguenot minority.[38] When she wrote to her nephew in 1566, Jeanne admonished Porcien not to listen to the many rumors of supposed hostile activity by their opponents. She entreated him to "compose himself" and to behave in such a way that no one could harbor suspicion about him or his intentions.[39] The strategies of the more powerful—such as Jeanne, Montmorency, and Condé—dictated that they keep their distance from this restive young nobleman at this point, although Porcien was doing no more than Condé had already done and would do again: assembling a private military force.

II

The actual behavior of Condé and his "followers" during the outbreaks of violence in the 1560s, then, reveals that they pursued interdependent but far from identical courses of action. Clearly, the conventional schematization of the civil wars, which depicts distinct wars spanning clearly demarcated dates, distorts the actual participation of the nobility. That model in fact reflects only a portion of the actual conflicts that occurred—that portion in which rebel power, focused in the body of troops commanded by Condé, directly challenged royal forces. This schematization is self-reinforc-

38. Nancy Lyman Roelker, *Queen of Navarre: Jeanne d'Albret* (Cambridge, Mass., 1968), chaps. 5–8.
39. BN, MS fr. 3196, fol. 76, Jeanne d'Albret to Porcien, 28 May 1566, Paris.

ing to a large extent, in that the sources that describe the activity of
Condé and the Huguenot leadership are of course the best known.
The strategies of these leading nobles, then, seems to distinguish
them as leaders and policy makers from the hordes of their "followers." Yet the behavior of Genlis, Morvilliers, and even such
lesser nobles as Jumelles reveals them to have been policy makers as
well. Within certain limits and at certain times, each acted independently of the strategy represented by Condé. Indeed, as the examples of Cocqueville and Porcien suggest, it could well have been in
Condé's interest to maintain his own independence from his supposed supporters. The behavior of these "followers" during the
years of civil war indicates that Condé was an important focus of
their attention but hardly the only means by which these nobles
defined their political lives. Particular conditions and individual circumstances prescribed their association with him—but these very
structures also dictated the limits of that association.

These conditions included the nobles' desire to defend their own
estates and the surrounding territories. The sire de St-Simon's
concern for the security of the Provins region prompted him to try
to influence the Huguenot army's strategy in 1567. Further, it is
interesting to note, the sire de Genlis's campaign in the second war
was directed toward controlling the Noyonais and the Soissonais—
regions that encompassed his principal family landholdings. Such
efforts to protect and control local power bases were reflections of
that regionalized power, particularly in the case of the most prominent nobles, such as Genlis. This power is clearly visible in the
crown's need to rely both on the former rebel Genlis and on the
royalist Chaulnes to maintain peace in the region south of La Fère as
the "second" civil war drew to a close in 1568. The decentralized
pattern of provincial military government was reproduced during
these early civil wars; there was no effective provincial order for
royal purposes without the cooperation of such noblemen. Their
bargaining power with the crown was consequently very considerable. When Louis de Halluin, sire de Piennes, quit the rebel forces in
the summer of 1562, he returned to Picardy not merely unmolested
but also with a new command of a compagnie d'ordonnance in
hand. Once having rewarded him in this way, the crown had limited influence over him. Back in Picardy, Piennes and his followers
began to harass local enemies, and Catherine de Médicis wrote to

him, begging him to put a stop to it. The Queen reminds him of the good bargain he has struck. She asks him to help "fermer la bouche à tout le monde"—stop the complaints of those who disagreed with her decision to award him the company. In other words, she asks him not to make a fool of her.[40]

The means to subdue independent forces such as those of a Genlis or a Piennes did exist in theory. Each of these men held at least one fortified château to which he could withdraw. While these châteaux could withstand raiding parties, they could not hold out against a determined siege. In fact, the large armies that could now be fielded made the holding of a single fortified site virtually worthless for strategic purposes, since any single fortress could be merely out-flanked—in effect, a successful siege without the bother. Nobles' awareness of the uselessness of expensive heavy fortifications is re-flected in the kinds of renovation work they had carried out instead; when they undertook major work on their châteaux, they tended to scale down walls and keeps, build more comfortable residential rooms, and design open parks and gardens.[41] The nobles continued to use their homes as refuges, however, because the means to breach their protection existed only under extraordinary circumstances. The crown could manage to field large, effective fighting forces, but only occasionally and never—even then—in more than one or two regions simultaneously. The crown decided to make the extraordi-nary effort required to "secure" Picardy in 1568, when fighting, beginning what we have since termed the third civil war, broke out again. Particularly in the wake of simultaneous unrest in the Low Countries, the crown wanted to take no further chances with the security of this province, which was rich in agriculture, manufactur-ing, and commerce and was strategically vital as the northeastern border of the kingdom. In the years after this effort was mounted, royal control of the province broke apart again.[42]

40. BN, MS fr. 3187, fol. 30, Catherine de Médicis to Louis de Halluin, sire de Piennes, 20 October 1562, "camp devant Rouen."

41. J.-F. Fino, *Forteresses de la France médiévale* (Paris, 1977), chap. 5; Pierre Hé-liot, *Les Demeures seigneuriales dans la région picarde au moyen âge: Châteaux ou manoirs? Recueil des travaux offert à M. Clovis Brunel, extrait* (Paris, 1955); H. Dusevel et al., *Eglises, châteaux, beffrois et hôtels de ville les plus remarquables de la Picardie et de l'Artois,* 2 vols. (Amiens, 1846–49); Lefevre, *Senarpont et ses seigneurs* (Amiens, 1876); A. Challe, "Valléry," *Extrait de l'annuaire de l'Yonne* (1842), pp. 145–85.

42. The efforts to subdue the province in 1568–69 led by the maréchal de Cossé can be viewed through correspondence; for example: BN, MS fr. 3244, fols. 1ff,

An effort to account for this balance of power, as it might be called, requires an understanding of the resources with which nobles could wage war—and which the crown both had to rely on and fight against. We can glimpse some of these resources in the same documents that reveal their independent warmaking. One such resource was their very familiarity with the territories they tried to protect. Genlis's help in guarding the passages over the river Oise against the sire de Vendy was important to the crown partly because a certain number of detachments of troops were required to guard all possible crossings of the river. In the absence of modern communication and transportation, well-dispersed manpower was indispensable to guard a stretch of territory effectively. The security of the province during the Imperial Wars had been achieved by similar means—the scattering of many garrisons in towns and fortresses throughout the province. But equally important to Genlis's and Chaulnes's success in guarding the river was their knowledge of the river and how and where it could be crossed. As Condé's rebel force moved from region to region, it had to depend on local sympathizers for this kind of knowledge. Even in peacetime, noblemen regularly employed local guides when their travels took them into unfamiliar areas.[43] There were no maps, after all, to guide them.

Another resource commanded by provincial noblemen was manpower. Contemporaries' comments about troops associated with such men as Piennes and Genlis, as well as muster rolls of their companies of gendarmerie, indicate that the ordinance companies they commanded included a core of men with whom they had longstanding and ongoing relationships. Some of these men joined their commanders in war and followed them into their private truces. One-fourth of the men enrolled in Genlis's company at a routine muster held before the first war (February 1562) were still in the company almost three years later.[44] The historian De Thou specifi-

---

correspondence between Cossé and Jacques d'Humières, June 1568–March 1569. Cossé had briefly served as governor of the province before Condé had been appointed in 1561, but his own family's property was not in Picardy. He had served the crown as a negotiator in previous civil wars and hence undoubtedly appeared well suited to this delicate task.

43. AN, 90 AP 23, Mise extraordinaire de Monsieur et Madame de Mareuil, April 1567, St-Fargeau and Paris.

44. BN, MS fr. 25800, p. 72, "Rolle . . . de 30 lances des ordonnances . . . de M. de Genlis," 23 February 1562, Noyon; BN, Clair. 260, p. 1683, "Rolle . . . de 30 lances des ordonnances . . . de M. de Genlis," 26 November 1564, Péronne.

cally locates one of the officers of his company with Genlis in the rebel encampment in 1562—although, according to De Thou, Genlis was unable to persuade him to abandon the fight at the same time he chose to do so.

Understanding the power that enabled someone like Genlis to function as a fairly independent agent requires more than a mere list of the resources he could use, however. Simply to list "man-power" as one of Genlis's resources, without further scrutiny, would be to renew the error of accounting for Condé's power simply by listing the Picard troops who appeared beside him in battle. Some men may have joined the rebellion in 1562 with the notion that they were joining Genlis specifically, but that does not mean that their behavior was therefore predictable or that it can be described as an expression of "loyalty." One of the officers of his company, after all, remained with the rebel forces after Genlis himself decided to leave and despite Genlis's deliberate efforts to persuade him to withdraw. The men who first enrolled in Piennes's newly awarded company when he abandoned the rebellion in 1562 had themselves joined the rebellion, but had most likely fought alongside several other noble commanders within the larger rebel force. This circumstance is suggested in Catherine de Médicis's angry letter to Piennes after his return to Picardy.

> Monsieur de Piennes vous avez bien peu entendre que ce n'a pas esté sans mescontentement de beaucoup de personnes que je vous ay accordé la compaignye d'homme d'armes que je vous feis despecher dernierement que vous estiez icy de sorte que pour fermer la bouche à tout le monde il est necessaire que ceulx que vous recepvez pour estre de votre dict [sic] compaignie se comportent avec telle doulceur et modestie que l'on congnoisse plustost en eulx une repentance d'avoir porté les armes à la devotion de ceulx ausquels ils ont cy devant adherés et une prompte volonté de reparer ceste faulte par leurs bons services que ung desir de se vanger de ceulx desquels ils peuvent avoir esté en aucune chose offenséz pendant qu'ils estoient à Orléans.[45]

> Monsieur de Piennes, you know that it was not without the displeasure of many people that I awarded you a company of men at arms

45. BN, MS fr. 3187, fol. 30, Catherine de Médicis to Louis de Halluin, sire de Piennes, 20 October 1562, "camp devant Rouen," copy.

. . . to stop all complaints it is necessary that those whom you receive
to be in your said company behave with such calm and propriety that
one could recognize in them repentance for having carried arms in the
devotion of those to whom they have previously been attached and a
ready will to make up for this fault with eager service rather than a
desire for vengeance against those who may have offended them in
some way while they were at Orleans.

Many individuals, then, had made decisions about joining and
leaving the rebellion. The fact that they exercised these choices
means that they cannot be simply counted as Genlis's or Piennes's
followers any more than those greater nobles can be counted as
Condé's followers. Their behavior, like that of Piennes and Genlis,
requires further scrutiny. What assumptions about their behavior
underly these relationships, and the relationships among Genlis,
Piennes, and Condé, if those relationships could accommodate both
alliance and opposition? What could "devotion" mean in such circumstances? What were the rules or assumptions that governed such
behavior?

One element at the heart of this behavior was an acceptance of
both the right and the responsibility of self-defense. Evidence from
household inventories and inventories after death indicates that
prominent noblemen owned personal supplies of swords, daggers,
and firearms with which they could arm themselves and a handful of
other men to defend them at any time.[46] More modest nobles, such
as Jumelles, also provided themselves with the means to make war.
An unusually detailed record of an attempt to hold a fortified site in
1580 by Jumelles and a group of other Picard noblemen reveals that
they commandeered supplies in the surrounding area as a matter of
course. Sometimes they paid for the supplies, sometimes not. They
paid for horses that they took for their own use but commandeered
the labor of nearby villagers without recompense.[47] It would be
very interesting to have a precise understanding of their notions of

46. "Inventaire fait au château de Folleville . . .," 5–6 May 1571, Folleville, in
Recueil de documents inédits concernant la Picardie, ed. Victor de Beauvillé, 4 vols.
(Paris, 1860–82), 4:325; AN, 90 AP 23, "Inventaire de accoustremens et aultres
hardes de Monseigneur le prince dauphin [François de Bourbon-Montpensier] . . .
baillés en garde à . . . St-Fargeau," 26 September 1576, St-Fargeau.
47. BN, MS fr. 4047, fols. 94ff, "Registre des expeditions du conseil estably à La
Fère pour Msgr. le prince de Condé," May 1580, La Fère.

justice in these matters. Who deserved recompense, and for what? A similar sense of what was right and what was unacceptable governed the sire de Vendy's justifications of his actions in 1568. He and his men had taken grain and wine in the area around Soissons, he confessed to the crown, but "not so much that we were not still short of supply ourselves." His troops, he insisted, had not been responsible for the devastation of the countryside. Undoubtedly, what was felt to be just varied with the circumstances. We will recall that Vendy said that he owed the sire d'Estrées (a Huguenot, but one who had not rebelled against the crown) for grain he had taken from his house. A hostile Catholic noble, or one less powerful than the sire d'Estrées, might not have been treated with so much consideration. In any case, what is most significant about these rules is simply the fact that they existed. They reflected an assumption of a right to the means to undertake private war and individual self-defense.

Noblemen such as these might even traffic in arms. One middling nobleman, Pierre de St-Deliz, sire de Bernapré, accumulated forty-eight corselets and sixty morions (breastplates and crested helmets for infantrymen) in his rented house in Amiens, which he then sold to the commander of a royal infantry company. Men enrolled in the prestigious companies of the gendarmerie were required to arm themselves—with horse, sword, body armor, and whatever else was necessary. The commanders of other royally funded troops, such as infantry companies, were responsible for arming their men. Both cases represent a blend of private and public responsibility for warmaking, in which nobles' access to weapons is crucial. The private transaction between Bernapré and the infantry commander mimicks the practice by greater nobles of keeping personal stashes of weapons. In storing arms in their own households or in making sure of their access to provisions and armaments, they were expecting to fight and accepting the responsibility to do so. Indeed, the aldermen of Amiens, ignorant of the sale, expected that Bernapré would use his arms for his own purposes; while he was fighting with the Huguenot armies in 1562, they confiscated his stash of armor.[48]

Nobles' behavior in the civil wars, in short, reflects not merely a

48. AC Amiens, BB35, fols. 124v–126r, 8 October 1562.

material ability to act independently vis-à-vis royal authority but also an acceptance of warmaking as a legitimate and familiar activity. This does not mean that noblemen embarked on full-scale war against the crown lightly or casually. The kind of violence for which they were best prepared was small-scale and immediate; this fact, however, reveals the significance of violence for them. Violence was not simply an instrument to achieve a specific strategic goal; it had a broader and more elemental significance. Violence was also an essential prerogative, an attribute of their status, a form of behavior that delineated who they were. Consequently, noblemen did not always need to resort to actual physical combat to defend or aggrandize themselves.

The details of the disturbance that occurred in 1570 as the sire de Jumelles returned to Amiens from Huguenot worship are interesting in this regard. As Jumelles and a small entourage accompanying him passed through one of the city's gates, the townsmen on guard there took away their sidearms and shouted insults at Jumelles. Specifically, they mocked him by being too familiar with him, calling him something equivalent to "buddy" or "mate." They also directly insulted his stature as a warrior by calling him a name that meant "old foot soldier," with the connotation of "bum." Jumelles did not let this affront go unchallenged. Two or three of his men sought out a member of the town council and informed him that the sire de Jumelles demanded satisfaction for these insults. This councilman relayed this demand to the council the next day, and also reported on another disturbance that had taken place at the Huguenot worship site outside town. The councillors ordered, in response, that "by the sound of the horn" it would be proclaimed once again throughout the town that "it is prohibited to injure others either by deeds or by words."[49]

Another vivid example of reliance on posturing and on verbal self-defense occurred during the third civil war. In December 1568, in a letter to a kinsman, the Catholic duc de Montpensier, Condé relied on verbal posturing as a form of self-defense. One of his châteaux had just been stormed and its garrison massacred. The Prince wrote from his rebel encampment in western France, all of his estates now being in the hands of his enemies. He begins his letter with a de-

49. AC Amiens, BB39, fol. 172r–v, 13 November 1570.

scription of the rapes and murders that were said to have followed the taking of the château. He continues:

> Toutteffois, le lien dont je suis issu, la vertu qui m'a tousiours accompagnée et les moyens que par les armes dieu m'a mis en main m'asseurant qu'il n'est en la puissance de tous mes ennemys me rendre pauvre et souffreteux.

> However, the bond of which I am the issue, the virtue that has always accompanied me, and the means with which God has equipped me through arms assure me that it is not within the power of all my enemies together to reduce me to poverty and suffering.

Condé then offers a contrasting picture of the gracious and restrained manner in which he has treated the occupants of Champigny, a château belonging to the Duke which Condé's forces have just taken. He closes the letter:

> Vous pryant croyre que je ne faicts aulcun estat des revanches mantionnées en votre lettre, tant pour estre mesdicts maisons en telle disposition qu'il est mallaisé qu'elle puisse empirer, que pour estre dieu gracée [sic] de telle qualité et accompagné de tant de moyens qu'il a peu de personnes en France qui aye moins d'occasion de craindre et plus de commodité pour presenter et porter semblables menasses que moy.[50]

> Praying you to believe that I have taken no account of the revenges [on my property] mentioned in your letter, both because my said residences are in such condition that it would be hard for it to be worse and because I am by the grace of God of such quality and accompanied by such means that there are few people in France who have less reason to fear and more capacity to afford and bear such threats than I
> . . .

At the moment this letter was written, the Prince was in fact in the most vulnerable position he would be in at any time during the civil

---

50. BN, MS fr. 3950, fol. 39, Louis de Bourbon, prince de Condé, to Louis de Bourbon, duc de Montpensier, 8 December 1568, "camp à La Fontaine," copy.

wars. He relied on the currency of honor and on an effective verbal defense of that currency to sustain his power.

In both of these incidents, the noble involved defended himself with a particular posture, fashioned largely with words rather than with arms. Jumelles's need to defend himself with words is reflected in the fact that he could not allow mere words hurled at him by townspeople to pass unchallenged. In neither of these cases, of course, was physical violence actually an option. Jumelles had been disarmed and undoubtedly was vulnerable as a result; Condé could exact no revenge against Montpensier at the time he composed his letter, and both he and his kinsman knew it. Yet both Jumelles and Condé exerted considerable energy to demonstrate their power in symbolic terms. Jumelles confronted the town council and forced it to take action; Condé portrayed himself as the superior of his cousin in force and character. The appearance of power, and not merely actual violence, was important to them, but the two were tightly linked. In their projections of the image of power these men were defending their right to the power that they were trying thereby to assume. What Jumelles was defending was his right to arm himself, to travel about guarded by his followers—in short, his right to be the kind of person whose identity was constructed in part by the privilege of violence. It is this right that the townsmen challenged by insulting him with familiarity and calling him a common soldier. It is this right that Condé assumes when he declares that God has armed him, and that the ability to defend himself against his enemies is rooted in his identity—it issues from his virtue and from that of his forefathers.

Precisely why verbal sparring of the sort examined here was felt to be an effective means of self-assertion is a complex question, which will be considered further in later chapters. We can understand why and how words worked to accomplish these ends only by examining practices of speaking and relating to language in general terms. We may speculate here that Jumelles's and Condé's words worked because of an assumption about the nature of the person who uttered them. In a very real sense, their words were not claims to power but rather displays of power. They reflected a deep-seated assumption about the empowered identity of the person who uttered them; that person has power, hence his words have power. The fact that both men could choose words to defend themselves, in other words, betrays not a lack of power or a feeling of powerlessness but rather the presence of power in and the assumption of power by that person. Thus the sort of people these noblemen felt themselves to be lies at the heart of their familiarity with violence and their claim to the right to engage in it.

The pattern of violence during the early civil wars thus reflects the choices of many noblemen to pursue independent strategies of aggression and self-defense. Influencing their choices of where and how to act, and in concert with whom, were a variety of immediate circumstances, such as the amount of arms they could afford, the numbers of men they could pay, the momentary strength of their opposition. The readiness to choose armed conflict, however, existed independently of the specific circumstances that informed their choice on any given occasion. The choice of violence had not only strategic roots but profound psychological and social roots as well. The conduct of Jumelles and Condé reveals that belligerence and actual violence were acceptable and expected kinds of behavior. Hence their ready acceptance of violence not only was a readiness to act on other interests but represents an interest as well. We should thus expect other aspects of their public lives to reflect the sense of identity that their proclivity for violence reveals. In the following chapters we will analyze more closely noblemen's assumption of the right to an independent public posture and explore the flexible and very elastic ties to other noblemen which were based on this assumption.

— 3 —

The Exchange of Favor: The Claim to
Honor and the Meaning of Relationships

I

A BUNDANT evidence concerning nobles' relationships in times of
peace is provided by their surviving correspondence. Here we
see the jostling for favor and security, the workings of the so-called
patronage system in its routine and nonviolent guise. And these
relationships, like the behavior of nobles during the civil wars, are
strikingly at odds with the clientage model. Consider, for example,
this request from Jean, sire d'Humières, one of the chief Picard
commanders during the Imperial Wars, to François de Lorraine, duc
de Guise, sometime during the 1550s:

> Monsieur, j'ay sceu la mort du chancellier d'Allencon. Il avoit pleu à
> Madame luy bailler la tere de Remy tout tel droict que elle y avoit. . . .
> Vous scavez Monsieur que c'est la tere du monde qu'il me doyt le plus;
> sy s'etait le bon plesir de Madame de me baller le droict que avoit
> ledict chancelier je luy en suplie tres humblement. . . . J'espere aller en
> la court . . . . Je vous suplye Monsieur que sy quelcun le demande à
> madame retarder la chose jusque à ce que je soye la, ou sy venoit à
> propos qu'il vous plest en dire ung mot à madicte dame . . .[1]

Sir, I have learned of the death of the chancellor of Alençon. It had
pleased Madame to grant him the territory of Remy, with all the

---

1. BN, MS fr. 3155, fols. 51–52, Jean d'Humières to François de Lorraine, duc de
Guise, n.d., Compiègne.

rights she had there. . . . You know, sir, that it is the land in all the world I most deserve; if it is the good pleasure of Madame to grant me the rights the chancellor had, I will humbly ask this of her. . . . I hope to come to court. . . . I ask you, sir, that if anyone asks this of Madame, please put them off until I get there or if it is appropriate, say a word to Madame about it.

Although a patron–client tie seems to be revealed here, a second letter suggests that Humières was also closely tied to Guise's supposed rival, the Constable, Anne, duc de Montmorency. The Constable writes to Humières in 1552:

Suivant ce que je vous ay cy devant promis, j'ay eu si bonne souvenance de vous que le Roy à ma requeste vous a donné la charge de cinquante hommes d'armes. . . .[2]

According to what I have previously promised you, my consideration of you is such that the King, at my request, has granted you the charge of a company of fifty men-at-arms.

The surviving correspondence of Condé presents similar evidence of plural dependence and loyalty. One of Condé's letters to Guise during the 1550s includes this explicit request:

Monsieur ayant entendu par mon fraire d'Anguin les propos de la guerre qui se tiennent à la court j'ay despeché se gentilhomme expres acompaigné de cest[e] lectre pour vous supplier bien humblement me faire ce bien de dire au Roy et le supplier tres humblement de ma part que, veu que je n'ay encore compagn[ie] de sinquante hommes d'armes, il luy plaise me faire tant d'honneur de me vouloir donner deulx cens chevaulx legers . . . et vous supplier bien humblement monsieur que si c'est le bon plaisir du Roy de me le accorder de le me vouloir mander par ce porteur à celle fin que je y puisse prevoir faire belle compagnie, vous asseurant Monsieur me faisant tant de bien vous n'aures jamais [parent] qui mieulx vous hobeisse en tout ce quil vous plai[ra] me commander.[3]

2. BN, Clair. 341, fol. 135, Anne, duc de Montmorency, to Jean d'Humières, 13 November 1552, Châlons-sur-Marne, copy.
3. BN, Clair. 307, fol. 237, Louis de Bourbon, prince de Condé, to François de Lorraine, duc de Guise, 7 May 1551, Paris.

Having heard from my brother Enghien the proposals for war now being discussed at court, I have sent the present bearer directly to you with this letter in order to beg you most humbly to do me the good turn of telling the King and asking him most humbly on my behalf that, in view of the fact that I do not yet have a company of fifty men-at-arms, may it please him to do me such honor as to . . . give me two hundred light horse. . . . And I also ask you, sir, if it is the good pleasure of the King to give me this command, please send me news of it by this bearer, so that I will be able to raise a good company, assuring you, sir, that in doing this for me you will never have a relative who obeys you better in all that it pleases you to command me.

Yet this letter was written just before Condé's marriage to Eléonore de Roye, the grandniece of Anne, duc de Montmorency. Indeed, a letter from Condé to the Constable's wife a few years later (Condé's correspondence survives very scantily for these years) appears to support the view, shared by certain historians of the nobility, that the young Condé was in fact closely tied to the Montmorency family:

Madame, oultre le nombre infiny des anciennes obligations dont je vous suis de si long temps attenus, le bien que j'ay receu de l'augmentation de ma santé en ceste votre maison pour m'y estre trouvé beaucoup dispost et deliberé que je n'avois faict depuis ma maladie, estant mesmement à ce soir monté à cheval pour me promener et chasser dans votre parc, me faict davantaige accroistre et resentir le devoir et l'obeissance que je vous veulx toute ma vie porter.[4]

My lady, in addition to the infinite number of obligations through which I have been for so long tied to you, the benefit I have received from the improvement of my health in this, your house, now that I feel better disposed than I have since my illness began, having even this evening ridden and hunted in your park, makes the duty and

4. BN, MS fr. 20507, fol. 7, Louis de Bourbon, prince de Condé, to Madeleine de Savoie, duchesse de Montmorency, 26 June 1558, Fère-en-Tardenois. Two historians who have viewed the Condé-Montmorency tie in virtually mechanical terms, as a product of Condé's marriage, are Lucien Romier, *Les Origines politiques des guerres de religion*, 2 vols. (Paris, 1913–14), 1:78, and Eugène Saulnier, *Le Rôle politique du cardinal de Bourbon* (Paris, 1912), pp. 48ff.

obedience I want to show you all my life grow and be more deeply felt by me.

Such competing claims for attention and professions of loyalty indicate that Condé's—or Humières's—relationships with these two courtiers must have been limited and not mutually exclusive. Scrutiny of a large sample of nobles' correspondence sheds light on the nature of these limitations and loyalties by revealing general patterns of interaction. By considering collective evidence of nobles' behavior, indeed, we can move beyond questioning the clientage model to construct an alternative understanding of the social regulations that informed all interactions among nobles. The sample of correspondence used here includes approximately fifteen hundred letters written between 1525 and 1590. The majority were written by or addressed to Picard nobles and are concentrated between 1550 and 1570—the two decades that coincided with Condé's adult life. Also included in the sample were all available letters either by or to Condé and, in addition, a portion of the correspondence of members of his family and other leading families, such as Montmorency, Châtillon, Clèves, and Lorraine.

The most striking feature of this correspondence is not the appearance of certain individual transactions, such as those of Condé and Humières, but the very fact of transaction itself—transactions of all kinds. Letters between nobles are arenas for exchange. Their exchanges include courtesies as well as the seemingly more concrete favors—what is usually regarded as patronage. Exchanges of both kinds are vitally important to an understanding of nobles' relationships, and each demands scrutiny. The fact that so much space is devoted to ritual courtesy would alone require one to speculate about its significance. Routine acknowledgments of receipt of letters and professions of esteem and friendship crowd all correspondence, in addition to the ever-present formulaic salutations and other courtesies of address. Occasional entire letters are devoted to outpourings of esteem for the recipient. Or a letter accompanies a ritual gift, such as a rare foodstuff, a length of fine cloth, or ornamental or hunting birds. The sire de Genlis writes to Anne de Montmorency, for example, to present a gift of two hawks. A letter from Coligny to François, duc de Guise, stands in the stead of Coligny's intended gift; he explains that the fruit he had hoped to offer Guise had been ruined by rain.[5]

These exchanges cannot be dismissed as being merely the "style" of noble relationships, distinct from their "substance." It proves impossible, first of all, to make hard-and-fast distinctions between empty exchanges of words or objects and supposedly significant exchanges of loyalty or favor. "Meaningful" offerings of loyalty, for example, cannot readily be distinguished from "meaningless" ones in the give-and-take of nobles' letters. Formal courtesies and concrete favors were linked by the nobles themselves in that one was offered in exchange for the other. This equivalence is most obvious in the exchange of a profession of loyalty by a lesser noble-man for a favor received, of which Condé's letter to the duchesse de Montmorency is an example. But this kind of exchange is also an exchange on a simpler, more mechanical level; it is an exchange of words in return for an object (or something else tangible, in this case bed and board). Another example of such exchanges is provided by a letter from one nobleman to another in 1553, when both men were commanding large companies in defense of Picardy against Imperial troops. The letter writer justifies his hoarding of available man-power in his own sector of the fighting by presuming his colleague's acquiescence and his own eventual reciprocation of the favor; he closes the letter by stating, "I hope I can do a comparable favor for you someday."[6] These words, typical of many of the courtesies in nobles' correspondence, are an acknowledgment of a debit out-standing. Such references to a credit or debit outstanding—some family tie, some reserve of favor established by previous service, some reminder of unresolved obligation—ensured that communica-tion and exchange between the two correspondents must continue.[7] Courtesies in their letters functioned to nurture the link that the

5. MC, Correspondence L–I, fol. 178, François de Hangest, sire de Genlis, to Anne, duc de Montmorency, 28 February 15??, Genlis; BN, Clair. 344, fol. 210, Gaspard de Coligny to François de Lorraine, duc de Guise, 14 August 1551, Châtillon.

6. BN, MS fr. 3128, fol. 54, Robert de La Marck to Jean d'Humières, 25 June 1553, Hesdin.

7. Jeremy Boissevain has analyzed this credit-debit process, particularly as it operates in certain contemporary societies, in *Friends of Friends* (New York, 1974), especially pp. 159–62. The terms "credit" and "debit" are Boissevain's.

letter itself represented. The written words were a substitute and a supplement for what could be exchanged face to face. In a 1562 letter, the cardinal de Bourbon, Condé's brother, thanks the sire d'Humières for his cooperation in peacekeeping duties in the province during the year with a letter and a gift of fruit. He states that he is thanking Humières now by letter and with the gift, and that he will thank him further in person when they next see each other.[8]

Moreover, courtesy perpetuated exchange between nobles, not only by describing and acknowledging but also by creating credit and debit. Courtesy, in other words, was in itself substantive exchange. Gestures of courtesy and esteem—whether or not any object, such as a gift, changed hands—were exchanges of substance in that they were exchanges of recognition of status. Recognition was offered by the initiator of the contact, and was exchanged automatically, since the ability to bestow honor on another implied honorableness in oneself. The rush to offer congratulations to the duc de Guise, for example, which fill all nobles' letters to him in the months after his victory over the English at Calais in 1558, is explained in part by the reciprocity implicit in such acts of recognition.[9] To recognize Guise's stature publicly was to be actively associated with it. When honor was recognized with a ritual gift, we are left an even more visible record of the mutual sustenance of honor which was initiated; the worthiness of the giver is acknowledged through the graceful acceptance of the gift. The bishop of Amiens accompanies his gift of swans to the cardinal de Lorraine with the words "I hope these are accepted with the good feeling [bon coeur] with which they are offered."[10]

This continual exchange of recognition with others was fundamental to a noble's identity. It was a function of and a way of securing that identity. This accounts for the continual effort to nurture existing relationships through the exchange of courtesy which

8. BN, MS fr. 3187, fol. 28, Charles, cardinal de Bourbon, to Jacques d'Humières, 9 September 1562, Abbeville.

9. See, for example, BN, MS fr. 20645, fols. 16–17v, Jean d'Estouteville, sire de Villebon, to François de Lorraine, duc de Guise, 2 January 1558, Compiègne; ibid., fol. 28, Antoine de Bourbon, duc de Vendôme, to François de Lorraine, duc de Guise, 31 January 1558, Saintes. Cf. Roger Sablonier, "The Aragonese Royal Family around 1300," in *Interest and Emotion: Essays in the Study of Family and Kinship,* ed. Hans Medick and David Warren Sabean (Cambridge, 1984), p. 229.

10. BN, Dupuy 549, fol. 70, Antoine, cardinal de Créquy, to Colin, chanoine et trésorier de l'église de Reims, 2 August 1573, Amiens.

we see reflected in all of their letters. Letters also reveal the fear of losing contact; particularly when great or enforced distance separated them, a fear of being left out of the process of exchange surfaces in nobles' letters. Letters between commanders in the scattered northeastern fortresses in the 1550s were quite often pointed in their reminders of previous contact. One such commander wrote Guise in 1558 from Montreuil: "I am pleased that you received the packet of information I sent you and I hope that you and the King found things of use to you in it."[11] Antoine de Bourbon wrote Guise from another Picard stronghold in 1553 with even more directness and anxiety. "Please do me the good turn of sending me your news," he asks, "because this is the third letter I've written you without receiving any." "Waiting for news," he closes the letter.[12] A refrain of many letters from modest and great nobles alike is the direct and plaintive appeal "Send me news of yourself!"[13] And the writers express relief when contact is reestablished; when the cardinal de Bourbon was sent to pacify Amiens and Abbeville during the first civil war, he wrote gratefully to another local commander on whom he had to rely for information and military cooperation: "I have received your dispatches, which make me see that absence does not make you forget your friends."[14] When a noble facilitated contact by forwarding letters between two fellows, he invariably called attention to this service by formally describing his quite obvious action in a covering letter. The importance of maintaining contact made this brokerage service valued by his fellows and hence valuable to him as a source of credit.[15] Simple information about a

11. BN, MS fr. 20471, fol. 171, René, sire de Mailly, to François de Lorraine, duc de Guise, 10 October 1558, Montreuil.

12. BN, Clair. 346, fol. 282, Antoine de Bourbon, duc de Vendôme, to François de Lorraine, duc de Guise, 22 May 1553, Auxi-le-Château.

13. BN, MS fr. 3128, fol. 25, Odet, cardinal de Châtillon, to Adrien d'Humières, 22 February 1550; BN, MS fr. 3124, fol. 48, Louis de Bourbon, prince de Condé, to François de Clèves, duc de Nevers, n.d., Villers-Cotterêts.

14. BN, MS fr. 3187, fol. 25, Charles, cardinal de Bourbon, to Jacques d'Humières, 4 September 1562, Abbeville.

15. See, for example, Robert de La Marck to Jean d'Humières, BN, MS fr. 3128, fol. 48, 24 April 1553, Abbeville. Cf. Sharon Kettering, *Patrons, Brokers, and Clients in Seventeenth-Century France* (Oxford, 1986), chap. 2. In common with the brokers Kettering describes, these noblemen gained credit from the exchange, but also contributed their credit to the success of the exchange. Unlike the seventeenth-century examples, nobles' "brokerage" in these and other situations did not constitute a position occupied in a political system but rather a temporary *role*.

fellow noble could convey prestige; a nobleman relished being privy to important news, such as the outcomes of battles and the fates of participants. In Antoine's letter of congratulation to Guise after the victory at Calais, he boasts that he learned of the victory before the king himself. Writing on Christmas Day in 1562, the sire de Chaulnes methodically names for his correspondent the participants in the battle at Dreux.[16]

The exchange of courtesy which abounds in nobles' correspondence, then, was an expression of their need continually to be acknowledged as honorable by fellow nobles. Letters were a medium for the mutual recognition by which nobles defined and defended their inclusion in a privileged community. Every letter carried, on a routine and less strident level, the same kind of message that Condé had conveyed, in very dire circumstances, in his letter of 1568: "I am an honorable man, and proof of that lies in the very words with which I assert my honor." Further, these exchanges of words cannot be separated, or even wholly distinguished, from the exchange of tangible favors. The exchange of symbolic favor (courtesies and gifts) and the exchange of concrete favor (what is usually termed patronage) were not distinct from each other, since even simple recognition was substantive and, as such, could be offered in return for tangible reward. Patronage, therefore, was always part of a process of exchange: favor in return for recognition, favor in return for a promise of a future favor or of continued esteem. All professions of loyalty and friendship, all solicitations and grants of largesse were encompassed by this habit of exchange revealed in their letters—a habit structured by the demands of honor.

Historians' and anthropologists' studies of systems of honor in past and present European communities have suggested that while qualities attributed to honor vary from society to society, the processes of inclusion and exclusion of individuals from the group and the dynamics of social relations dependent on honor within all such societies are strikingly similar. Honor is accorded through the recognition of the community. The process of endowing persons with honor distinguishes members of a community from nonmembers: aristocrats from commoners, villagers from outsiders, one ethnic

16. BN, MS fr. 20645, fol. 28, Antoine de Bourbon, duc de Vendôme, to François de Lorraine, duc de Guise, 31 January 1558, Saintes; BN, MS fr. 3187, fol. 36, Louis d'Ongnies, sire de Chaulnes, to ?, 25 December 1562, Chaulnes.

group from another. Honor creates and binds together a privileged group; it classifies people for the purposes of the group.[17]

In effect, because it is a way of defining a community, the honor of an individual antedates the attributes of honor themselves. Attributes of honor, such as physical courage, are regarded in such societies as proofs of honor, not as its causes. It is the recognition of these proofs by the community—the visibility of honor—that counts. A principal motive of behavior, then, is not necessarily to do "objectively" honorable deeds but to have one's behavior judged honorable. The distinction is an important one; several implications that follow from it are reflected in the lives of sixteenth-century noblemen. One implication is that seemingly trivial, commonplace situations can become charged with the possibility of displaying or impugning honor. Another related implication central to the present analysis is that a member of a community of honor is preoccupied with the notice of his fellows. As one anthropologist puts it, "he is constantly 'on show,' he is forever courting the public opinion of his 'equals' so that they may pronounce him worthy."[18]

The language of credit and debit used in their letters reflects the fact that every instance of contact between noblemen was automatically a potential source of recognition or failure of recognition. Their letters are artificial arenas for exchange in many ways. However, the intertwining of courtesy and concrete favor in their letters suggests that in these highly stylized exchanges we can nevertheless glimpse the full range of lived relationships of which their letters are artifacts. Specifically, the importance and the variety of contact, the recognition and exchange of favors in their letters suggest that multiple relationships with fellow nobles were sought and continually nurtured as a matter of course. Men and women of the nobility worked to sustain broad and inclusive networks of relationships. These networks included blood relations and relations by marriage,

17. A useful survey of the operations of honor is J. G. Peristiany, ed., *Honour and Shame: The Values of Mediterranean Society* (London, 1965). Concerning the similarity of function of all systems of honor, see Julian Pitt-Rivers, "Honour and Social Status," in ibid., p. 21. The operation of honor codes among English gentry and nobility during this period is strikingly similar: see Mervyn James, "English Politics and the Concept of Honor," in *Society, Politics, and Culture* (Cambridge, 1986), pp. 308–414.

18. J. G. Peristiany, "Introduction," in ibid., p. 11. The intersubjective nature of honor in the sixteenth century is noted also by A. Jouanna, "La Notion d'honneur au XVIe siècle," *Revue d'histoire moderne et contemporaine* 15 (1968): 607.

members of the household where a noble passed his or her youth, fellow nobles in the region of his own estates or in the region of any governorship or captaincy he might assume.

II

From birth, a noble was enmeshed in an extensive web of family relationships. Of course, these people did not speak of or have a notion of the family in the same sense that we do. Several conceptions of the family operated simultaneously, and not necessarily consistently. The patriarchal family line was valued. Preserving the patrimony through judicious financial arrangements and through the birth of heirs was a major preoccupation of marriage agreements. Yet relationships between spouses and between parents and their children do not seem to have been distinguished by affective or material ties unique to them. Significant affective and practical ties were extended to a larger kin group as well, reflecting a somewhat competing sense of family as a horizontally structured group less connected to generations past and to come. The precise boundaries of these kin networks are not fully understood, though they were certainly far narrower than the extensive clans of the early medieval period, in which family identity extended laterally to distant cousins. There is some evidence that aunts, uncles, and first cousins, together with parents, constituted a particularly significant group in the sixteenth century.[19]

Certain evidence suggests that paternal relatives were particularly important. Robert Muchembled has noted the role of paternal male kin—father's brothers, nephews, and cousins—in the crucial work of arranging and witnessing marriages in minor noble families in Artois.[20] However, there are also many examples of noblewomen—mothers, sisters, aunts—arranging marriages and supervising the management of family resources. Noblewomen seem to have rou-

19. Natalie Z. Davis, "Ghosts, Kin, and Progeny: Some Features of Family Life in Early Modern France," *Daedalus* 6 (1977): 87–114; Robert Wheaton, "Introduction: Recent Trends in the Historical Study of the Family," in *Family and Sexuality in French History,* ed. Robert Wheaton and Tamara K. Hareven (Philadelphia, 1980), pp. 3–26.

20. R. Muchembled, "Famille, amour et mariage: Mentalités et comportements des nobles artésiens à l'époque de Philippe II," *Revue d'histoire moderne et contemporaine* 22 (1975): 247–55.

tinely overseen household accounts, dealt with creditors, and carried out transfers of property. Such activities make their involvement in major property settlements, such as marriages, both logical and understandable. In fact, male relatives' signatures on marriage contracts, which Muchembled finds significant, may obscure the participation of female kin.[21] In daily life, the activities of noble men and women overlapped; men as well as women helped to provision the household with foodstuffs and furnishings; women as well as men kept horses, went hunting, laid in supplies of gunpowder. In the large households of prominent families, women as well as their husbands might be served by young male pages, some of whom were their young kinsmen. Thus bonds of personal familiarity could form between aunts and nephews as well as between mothers, daughters, and nieces or fathers, sons, and nephews.[22]

Much, in short, is still unclear about the precise roles of close kin in each other's lives. Individual examples of relationships are difficult to interpret as a result. The fact of kin relationships—whatever the precise boundaries of such networks—is indisputable, however. The importance of ties between individual kin varied not only according to the personal familiarity that might develop between them but also according to positional factors: the sex of individuals and their position within the family; their stature outside the family; the existence of other relationships on which they might depend; the role they could play in larger family strategies. Some of the varied ways family relationships might operate, and both affect and be affected by a noble's wider acquaintance, can be glimpsed in the family of the prince de Condé.

Condé's father, Charles, duc de Vendôme, died in 1537, before Condé's seventh birthday. Though he was not a continuing personal presence in Condé's life, the legacy of the Duke's adult life was significant for all of his children. The Duke had pursued a career of

21. The wife of the sire de Jumelles, for example, sold *rentes* and supervised property divisions between their children: AD Somme, B69, fols. 4–5v, October 1585. Great noblewomen directly supervised household accounts, negotiated with creditors, and secured loans: see the activity of the marquise de Mezières in dealing with Parisian merchants, Min C XLIX-121, 1 June 1567.

22. The household accounts of the marquis and marquise de Mezières, their daughter Renée d'Anjou and her husband, François de Bourbon-Montpensier, reveal close connection and daily familiarity among ladies of the household, attendant noblemen, and young pages: AN, 90 AP 21-24. These records are discussed more fully in chap. 5.

often unglamorous but nevertheless unstinting military service which had enabled him to weather the crisis of the treason of his cousin, the connêtable de Bourbon.[23] His steady career meant that he was survived by several well-established relatives—among them his mother, Marie de Luxembourg; his brothers François, comte de St-Pol, and Louis, cardinal de Bourbon; and his sister Antoinette, duchesse de Guise—whose status could help ensure the security of his children.

Antoinette, duchesse de Guise, would be a lasting figure in Condé's world; in fact, she outlived most of her nieces and nephews and several of her own children, dying at the age of eighty-eight in 1583. Owing to the favor enjoyed by her husband and son, Antoinette was one of the preeminent noblewomen in the kingdom, and was a useful contact for any noble to cultivate. Not only was her influence continually solicited, but she was also kept well informed of news of wars, marriages, deaths, and personal affairs by her many acquaintances among the nobility. A letter from Robert de La Marck, duc de Bouillon, in 1551, for example, chats about war news and discusses another noblewoman to whom, he tells Antoinette, he is obliged for a favor—presumably in an effort to draw Antoinette's attention to her case.[24] Other surviving letters document her involvement with her Bourbon kin—her concern for their health, their financial affairs, their successes in battle. Her special efforts on behalf of one grandniece are very well documented. This young woman, Catherine de Clèves, had been orphaned by the early deaths of her father, François de Clèves, duc de Nevers (d. 1560), and her mother, Marguerite de Bourbon, Antoinette's niece and Condé's eldest sister (d. 1559). Marguerite's younger children were virtually adopted by various relatives after her death, and Antoinette assumed the protection of the teenaged Catherine. She later assumed responsibility for negotiating Catherine's marriage to the prince de Porcien and remained closely involved in the young couple's life.[25]

Condé's uncle François, comte de St-Pol, was a particularly important figure in the lives of Condé's brothers. François's elder brother, Charles, had inherited the duchy of Vendôme and the

---

23. Saulnier, *Cardinal de Bourbon*, pp. 2–3.
24. BN, MS fr. 20550, fol. 23, Robert de La Marck to Antoinette de Bourbon, duchesse de Guise, 25 May 1551, Sedan.
25. Jules Delaborde, "Antoine de Croy, prince de Porcien," *Bulletin de la société de l'histoire du protestantisme français* 18 (1869): 127.

Bourbon family holdings in Picardy; François had received his mother's inheritance of the county of St-Pol, in Artois. St-Pol had been the principal seigneurie of one branch of the Luxembourg family. It had been stipulated in the contract for the marriage of Marie de Luxembourg and François de Bourbon (d. 1495), parents of Charles and François and grandparents to Condé, that the second son of that marriage would inherit St-Pol and perpetuate the title in his line.[26] This son, François, duly was given the seigneurie at the time of his marriage. His household thereafter became a secondary focal point for his Bourbon kin, after Vendôme and the Picard seigneurie of La Fère, where Marie de Luxembourg had established her principal residence.[27] Two of François's nephews, Condé's older brothers François and Jean, lived in their uncle's household in their youth. And as the comte de St-Pol's marriage produced only one child, a daughter, one of these brothers was later married to his first cousin, François's child.[28]

Condé, the youngest son of the family, was not considered for these liaisons with his uncle and the St-Pol inheritance. Like all of his siblings, however, he was supported as a youth with small allotments of money from his parents' revenues. These allotments were probably supplemented by gifts from other relatives.[29] For example, their father's remaining brother, the immensely wealthy prelate Louis, cardinal de Bourbon, may have helped to support his nephews from time to time with proceeds of sales of some of his property. His wealth would directly benefit Condé when he was old enough to marry; the two major seigneuries settled on Condé at his marriage (1551), Condé-en-Brie and La Ferté-sous-Jouarre, had been in the family only a short time. Fortunately for Condé, however, in that time his uncle had substantially enlarged and remodeled the château at Condé for his own use.[30]

The stature of each of Condé's brothers and sisters was, in turn,

26. BN, MS fr. 4643, fols. 224–232v, "Contrat de mariage de Marie de Luxembourg et François de Bourbon," 8 September 1487, château de Ham.

27. M. Poissonier, "Marie de Luxembourg, dame de La Fère," *Société académique de Chauny* 6 (1900): 38–43; Saulnier, *Cardinal de Bourbon*, chap. 1.

28. Le duc d'Aumale, *Histoire des princes de Condé pendant les XVIe et XVIIe siècles*, 6 vols. (Paris, 1863), 1:19–20.

29. AN, KK 278, "Recette des terres du duc de Vendôme en Pays-Bas et Picardie, 1548–49," fols. 67–68, 11, 13, and 21.

30. Claude Haton, *Mémoires*, 2 vols. (Paris, 1857), 1:46; Saulnier, *Cardinal de Bourbon*, pp. 4–5; Xavier de Sade, "Le Château de Condé-en-Brie," *Vieilles Maisons françaises* 53 (July, 1972): 17.

an important element in determining the nature of their relationships with kin, including Condé. Simultaneously, it structured their relationships with outsiders.[31] Condé's own stature was enhanced as each of his siblings became, in the course of the 1540s, a recognized and distinct figure in the community of the nobility, exactly as his aunt and his uncles had become. Antoine, the eldest, was nearly nineteen years old when their father died in 1537; he was a young nobleman already engaged in routine competition with his fellows for recognition and reward. In succeeding years, like many young nobles, he brought himself credit through demonstrations of courage and resolution in battle. In 1548, his relations with his closest peers were punctuated by his success in winning the hand of the coveted heiress to the throne of Navarre, Jeanne d'Albret. He had been named governor of Picardy in 1537 and, particularly between 1548 and 1555, was fully involved in the defense of the province. This activity necessarily added a dimension of constant cooperation for the war effort to his relationships with prominent fellow nobles—Guise, Montmorency, Robert de La Marck, and others—with whom he already corresponded concerning more routine and personal matters.[32] Antoine's new stature undoubtedly was a factor in the marriage he was able to negotiate for his youngest brother in 1551. When Condé married the eldest daughter and principal heiress of Charles de Roye and Madeleine de Mailly—both of whom were themselves the last surviving members of old Picard families—the Bourbons established a firm link with the leading Montmorency family, as Madeleine de Mailly was one of the Constable's favorite nieces.

31. See the discussion of the interconnection of external status and family relationship in Medick and Sabean, "Interest and Emotion," in *Interest and Emotion*, pp. 15–18.

32. Numerous letters documenting Antoine's activities and his interaction with his fellows have survived. See, for example, some of the many letters from Antoine to Jean, sire d'Humières, in BN, MS fr. 3131: fol. 7, 11 January 1552, Coucy; fol. 25, 5 February 1551, Amiens; fol. 31, 10 August 1551, La Fère; fol. 35, 7 September 1551, Coucy. See also the regular war-related correspondence with Guise in BN, Clair. 346: fol. 279, 19 May 1553, Auxi-le-Château; fol. 282, 22 May 1553, Auxi-le-Château; fol. 284, 25 May 1553, camp de Dampierre. Among the more personal interchanges between Antoine and both Guise and Montmorency are BN, Clair. 346, fol. 315, Antoine to Guise, 14 June 1553, camp de Dampierre, and MC, Correspondence L-XVII, fols. 63–64, Antoine to Montmorency, 25 December 1551, Coucy. Concerning Antoine's marriage, see Nancy L. Roelker, *Queen of Navarre: Jeanne d'Albret* (Cambridge, Mass., 1968), pp. 71–75.

Between Antoine and Condé in age, their brother Charles was groomed for a career in the church and eventually succeeded their uncle Louis as cardinal de Bourbon. Circumstances dictated that Charles would develop a close association with his cousin Charles, cardinal de Lorraine, and would act as a broker for the interests of his own brothers and sisters with the powerful Lorraine. The two future cardinals had studied together for a number of years in preparation for their future positions. Lorraine, who would gain the cardinalate first because of his family's greater influence at the time, and who possessed a more forceful personality than Bourbon, would consistently be the more powerful of the two men.[33] Charles de Bourbon can be observed cultivating his ties with Lorraine in succeeding years. In 1551 he wrote to Guise, thanking the young duke for having been instrumental in procuring the cardinal's hat for him. Charles adds that he is sure that he received this honor "because of the great solicitousness and friendship [par la grande instance et amitié] that your brother, monsieur the cardinal, bears me."[34] He had also written to Guise (then duc d'Aumale) in the 1540s:

Monsieur, encores que je sache bien le plaisir qu'avez faict à mon frere d'Anguhien en l'affaire qu'il a pu pour monsieur le prince [de La Roche sur Yon] notre cousin, viengne d'ung naturel de vray frere parent et amy, toutteffoys pource qu'il m'a faict entendre s'en sentir grandemment vostre obligé et que ceste obligation m'est commune avecques luy, je n'ay voullu faillir vous remercie par ceste presente. . . .[35]

Monsieur, although I know very well that the pleasure you have given my brother Enghien in the affair concerning monsieur the prince [de la Roche sur Yon] our cousin comes naturally [from you] as a true

---

33. Concerning Charles de Bourbon's education and association with Lorraine, see Saulnier, *Cardinal de Bourbon*, especially pp. 5–7. Saulnier is the only historian of the Bourbon family to detail these Bourbon-Lorraine connections, and is one of the few historians of the nobility in general to give credence to the plurality of nobles' relationships.

34. BN, Clair. 345, fol. 137, Charles, (then) cardinal de Vendôme, to François de Lorraine, duc de Guise, 26 January 1555?, Montargis.

35. BN, MS fr. 20394, fol. 8, Charles, (then) cardinal de Vendôme, to François de Lorraine, (then) duc d'Aumale, n.d., n.p.

brother, relative, and friend, nevertheless because he has let me know that he feels himself greatly obliged to you and [because] I have this obligation in common with him, I did not want to fail to thank you with this present [letter]. . . .

The process of favor and obligation here linked three individuals, and Charles de Bourbon enhanced his credit by identifying himself with his brother's gratitude.

Jean, comte d'Enghien, was the remaining son of the family who lived into Condé's adulthood. He died at the battle of St-Quentin in 1557, shortly after his marriage to his cousin, the heiress of St-Pol.[36] Unlike his relationship to Antoine, particularly, Condé's ties to his brother Jean probably grew to include the companionship and trust that could come of familiarity. These two youngest sons of the family seem to have been frequently in each other's company during the 1550s. References to them in letters and memoirs show that they not only fought in the same regions concurrently but often in the same isolated actions against the enemy during the Imperial Wars.[37] Antoine and Condé, in contrast, had spent relatively little time together up to this point, separated as they were by twelve years in age. Moreover, their relationship may have been more distanced by Antoine's position as his father's heir and controller of family property. Even after Condé had reached adulthood and married in 1551, he and Antoine could only infrequently have been in physical proximity, since Condé fought in Italy for part of the period of Antoine's governorship of Picardy, and in Picardy when Antoine resided in the Albret estates in the south, for the most part, after 1555.

Relationships with cousins, uncles, aunts, siblings, and parents could thus vary greatly. Each was minimally shaped by the basic facts of blood relationship, family position, and the simultaneous existence of other relationships within and outside the family. The content of individual relationships among kin might vary, but the necessity for such links did not. A young noble entered a world

36. The fifth brother of the family—the second eldest, François—had also held the title comte d'Enghien. He had been killed at the battle of Cerisoles in 1544. It may have been this comte d'Enghien to which the preceding letter refers.

37. BN, MS fr. 20394, fol. 2, Louis de Bourbon, prince de Condé, to François de Lorraine, duc de Guise, 6 October 1551, Turin; Jacques-Auguste De Thou, *Histoire universelle*, 16 vols. (London, 1734), 2:137, 311–12, 588–89.

where reliance on a range of kin relationships was taken for granted. It is important to remember that this world was a concrete world—that the interactions across distances which are embodied and preserved in letters were not the normal arena for relationships. A young noble's first actual world was the household of his birth. Perhaps even more important to his socialization was the household where he was placed to be *nourri* (nourished). In these households, noble youths lived on familiar terms with other nobles of various ages and stature. It was here that they began the lifelong habit of cultivating relationships with a number of other nobles, both within and outside the family.

Before adolescence, a noble boy or girl would often be sent to live in another noble household for what was, for all intents and purposes, a period of apprenticeship in being noble. This household of *nourriture* might be that of a near or distant relative. Condé's brothers were sent to the household of their uncle at St-Pol, while Condé himself may have been placed in that of the Breton duc de Rohan, a distant relative by marriage.[38] The young men and women in these households would become familiars not only of the heads of the household but also of the other adults resident there—the five or ten men and women of varying noble ranks who routinely lived there. In addition, the youths would meet dozens of noble guests, each usually accompanied by a small number of hangers-on, who took meals at the château and stayed overnight from time to time. Such parties of guests could also meet up with the household when it was traveling, and accompany it along its route. During the day, a young nobleman always found himself in the company of others as he took part in the household's daily activities (most likely directly serving its head): when householders went hunting a young page might help to prepare his lord's equipment and ride alongside him; when members of the household journeyed to court, the page might pack his lord's belongings and travel with him there; wherever the lord might be, the youth could carry letters and messages to and fro at his request. At night, whether on the road or in a residence, these young men shared a single room and at times single beds, or shared a room with adult noblemen. Unless they were sent to carry letters some distance or to purchase some article or supply for the house-

38. Aumale, *Princes de Condé*, 1:19–20.

hold at a nearby market or town, neither they nor any other member of the household was ever without the company of a fellow.[39]

The experience of a young nobleman in another noble household would thus have introduced him to the demands and expectations of adult life, particularly to the public character of life and to the habit of cultivating many simultaneous, even intimate relationships. Relationships begun in a noble's youth might remain as touchstones of status and familiarity throughout later life. In a letter to Guise announcing the birth of his   son, Antoine de Bourbon expressed the hope that their young sons could be "nourished" together "as we were when we were young."[40] He thereby reinforced his tie with Guise in the present both by reminding him of their early association and by adding a potential further strand to that tie through the persons of their sons. The tie of nourriture is invoked in similar ways in a surviving letter to Condé's aunt Antoinette de Bourbon. One Marie d'Eternay, a Champenois noblewoman, wrote to Antoinette in 1551 to solicit a military post for her son. Marie mentions that she "was nourished" in the house of Antoinette's mother as one of several ways of identifying herself and recommending herself and her request to the Duchess. She closes the letter by invoking another, more immediate tie:

> J'en ay parlé [de cette requête] à Monsieur le bailly de Marle quy est de voz treshumbles serviteurs et luy ay prié vous en escripre pour la congnoissance qu'il a de moy ce qu'il m'a promys de faire.[41]

> I have spoken of this to monsieur the *bailli* of Marle, who is one of your most humble servants, and have asked him to write to you because of the knowledge he has of me, which he has promised to do.

Marie's letter suggests that the associations initiated during the period of nourriture would, at the very least, serve as continuous

---

39. This discussion of noble households draws on evidence presented more fully in chap. 5.

40. Cited in Alphonse de Ruble, *Le Mariage de Jeanne d'Albret* (Paris, 1877), p. 240, n. 3.

41. BN, MS fr. 20649, fol. 99, Marie d'Eternay to Antoinette de Bourbon, duchesse de Guise, 20 February 1551?, La Fère.

demarcations of one's identity and stature and potentially could later be cultivated for concrete support.

Like a noble's ties to his immediate family, the ties formed in the household were predetermined in the sense that all nobles experienced such interaction, but they were not predetermined in content. Nor were they at any time even *determined* in content. If Marie d'Eternay's request of Antoinette bore fruit (a matter that cannot be ascertained), then her ties to the Duchess would have been reinforced; the past family tie and her credit with the bailli would be legitimated and future exchange between the two women made more likely. A relationship changed value to the two participants with every transaction. The potential value of any relationship could also, of course, be affected by factors external to it. For example, Condé's personal credit was directly enhanced when his brother the comte d'Enghien died in 1557. Attention was focused on the Prince in a particularly dramatic fashion, since he had survived the battle in which Jean was killed, and was one of the few survivors not to be captured. Condé became the only remaining male in the family in lay life, after his brother Antoine. The credit of all three surviving brothers was greatly increased when their status as Princes of the Blood became important upon the accession of a minor king in 1559.[42] Antoine and Condé were catapulted into a closer interaction than they had ever previously experienced; in addition, their relationships with many of their fellows became more competitive. The competition with the Lorraine family, allegedly a cause of the civil wars that erupted within three years, did not develop until this point. This especially bitter competition was neither an inevitable nor a permanent characteristic of the relationships between the Bourbon and Lorraine family members. Condé, for example, lived less than seven years after the outbreak of the first civil war, yet his adversary relationship with members of the Lorraine family already may have begun to ease within that time. Certainly his brother the cardinal worked during these years to ease the tensions between them. In 1564, while Charles IX was making his long tour of the

42. See a helpful discussion of *crédit* by Kettering, *Patrons and Brokers*, pp. 43–44. In contrast to the subjects of Kettering's study, however, the term "credit" is not used by those sixteenth-century warriors themselves. See below, pp. 118–30, concerning nobles' terminology about their own relationships.

kingdom, it was reported to the court (then at Arles) that Condé and Lorraine had met with each other at Soissons and that, shortly thereafter, Condé had accepted the cardinal's invitation for a visit to one of the family's châteaux.[43] These amicable gestures would have been unthinkable had Lorraine or Condé felt and wished to display only bitterness or hostility. Condé's actions evince the possibility of a more accommodating relationship with his cousins. Relationships were always in flux, and events within and outside the relationship could alter their meaning.

Another of the prince de Condé's closest ties also reflected the continuous process of relationship. The tie in question is that between the Prince and his sister Marguerite, duchesse de Nevers, and her children. The letters exchanged between Condé and his wife and Marguerite and her family are among the most intimate and effusive in the entire sample of correspondence.[44] Marguerite's eldest son evidently considered—and considered seriously—joining Condé in rebellion in 1562, but was dissuaded from doing so by other, staunchly Catholic relatives and friends. This nephew died during the war. But after the war Condé was again closely associated with the family. In 1563, he and his brother the cardinal were helping their surviving nephew, now duc de Nevers, manage certain family debts.[45]

---

43. *Calendar of State Papers, Foreign Series*, 1564–65, 24 November 1564, 248, cited in Saulnier, *Cardinal de Bourbon*, pp. 48ff.

44. A number of surviving letters attest to the warmth of the tie between Condé and his oldest sister and her family. See BN, MS fr. 3124, fol. 47, Condé to Marguerite de Bourbon, duchesse de Nevers, n.d., n.p.; ibid., fol. 48, Condé to François de Clèves, duc de Nevers, 3 September 155?, Villers-Cotterêts; BN, MS fr. 3136, fol. 63, Condé to Marguerite de Bourbon, 30 August 1558, La Ferté. The particular quality of these letters raises the question of whether noblewomen, and hence female family members in general, were considered to be guardians of emotions and nurturers of bonds in ways that anticipate modern gender roles. We lack adequate evidence to sustain such an interpretation. See my forthcoming article on the importance of analyzing gender roles: "A Cannon in the House: Noble Women and Noble Men in Early Modern France." See also Muchembled, "Famille, amour et mariage," pp. 240–47.

45. BN, MS fr. 5121, fol. 86, Louis de Bourbon, prince de Condé, to Jacques de Clèves, duc de Nevers, 1563, n.p. The involvement of the Bourbon uncles is also revealed in the Nevers accounts: see Denis Crouzet, "Recherches sur la crise de l'aristocratie en France au XVIe siècle: Les Dettes de la maison de Nevers," *Histoire, économie et société* 1 (1982): 16.

Condé's relationships with the members of his family, though always potentially major sources of recognition and support, were fluid, as were all of his other relationships. A noble's family formed the core of a broad personal network of associations, but no clear line separated family from nonfamily relationships because of the breadth of kin networks. Marriage, blood relationship, and practical familiarity created complex and overlapping ties. Consider, for example, the kinship ties that Jeanne d'Albret invoked when she argued on behalf of her cousin Françoise de Rohan in a suit against the duc de Nemours. The Duke, Françoise claimed, had seduced her—and now, still unmarried, she was pregnant. In arguing that the matter should be handled by the Parlement of Paris and not by the King's council, Jeanne listed reasons why each member of the council should be disqualified from judging the matter—and she included her Bourbon brothers-in-law by reason of their kinship with Nemours. She noted that the Bourbons' grandmother and Nemours's grandfather had been sister and brother and hence the Bourbons and the duc de Nemours were second cousins; further, Eléonore de Roye, as it happened, was Nemours's first cousin. Finally, Jeanne mentioned that the Bourbons were first cousins to the cardinal de Lorraine, who was "an advocate in this matter on behalf of the seigneur de Nemours."[46]

This document does not, of course, prove that the Bourbon brothers in fact had any sympathy for Nemours's situation or were eager to defend him for that reason or any other. It is the almost mechanical reference to the kinship ties between Lorraine and the Bourbons, in fact, that leads us to suspect that Jeanne made this argument not because she wanted to disqualify her brothers-in-law, much less because she thought their actual relationship with Nemours made them suspect, but rather to help accomplish her larger goal of removing the case from the purview of the council—where voices likely to be sympathetic to her, and hence to Françoise, were outnumbered. This document outlines in a very straightforward fashion how relationships were expected to mobilize attention and obligation. Revealed here is the notion that kinship was, naturally, a tie of potential significance. The precise

46. BN, MS fr. 6606, fol. 31, "Recusation au Roy," n.d., n.p.

weight of a kin relationship—even a very distant one—could not be known, but the assumption in this document is that such a tie could at any time become active rather than merely potential.

It was not possible to fix the content of a relationship, nor was it ever possible to view one relationship in isolation from the others in a noble's life. If a noble's honor was supported and reflected by his relationships, then his identity as a nobleman was the product of all his relationships. A noble's various ties were a source of credit to be used in individual transactions. In her letter to Antoinette de Bourbon, Marie d'Eternay invoked her ties both to Antoinette's mother and to the bailli of Marle in order to press her request. Louis de Lannoy, sire de Morvilliers, was the probable author of a 1548 letter to Guise (then duc d'Aumale) in which several noble connections are invoked. He begins by saying that he accompanied the duc de Nevers to St-Dizier, in accordance with royal instructions, and there he learned that the appointments of all commanders in the frontier towns would have to be reconfirmed, owing to the death of François I. He asks Guise to make sure that his charge is renewed, and adds, "You know, my lord, that I was placed in this town [St-Dizier] through my lord your father." Then he mentions that he has spoken with Guise's sister about his request and that she has assured him that she will write to Guise herself so that everything will be taken care of.[47]

Relationships among nobles were thus nonexclusive; indeed, they were mutually inclusive. Nobles relied on a wide variety of ties among kin and acquaintances for recognition and support. Condé's simultaneous relationships with Guise and Montmorency are now more easily interpreted, since it is not necessary to view either set of contacts as an exclusive tie. Condé's relationships with these two men can be thought of as processes—processes not exclusive of each other or of the dozens of other contacts in Condé's daily life. Unfortunately, no correspondence between Condé and Montmorency has survived from the 1550s to suggest the tone of the relationship or the nature of the exchanges between them in the several years after Condé's marriage to the Constable's grandniece. But Condé's let-

47. BN, MS fr. 20548, fol. 68, Louis de Lannoy, sire de Morvilliers, to François de Lorraine, (then) duc d'Aumale, 12 April 1548, St-Dizier.

ters to Guise in the 1550s, it is clear, differ little from numerous other letters written to the Duke by other junior commanders during the Imperial Wars—all reporting military news and asking for the honor of further orders, all assuring Guise of their desire to serve and requesting a more prestigious command with which to do so. Peculiar to Condé's letters are his invocation of his own kinship tie to Guise (he and the Duke, it will be remembered, were first cousins) and an anxiety reflecting in part the insecurity of a young warrior concerned with establishing his reputation and the uncertainty of depending on the favor of so exalted a cousin.[48]

We can also notice noblemen continuously soliciting and receiving favors from their peers. Jean, sire d'Humières, was only one of the dozens of nobles whose solicitations of Guise and the Constable abound in archival collections. Yet as Humières wrote to them in the 1550s, he was also soliciting favors from other nobles. A letter of Antoine de Bourbon in 1552 indicates that Humières had asked a favor of him; "I have not forgotten," says Antoine, "to ask the King for the payment of your pension . . . knowing the expenses you are constrained to meet."[49] A year later, Gaspard de Coligny responded to Humières concerning a man under Coligny's command. Coligny states that he has received Humières's letter concerning "Capitaine Aginore and the post you wish to grant him." He continues:

Et vous asseure pour responce que ce m'est tousiours plaisir que ceulx que j'ay aupres de moy soyent pourveus de charges qui leur soyent honorables comme sera audict Aginore celle que luy baillez, pour laquelle je vous avoys aussi accorder le cap[i]t[aine] La Castelle, ne sachant que l'autre l'a voulust, et desirant à tous deux les veoir pourveus pour les avoir congneus tels qu'ils sont, c'est à vous de prendre celuy que vouldrez, car je vous ottroye d'aussy bon cueur l'ung que l'autre.[50]

48. BN, Clair. 307, fol. 237, 7 May 1551, Paris; BN, MS fr. 20460, fol. 51, 7 July 1551, n.p.; BN, MS fr. 20394, fol. 2, 6 October 1551, Turin, and fol. 3, 10 November 1551, Lyon; BN, Clair. 307, fol. 239, 20 November 1551, St-Denis; BN, MS fr. 20472, fol. 65, 16 July 1558, Roucy.

49. BN, MS fr. 3131, fol. 17, Antoine de Bourbon to Jean d'Humières, 27 January 1552, Corbie.

50. BN, MS fr. 3128, fol. 53, Gaspard de Châtillon, amiral de Coligny, to Jean d'Humières, 24 May 1553, Paris.

In reply, I assure you that it always pleases me that those I have close to me should be provided with posts that are honorable for them, as the one you are giving the said Aginore will be for him, [a post] for which I also granted you Captain La Castelle, not knowing that the other one wanted it, and wanting to see both of them provided for, knowing them both as I do, it is for you to take the one you want because I grant you either of them with equal good feeling.

In this exchange, couched in terms of accommodation and companionship, Coligny is attempting to ingratiate himself with Humières. Simple requests for information and assurances of goodwill are continually exchanged by Humières and dozens of fellow nobles. Typical is a letter to Humières's father from the cardinal de Châtillon in which he says that if he is forced to stay longer in Paris (where presumably he was conducting personal business), he will not do so without visiting the elder Humières.[51]

After such assurances of esteem, simple information was most commonly exchanged. When victory in battle enhances personal power, even the simplest information about the disposition of enemy forces is a vital resource. Nobles' letters are filled with appeals for military information. Where are the enemy's troops? Where are cannon and shot available? Are any major rivers running high and therefore impassable? Exchanges of this kind of information are common in Picard letters before 1559 and afterwards, during the civil wars, as are complaints, often anxious ones, when such information does not arrive.[52] The better informed a commander was, the more effective he could be and the more credit he could bring himself. More immediately, he could ensure his own security. In any case, the exchange of information reflects the very real power that local commanders could wield; routine provincial government and defense depended on the cooperation of widely scattered, necessarily independent noble warriors. A graphic demonstration of this reliance is provided by the sire de Genlis, who was assigned peace-

51. Ibid., fol. 24, Odet, cardinal de Châtillon, to Adrien d'Humières, 22 February 1550, Paris.

52. BN, MS fr. 4717, fol. 79, Louis d'Ongnies, sire de Chaulnes, to Jacques, sire d'Humières, 19 October 1567, Brussels; BN, MS fr. 3187, fol. 118, Antoine de Bayencourt, sire de Bouchavannes, to Jacques, sire d'Humières, 31 July 1568, Bouchavannes.

keeping duties within the province shortly after making a separate peace with the crown in 1568. His case has been a focus of attention because he had rebelled against the crown; his position of authority, however, was not unique. Hence, in times of peace as well, the king (or Catherine de Médicis) commonly communicated with local commanders directly, and those nobles, from men of the stature of Genlis and Humières to more modest commanders, addressed the crown without intermediary. One nobleman, stuck with an unenviable frontier command in the town of Ardres, writes to Catherine in 1567 to complain of neglect. Other town governors are receiving more recompense than he, yet "my devotion to the service of your majesties is not less than that of my companions," he says. A few days later, a captain of some troops at Abbeville writes to the Queen Mother, in the hope of joining the ranks of fortress governors. He has just heard of the death of the governor of Corbie; may he be given that command, so that he will be able to continue to serve the crown?[53]

III

By insisting on the mutuality and nonexclusivity of nobles' relationships, I am not attempting to deny the obvious—that some nobles enjoyed more power and controlled greater resources than others; nor would I deny that lesser nobles depended on their relationships with greater nobles for maintenance. Yet it is a fact that great noblemen, even the great Guise and Montmorency, did not control all resources. Nor did they monopolize credit. The constant transactions in nobles' correspondence reflected the fact that every noble enjoyed some credit because every noble was an honorable person. Indeed, whatever the material bases of their credit vis-à-vis each other or the crown, their ultimate source of credit lay in the power of their personal honor. This quality of honor was their guarantee to the right to behave as self-justified and autonomous political beings. The assumption of this right enabled even very petty nobles to feel themselves to be autonomous beings.

53. BN, MS fr. 23193, fol. 107, Jean du Bies to Catherine de Médicis, 6 February 1567, Ardres; ibid., fol. 125, "Capt. d'Esme" to Catherine de Médicis, 18 February 1567, Abbeville.

Of course, lesser noblemen did not consider themselves the equals in honor of their contemporaries Guise or Montmorency, any more than they were their equals in wealth. Notions of honor did function, in certain respects, to create and reinforce hierarchical relationships among nobles. The greater honor of some, such as Guise, reinforced hierarchical distinctions because it became a source of honor to others. Lesser noblemen could bask in Guise's honor, for example, by associating themselves with him, and thereby enhance their own. Fellow noblemen of relatively exalted rank could gain from Guise's honor by helping to create it. They could, as many did, acknowledge and admire his successes in battle, such as his victory at Calais; as we have seen, even mere knowledge of this victory was a source of prestige.

The reflected honor that rubbing shoulders with the great brought to a modest nobleman is visible in rare surviving memoirs as well as in letters. One Champenois nobleman wrote of his life of warring and service, some of which was passed in association with Condé's brother-in-law, the comte de La Rochefoucauld. This Jean de Mergey reveals his assumptions about how he gained honor by the way he describes his career for his sons. The narrative consists almost entirely of a series of incidents in which he interacted with or was somehow associated with such worthy superiors as La Rochefoucauld. Mergey eagerly describes their notice of him and even his physical proximity to them. He proudly describes his activities during the early days of the French forces' captivity after the defeat at St-Quentin (1557), for example, and his concern for the fate of the Count at the time. Much like Antoine a year later, proud of his knowledge of Guise's battle victory, Mergey records his desire to know about La Rochefoucauld's fate. Had the Count been wounded? Had he been captured as well? Mergey then records an occasion of service to the Count with particular pride, and hence in particular detail. After realizing that La Rochefoucauld was also among the prisoners, Mergey feigned not to recognize him—hoping, he says, to help the Count avoid being saddled with the onerous ransom appropriate to his rank. He then reports that the Count acknowledged this service to him by looking at Mergey—thus publicly recognizing him as well as the effort he had been making—and telling him that he (Mergey) no longer needed to pretend, that his own identity had already been discovered. Mergey later describes the task of bearing some of the captives' ransom requests back to the French court, where friends and relatives were to take charge of them. This kind of individual service is what he considers worth noting for his sons' benefit, and he records these small incidents of mingling with the great in some detail. He mentions, for example, that when he bore La Rochefoucauld's requests to the cardinal de Châtillon at court, the King was present in the room when he delivered them into the cardinal's hands.[54] Without articulating it, Mergey is expressing his belief that service to, even contact with, the great enhances his own stature. Each incident of contact was noteworthy, and intimate contact was particularly noteworthy. Hence he takes the time to record in great detail the prison-camp scene in which La Rochefoucauld thanks him for his efforts.

Similarly, we can feel the young Condé's desire, early in his career, to be sustained by attention from the duc de Guise. As a young man, the Prince was in fact a noble of relatively modest standing. His stature as a Prince of the Blood carried little weight as yet. Wishing to demonstrate his eagerness to serve Guise, in 1551 Condé writes a letter explaining his efforts:

Monsieur, quant je sceu qu'estiez party de la court pour vous en venir par deça, j'envoiay l'ung de mes gentilhommes expres pour vous trouver à Orléans ou il sceut qu'estiez passé le soir devant et en s'en revenant en ce lieu . . . il s'est blessé en sorte qu'il ne peust achever son voiage quy est cause que je vous renvoye ce gentilhomme expres lequel je vous suplye croire de ma part ce qu'il vous dira et me faire ce bien de me mander ce qu'il se faict et ayant votre advis je ne fauldray à me trouver la où vous serez pour faire service au Roy et à vous, vous asseurant monsieur que me faisant ce bien et plaisir comme m'avez par cy devant faict vous m'obligerez de plus en plus à vous obeir . . .

My lord, when I learned that you had left the court to come here [south into Italy], I sent one of my gentlemen expressly to find you . . . but he learned that he had missed you by a day, and on returning here he was injured, so that he could not successfully carry out his

54. Jean de Mergey, *Mémoires du sieur Jean de Mergey, gentilhomme champenois,* Collection universelle des mémoires particuliers relatifs à l'histoire de France (n.p., 1785–90), 40 (1788): 33–49.

charge; which is why I have sent the present gentleman expressly to you now, whom I pray you to believe when he speaks for me, and I pray you to do me the good turn of letting me know what I am to do, and when I have news from you I will not fail to journey to where you are, where I can serve the King and you. Assuring you, sir, that in doing me this good turn and pleasure, as you have done in the past, you will oblige me further and further to obey you . . .

Condé then adds an ingratiating holograph postscript to beat his message home. Once again he says, "I am [begging] you most humbly to do me the favor of letting me know what it pleases you that I should do, and to give me the means to serve the King and you."[55] The means to serve, the means to honor, come from the great. This and other letters begging for permission to join Guise wherever he is parallel Mergey's pride in all his intimate experiences with La Rochefoucauld; physical proximity was felt to be a powerful guarantor of a useful, nurturing relationship. This letter, like Mergey's narrative, demonstrates that putting oneself in a dependent and supplicating position—that is, adopting the role of *serviteur*—was not necessarily to be feared. Rather, it was a means to honor for the relatively humble. Many of the routine offerings of recognition in nobles' letters are acknowledgments of the greater honor of the recipients, but they are exchanges of honor nonetheless. Condé's willing humility to Guise is an admission of Guise's stature. In that letter, and in his letter cited earlier to the duchesse de Montmorency, Condé is bolstering his own honor by depicting himself in a relationship of service to them. He is trying to evoke, by means of words on a page, the same reassurance for himself that Mergey gained from a knowing gaze from La Rochefoucauld.

The language of humility and service which figures so prominently in nobles' correspondence, and which has loomed so large in historians' insistence on patronage hierarchies, thus did reflect a hierarchical aspect of nobles' relationships. But it was only one aspect of those relationships; it was not their sole structure. On the contrary, the operations of the noble's code of honor also nurtured antihierarchical assumptions and behavior. The hierarchical aspect of nobles' relationships always operated within a broader context.

55. BN, MS fr. 20470, fol. 51, Condé to Guise, 7 July 1551, n.p.

Put simply, no nobleman, however modest, would have confused his own identity or his own self-interest with that of a great nobleman he might serve, however much his own stature might be sustained by that relationship. The center of any nobleman's world had to be himself, and all of his relationships functioned to sustain and to nurture his identity. Mergey did not confuse La Rochefoucauld's interests with his own, however fruitful his relationship with the Count may have been. Indeed, he reveals his awareness that La Rochefoucauld, in turn, is motivated by his own self-interest. Near the end of his memoir, Mergey warns his children that there is much truth in the proverb that "the service of great lords does not make an inheritance" ("le service des seigneurs n'est pas heritage") and he adds his hope that they will be "happier than I have been in the recompense for their services" ("plus heureux que moy en la recompense de leurs services"). He concludes these remarks by relating the experience of another "serviteur" to La Rochefoucauld who one day overheard the Count speaking rather baldly with two of his brothers. One of the Count's brothers observed that it was better to "maintain [a serviteur] in hopefulness [entretenir en bonne esperance]" than to "do him good [luy (faire) du bien]," for, once rewarded, a man will leave your service. But if he hopes for future reward, "you will always retain him [vous le retenez tousjours]."[56] Mergey presents this story with no further editorializing as a warning to his children.

There is no doubt that Mergey held La Rochefoucauld in great esteem, yet he is equally frank about his expectations of his relationship with the Count. Relationships are to be reciprocal; lesser noblemen have the right to expect reward in return for service. Moreover, they must be, as Mergey is, conscious of the conflicting self-interest of greater and lesser nobles. Mergey certainly did not expect his honor or power to equal that of La Rochefoucauld, but he claimed both his personal honor and his material power by right. He did not confuse his recognition of the precedence of the great with his right to his due.

Frank statements such as Mergey's are rare in the surviving evidence available to us. Not surprisingly, the kind of tension that Mergey verbalizes is seldom expressed in letters. One exception to

56. Mergey, *Mémoires*, pp. 107–9.

this pattern is a letter from an aged warrior to the young prince de Porcien. The letter writer had served Porcien's father, it seems, and his letter to the young Porcien appears to have been in response to a request for renewed service of some kind while Porcien was occupied with the reiters problem.[57] The old man uses the occasion to remind the young prince of his ill health and of exactly how he came by it. He begins by thanking Porcien profusely for the attention Porcien's letter bestowed on him, saying, "I do not know how I can thank you humbly enough . . . except by doing you the most humble service I possibly can." Yet his following remarks put this "humility" in a particular light. Like Mergey, he is willing to acknowledge his superiors' status but is simultaneously determined to protect his own interests. He thanks Porcien for two pistols the Prince had sent him as a gift:

> Je ne dys pas que si elles pouvoient servir à combatre une goutte qui me travaille infiniement comme vous dira ce porteur . . . mais je ne l'assaulx que avec . . . ung cueur bien foible et bien failly. Ce sont les principaulx fruictz de mes labeurs passez à la fin desquelz je me treuve vieil, pauvre et goutteux.[58]

> I don't know whether they will be able to combat the gout that is afflicting me terribly, as the bearer of this letter will tell you . . . but I [can] fight it only with a weak and feeble heart. Such are the principal fruits of my past labors [that] I find myself old, poor, and gout-ridden.

We cannot identify this man, since the portion of the page bearing his signature has been torn away. But we can surmise that it was a combination of his advanced age and ill health and what must have been Porcien's insistent—even desperate—request (revealed by the unusually costly gift) that enabled the old man to feel empowered to refuse Porcien's request with so frank a statement. Poverty and gout were the fruits of his past service; undoubtedly he would agree with Mergey that the "service des seigneurs n'est pas heritage." Indepen-

---

57. See above, pp. 53–58.
58. BN, MS fr. 3192, fol. 24, ? to Antoine de Croy, prince de Porcien, 16 June 1563, Paris.

dence was forced on lesser noblemen sooner or later; it was as well that they behaved in the light of that reality.

One's stature depended on the favor of the great. But the relationship was always, in the end, an exchange—the honor of both was enhanced by the relationship. Mergey and others like him received symbolic and concrete favors, while La Rochefoucauld's esteem and power were enhanced by their service. Mergey and the anonymous old man perceived the exchange as such, and demanded that it be a fair one. A kind of moral economy couched their attitude toward material favor. Recompense for services was what the elder Mergey wanted, and the "means to serve the King" was what the young Condé wanted. The status of the inferior in the exchange was not felt to be wholly dependent on the superior's power, since certain rules were felt to govern what the superior did. Modest noblemen may have drawn more attention to the actual material support than would nobles from more prominent families, but "playing by the rules" was vitally important to all of them.

In a letter to the connêtable de Montmorency (then still a *maréchal*), Condé's father, Charles, duc de Vendôme, complained about a violation of the "rules" which had undermined his brother's stature. His brother (François, comte de St-Pol) had been invested with the guard of one of the towns on the northeast frontier, but had been ordered by Montmorency to surrender his command to another (unnamed) captain should the enemy arrive at the gates. Vendôme protested that having to abandon his command in that way would be a great "reproach" to his brother, and that it would appear as though "neither the King nor I hold him in [enough] esteem to give him the defense of a town." Vendôme reported that he had therefore taken it upon himself to send his brother with new instructions to return to the town, with full powers to defend it, "because not for anything would I wish him to be shamed." His concern for his brother was so great that he was moved to menace Montmorency with an unusually strong statement of anger: "I have always held you to be among my friends and among his, [and] I pray that for such a thing this friendship may not be broken."

The fates of family members, as we have seen, could be tightly linked, and Vendôme was undoubtedly interested in his brother's stature for that reason. Most interesting here, however, are the precise terms of his protest. Vendôme argues that this predicament will dishonor his brother because a larger group of noblemen has so judged the circumstances. He begins the letter by reporting that his brother has "remonstrated in the presence of all the captains and gentlemen who are here [that his predicament will shame him]," and he adds that "the gentlemen who are here have decided that it is neither honorable nor reasonable for him to abandon the said town."[59] The "rules" governing the maintenance of honor were the responsibility of the entire community. The recognition of the community established and defended the honor and stature of great and petty noblemen alike, and led all of them to seek reassurance and support.

The importance of this recognition to them is perhaps best seen in an instance when that recognition was withdrawn. An incident in Condé's own life—his condemnation following the failed Amboise conspiracy in 1560—reveals that the withdrawal of that recognition could be disastrous. Condé, it was widely believed, had been the real force behind the Amboise plot. He was lured to court with his brother Antoine in the autumn of that year, and was arrested there in the presence of the King on October 30. Rather than being tried by the Parlement of Paris—a right that Condé claimed as Prince of the Blood—he was hastily tried by the royal council, which was dominated by the Lorraine family. Their ascendancy at court had obviously been directly threatened by the conspiracy; predictably, Condé was found guilty of lèse-majesté by the council members. It was only the death of François II on December 6, ten days after the verdict was announced, that saved the Prince's life.[60]

The facts of his arrest, unorthodox trial, and condemnation— particularly when several other nobles visibly associated with the uprising were not punished—might be explained by Condé's peculiar vulnerability. Condé was vulnerable because no one stepped in to support him; no one publicly defended his honor against such an outrage. Certainly his wife and a number of others protested his

59. BN, MS fr. 3006, fol. 26, Charles de Bourbon, duc de Vendôme, to Anne, (then) comte de Montmorency, 1 October 15??, Abbeville.

60. On the Amboise conspiracy, see Henri Naef, *La Conjuration d'Amboise* (Paris, 1922), and the summary of subsequent research by Roelker, *Queen of Navarre*, pp. 140–41. Concerning the details of Condé's arrest and his claims to right of trial by the Parlement, see Michel de Castelnau, *Memoirs of the Reign of Francis II and Charles IX of France* (London, 1724), especially bk. 1.

arrest after the fact, but it seems that when Condé appeared before the King in October 1560, no peer stepped forward with a word or an act that would have reinforced his honor.[61] What kind of word or act would have been required? An answer can be found in a series of incidents that occurred some months later, early in the reign of Charles IX. Antoine had begun to contest Guise's control of certain prestigious posts that he wanted for himself. In the climate of bitter competition and uncertainty as the new minor king assumed the throne, a gesture of support for Antoine by a prominent fellow could be highly significant; Anne, connêtable de Montmorency, made a great show of supporting Antoine, not by echoing his demands for offices but by escorting him daily with armed retainers from Antoine's lodgings at court to the royal apartments—a distance of only two hundred yards.[62] Such a gesture of recognition and support might well have saved Condé from arrest in 1560. Once his honor had suffered the affront of arrest in the presence of the King and his peers, nothing could save him, even from the extraordinary step of execution—nothing short of the death of the King himself. He had been stripped of political legitimacy—that is, of his identity—by his peers' withdrawal of their recognition.

Great and petty nobles alike, then, struggled to maintain their status as honorable men. Their honor was their publicly accorded identity; it was not the sum of all of their honorable offices, commands, or moments of recognition, but rather the proof of that status embodied in those rewards and in that recognition. A man's honor could be lost—despite his past status or even his current behavior—if he was successfully challenged or insulted in public. And loss of honor, we see, meant possible annihilation. Hence Condé vigorously defended his honor as all material support was pulled away from him when he fled to western France in 1568; by stridently insisting on his honor, he was refusing to acknowledge the insults he was suffering at the hands of Catholic forces. When he was cornered in the King's presence in October 1560, in contrast, he was forced to witness his own loss of identity.[63] He had no means, in

61. Castelnau, *Memoirs*, p. 42.

62. Pierre La Place, *Commentaire de l'estat de la religion et la république*, in *Choix de chroniques et mémoires sur l'histoire de France*, ed. J. A. C. Buchon (Paris, 1836), p. 110.

63. See the discussion of public recognition and personal witness of honor in Pitt-Rivers, "Honour and Social Status," pp. 24–28.

those circumstances, to maintain his status. Constant competition for proofs of honor—for commands, pensions, "patronage"—was thus the rule for noblemen, for the stakes were very high; but it was a competition that noblemen claimed in a positive sense, *by right*. It is a self-consciously proud Mergey who declares that he knows great lords may try to short-change him; he knows what is his due. Competition for and dependence on largesse thus coexisted with and supported an identity as an autonomous political being. As these noblemen jostled for favor and reward, it was not with a feeling of limitation or powerlessness but rather with anticipation of responsibility and possibility.

– 4 –

The Power of Words: Oral Culture
and the Definition of Events

I

IT IS impossible to distinguish style and substance in nobles' letters; formulaic expression operated to convey meaning. Nobles' language is a highly revealing window into their world because, like all uses of language, it both reflected and shaped the speakers' experience. Our own culturally bound uses of language, however, predispose us either to misinterpret or to overlook the significance of their expression.

The window onto the society of the nobles which their letters provide reveals certain forms of expression to which they were accustomed. Nobles were accustomed to face-to-face communication, and the language with which they perceived and expressed knowledge about their world was still largely an oral one. Its oral quality is revealed, in part, by some of the characteristics of language use within the written sources that have survived to us. We have noted that nobles' letters begin and end with courtesies that serve to recognize the status of both sender and recipient. But the entire body of a noble's letter is formulaic in another sense as well: its language resonates with the formulaic and repetitive construction typical of orally based composition.

To persons whose principal experience of language is oral, words are irretrievable sounds rather than objects; they exist only at the moment of expression.[1] Consequently, oral expression is typically made up of formulaic clusters of words rather than of infinitely varying combinations of words. Variety is random, and random thoughts are irretrievable thoughts. Hence description, for example, tends to be epithetic. In the *Iliad* and the *Odyssey*—both orally based compositions—we meet "wise Nestor" and "clever Odysseus" and see the "rosy-fingered dawn." A few aggregates are possible—Odysseus may also occasionally be "courageous"—but only a few. Proverbs, somewhat larger formulaic units, are also characteristic of oral expression. The rhythmic structure and fixed content of such statements as "to err is human, to forgive, divine" make knowledge formulaic and hence assimilable.

Lengthy oral utterance, particularly, also relies on redundancy. In the absence of retrievable words, sense cannot be made out of a succession of thoughts—indeed, and perhaps most important, a sequence of thoughts cannot even be constructed—unless the memory of what has already been uttered is kept alive by repetition. Formulaic devices aid recall for both speaker and listener, and sheer copiousness is required, particularly by speakers, to keep the flow of thought and speech going while the next idea is fashioned. A consequent feature of much lengthy orally based composition is the grafting of subsequent, often unrelated, thoughts to previous ones; as an oral composition moves forward, it does so slowly, with much

---

1. What follows is a summary of Walter J. Ong's compilation of a number of scholars' work (most notably that of Milman Perry and Eric A. Havelock) on the characteristics of oral thought and expression. See *Orality and Literacy: The Technologizing of the Word* (London and New York, 1982), pp. 20–28, 36–41. Ong does not note that the example of "to err is human . . ." was coined by the very literate Alexander Pope, but he does account for this possibility in general, first by discussing some of the ways in which proverbs and other formulas are most likely to be preserved in literate thought, and then by pointing out that while such expressions may exist in literate thought (particularly in certain contexts), they abound in, indeed form the very "substance of," oral expression (p. 35). Fundamental to our understanding of oral culture is the work of many anthropologists and, more recently, sociolinguists who examine the structuring of speech in both literate and nonliterate societies. See Jack Goody, *The Domestication of the Savage Mind* (Cambridge, 1977); Del Hymes, *Foundations in Sociolinguistics: An Ethnographic Approach* (Philadelphia, 1974); Richard Bauman and Joel Sherzer, eds., *Explorations in the Ethnography of Speaking* (Cambridge, 1974). See also the remarks and suggestions for application of sociolinguistics to the study of early modern European society by Peter Burke, "Languages and Anti-Languages in Early Modern Italy," *History Workshop*, no. 11 (1981), pp. 24–32.

backlooping and with much addition, rather than tight subordination, of ideas to one another.

Virtually any surviving letter from a noble can provide examples of such formulaic composition. In a letter we have previously examined, the sire de Morvilliers writes to the crown on the eve of the second civil war to report that Huguenots around Boulogne are so frightened for their safety that they have abandoned their homes and are gathering in the town for protection. In the following portion of the letter, Morvilliers reports what he has tried to do to calm the situation and asks for counsel:

> . . . mais considerant l'importance que c'eust esté en ceste frontiere et sachant bien aussy l'intention de vos majestés n'estre aultre que de faire vivre chacun en paix et tranquilité, je les ay asseurés et retenus tous aupres de moy sans les laisser plus effrayer ny courir deça et dela, cè de quoy il m'a semblé ne debvoir faillir de vous advertir incontinent par homme expres, tant pour ce que je scay bien qu'il y en a tousiours qui ne faillent poinct en tel temps de donner des advertissements à tors et à travers, comme aussy pour entendre de vos majestés en quelle sorte je me debveray conduire parmy tels deportemens et avoir les moiens pour ce faire selon mon desir au gré et contentement et pour l'etablissement du service de vos dictes maiestés en ce lieu de frontiere, ainsy que j'ay donné charge à ce porteur de vous le desduire plus particulierement sy ainsy le vous plaist entendre pour y remedier.[2]

> . . . but knowing the significance this would have on this frontier and knowing well that the intention of your majesties is only to allow everyone to live in peace and tranquillity, I reassured them and kept them here with me and have not allowed them to alarm or rampage around the countryside, of which it seemed I ought not to fail to inform you immediately by this bearer [sent] expressly, as much because I know well that there are always those who do not fail to spread evil rumors as to hear from your majesties how I ought to manage amidst such misconduct and to have the means to do so according to my desire and will and for the establishment of the service of your said majesties in this frontier region, as I have told this bearer more fully to

2. BN, MS fr. 15543, fol. 16, Louis de Lannoy, sire de Morvilliers, to Catherine de Médicis, 30 September 1567, Boulogne.

explain to you if it pleases you to listen to him so as to remedy the problem.

We can note, first of all, that the text flows from one point to the next as one long utterance, relying, at times, on very awkward connections ("ce de quoy") to keep the stream of prose going. We must also note that the narrative is constructed with groups of words rather than words standing alone: "paix et tranquilité," "asseurés et retenus," "effrayer ny courir," "deça et dela." These word pairs facilitate composition and comprehension by slowing the pace at which the prose moves forward and by giving it a rhythmic structure.

Similar features distinguish another letter written in the same year by Condé, in his capacity as provincial governor, to the sire d'Humières:

> Monsieur de Humyeres pour ce qu'il plaist au Roy monseigneur que toutes les compagnies qui sont en mon gouvernement tiennent garnison trois mois durant apres la monstre faicte, et que je desire que la myenne qui est ordonnée à Péronne soit accommodée et de logis et de vivre je vous ay bien voulu escrire ce mot de lettre et par icelluy vous prier voulloir incontinant que l'aurez receue donner ordre de tellement faire renger et ressayer les gens de pie qui y sont que les gendarmes puissent avoir place pour eulx, leurs gens et chevaulx, et au demeurant quant aux vivres enjoindre aux habitans des villages circonvoisins d'en apporter si competenment que aucun n'ont occasion d'aller fourager, ausquelz touteffois vous mectrez tel et si raisonnable taux que ny le soldat ny le paysant aient cause de se plaindre, mais que estans les uns et les autres satisfaicts de gré à gré ils vivent ensemble avecques telle doulceur et gracieuseté que chacquun soit contant et la volonté de sa majesté observée et executée.[3]

Monsieur de Humyeres, because it pleases my lord the King that all the companies that are in my government remain in garrison for three months after having mustered and I desire that mine, which is ordered to Péronne, be accommodated in both lodging and provisions, I wanted to write you this letter and by means of it pray you kindly imme-

---

3. BN, MS fr. 3187, fol. 80, Louis de Bourbon, prince de Condé, to Jacques d'Humières, 23 May 1567, Paris.

diately upon receiving it to give the order to have the pikemen who are there marshaled and disposed in such a way that the gendarmes will be able to have room for themselves and their horses, and as for the rest concerning the provisions enjoin the inhabitants of the surrounding villages to furnish them sufficiently so that there will be no reason to have to go foraging, for which however you will put such a fair price that neither soldier nor peasant will have reason to complain but rather that being both satisfied they will live together with such calm and graciousness that each will be content and the will of his majesty will be observed and executed.

Again the narrative is constructed as a single sentence. Distinct subjects are arbitrarily connected by the use of "and" and by means of more elaborate devices ("et au demeurant quant aux vivres"). Although the narrative seems cumbersome to twentieth-century readers, the weighted and rhythmic phrasing breaks it into chunks that a listener can manage. The pairs of words—"renger et ressayer," "doulceur et gracieuseté," "observée et executée"—create moments of emphasis which make the meaning easier to absorb. Often, as comparison with a large sample of nobles' correspondence reveals, such expressions prove to be minor variations on themes. They are among a limited number of stock phrases, and minor variations on those phrases, which are endlessly called upon to assemble description. The king's will (or will and intention), for example, is invariably observed and executed (or observed and obeyed).

An earlier letter from Condé to Humières provides a brief but striking example of the copiousness and backlooping common in nobles' letters.

Monsieur de Humières j'ay receu la lettre que vous m'avez escrit [sic] touchant la visitation qu'avez faict faire des murailles de Péronne dont j'advertiray ses majestés et leur feray tenir le memoyre que m'avez envoyé de ladicte visitation affin d'en scavoir ce qu'il leur plaira en ordonner.[4]

Monsieur de Humières, I have received the letter that you wrote me concerning the visitation [inspection] that you have had carried out of

4. BN, MS fr. 3209, fol. 5, Condé to Humières, 22 April 1566, Anizy.

the town walls of Péronne, of which I will inform their majesties, and [I] will have them given the memoir that you sent me of the said visitation in order to know from them what it will please them to order [done].

Rather than say, "I received your letter," Condé adopts the more elaborate "I received the letter that you wrote me." Rather than break his narrative to begin a new sentence after referring to the subject of Humières's letter, he links this information with what follows with a prepositional phrase ("dont j'advertiray"). He then continues with a phrase that strikes the modern reader as unneeded and redundant: "and will have [their majesties] given the memoir that you sent me of the said visitation." The phrase "of the said visitation" seems doubly redundant, as Humières presumably knew which memoir he had sent, and there could hardly be any doubt about which visitation was being referred to. However unneeded such reminders may appear, the use of "ledict" and "ladict" is constant in their correspondence, and obviously felt natural to them. Such devices keep the listener/reader, a few clauses into the narrative, from losing track of what has gone before, and for the same reason are helpful to the writer himself.

The interpretive problem that these letters present is not a simple question of whether or to what degree these noblemen were literate. The majority of these nobles were probably literate in a restricted sense, in that they were able to read and to write in some measure—although the measure is very difficult to specify. Their literacy may be inferred from their ability to sign their names, as they nearly always do. The ability to sign one's name has been correlated with the ability to read and write in nineteenth-century populations, and is explained by reference to the educational practice of teaching writing (including one's signature, to which no special importance was attached) only after reading; since the same order for acquiring skills prevailed in early modern schooling, it has been argued, the correlation between signing and at least minimal literacy may hold true in those centuries as well. Even scholars who rely on the evidence of signatures, however, point out its limitations. Even in modern centuries, the lack of a signature obviously can mask a subject's reading ability. This is even more likely to be the case in the medieval and early modern periods, when dependence on quills (and, in the Middle Ages, on parchments) made writing a difficult and distinct skill.[5]

Signing may not be correlated with writing skills among noblemen in the sixteenth century for a further reason: a nobleman might have valued his signature for its own sake and learned to produce it early on. Whereas a tailor, for example, could inscribe a rendering of scissors or a spool of thread in place of a signature, only a name could fill the same function for a nobleman. The power that these nobles claimed for themselves lay, simply and wholly, in their personal identity. A signature served to transmit, in writing, the power-through-identity so basic to their function.[6] Indeed, the very appearance of many handwritten postscripts and holograph letters reveals that skill with the pen varied considerably among nobles. Some holograph letters, for example, reveal the author's discomfort with the task of writing. Not only is spelling wildly erratic (far more so than was common even then) but the formation of the letters is also varied and irregular. Splotches of ink reveal lack of practice with the quill. Moreover, the words and lines on the page also lack uniformity; the lines of words rise at odd angles across the page. In general, there seems to be little relationship between the physical unit of the page and the words destined to appear on it.

Yet if some nobles seemed unaccustomed to writing, for others it seems to have been quite routine. The handwriting and composition of some letters are quite polished, and we have other evidence that a few noblemen—the sire de Gouberville is the best known—wrote methodically, every day, in *livres de raison*. We can assume that writing was a fairly routine undertaking for Louis de Lannoy, sire

5. On the use of signatures as an indication of literacy, see R. S. Schofield, "The Measurement of Literacy in Pre-Industrial England," in *Literacy in Traditional Societies*, ed. Jack Goody (Cambridge, 1968), pp. 311–25; François Furet and Jacques Ozouf, *Reading and Writing: Literacy in France from Calvin to Jules Ferry* (Cambridge and Paris, 1982), pp. 11–17; David Cressy, *Literacy and the Social Order: Reading and Writing in Tudor and Stuart England* (Cambridge, 1980), pp. 25–34, 54–55. For reservations concerning the limitations of signature evidence, see especially Schofield, "Measurement of Literacy," and Harvey J. Graff, *The Legacies of Literacy: Continuities and Contradictions in Western Culture and Society* (Bloomington, Ind., 1987), pp. 34–35.

6. For an interesting discussion of the importance of social and political contexts in shaping the significance of signatures, see Roger Chartier, Marie-Madeleine Compère, and Dominique Julia, *L'Education en France du XVIe au XVIIIe siècle* (Paris, 1976), pp. 87–89.

de Morvilliers, for among the contents of his château at Folleville were a portable writing desk and a supply of paper, ink, and sand; found in the desk at the time of the inventory after his death were several receipts Morvilliers had made out acknowledging his quarterly pension from the king as governor of Boulogne.[7] Writing was most certainly routine for another nobleman of similar stature, the comte de Châteauvillain, who commanded the town of that name near Chaumont, under the aegis of Louis de Gonzague, duc de Nevers. A description of the Count actually writing survives, oddly enough, in an account of his murder at the hands of a rival nobleman who coveted the Count's position.[8] A narration of the events compiled afterward by investigators recounts that the murderer, the sire de Meuse, began by lavishly entertaining the Count in order to build trust between them. Later, hoping to lure the Count alone into a chamber where he and his familiars would be waiting, Meuse one day sent one of his men to tell the Count that he was about to leave for Châlons, and that if the Count wanted to send any letters there, he would gladly carry them. "Immediately, the Count wrote" ("aussitot ledict sire comte escript"), the report of the murder records. The Count then told the man who had come to him that he would carry his letters to Meuse himself, in order to take his leave of Meuse before his departure. The Count thus walked spontaneously and alone into Meuse's room, and was stabbed to death by the men waiting there.

This story reveals the businesslike way in which the Count set himself to a task of writing. And the assumptions his murderer made about his behavior reveal facets of the larger patterns of communication among nobles. In plotting his act, the murderer planned on two things: that the Count would seize an opportunity to communicate with others via a reliable courier and that he would want to say good-bye to his "friend" face to face. From the story of his murder we learn both that the comte de Châteauvillain has mastered the art of writing to an impressive degree and also that he chooses face-to-face communication in certain circumstances. We would like to know more about those circumstances and what they mean.

7. "Inventaire fait au château de Folleville . . . ," 5–6 May 1571, Folleville, in *Recueil de documents inédits concernant la Picardie*, ed. Victor de Beauvillé, 4 vols. (Paris, 1860–82), 4:324–36.

8. BN, MS fr. 3632, fol. 1, "Discours sur la mort de feu Monsieur le comte de Chasteauvillain," n.d., n.p.

The interpretive issue is not simply the matter of measuring nobles' literacy—which is itself elusive—but rather of understanding their uses of literacy.

Recent studies of literacy in Europe over a number of centuries have shifted away from the notion that we can profitably study literacy by simply quantifying it; the reification of literacy which is implied by such studies distorts the actual meaning of literacy skills in any given context and oversimplifies the processes of historical change. "Literacy" becomes an agent, separate from human beings' experience of it. (And "orality," similarly overgeneralized, becomes a prison.) Historians' attention is now more profitably focused on the social, political, and cultural significances of particular historical uses of literacy skills.[9] Scholars have worked to appreciate the complex significance of both literate culture and the contemporaneous oral culture in which it was embedded—particularly in the medieval and early modern periods—and, further, the overlap and interaction between the two. Issues being considered currently include that of the cultural power of differing kinds of knowledge: the power of the literate state to enforce its modes of religious behavior or notions of community on a still oral populace, for example. On the other hand, historians have also documented the resilience of oral habits of exchanging and verifying knowledge—such as the collective "reading" of early printed books by oral-aural transmission in traditional group settings.[10] Central to the present discussion is the very rich and complex issue of the consequences for thought, expression, and social life of the different modes of communication. Dependence on oral communication fosters distinct habits of perception and be-

9. See Graff, *Legacies of Literacy*, for extended discussion of scholarship on the meanings of literacy and the "Introduction" to his *Literacy and Social Development in the West* (Cambridge, 1981).

10. Natalie Z. Davis, "Printing and the People," in *Society and Culture in Early Modern France* (Stanford, 1975), pp. 189–226; Carlo Ginzburg, *The Cheese and the Worms: The Cosmos of a Sixteenth-Century Miller* (New York, 1982); Robert Scribner, "Oral Culture and the Diffusion of Reformation Ideas," *History of European Ideas* 5 (1984): 236–54; Roger Chartier, "Culture as Appropriation: Popular Cultural Uses in Early Modern France," in *Understanding Popular Culture*, ed. Steven L. Kaplan (Berlin, 1984), pp. 229–54; David Warren Sabean, *Power in the Blood: Popular Culture and Village Discourse in Early Modern Germany* (Cambridge, 1984). Such evidence as we have of book ownership by nobles must be interpreted in this light. See the summary of research by Roger Chartier, "Le Pratique de l'écrit," in *Histoire de la vie privée*, ed. Philippe Ariès and Georges Duby, 3 vols. (Paris, 1986), vol. 3, *De la Renaissance aux Lumières*, ed. Chartier, pp. 126–31.

havior. It is precisely the many historical intersections of these habits with the uses of literacy which pose the greatest challenges for social historians—especially, perhaps, to our understanding of the development of the early modern state.

A study by M. T. Clanchy examines the growth of record keeping and reliance on written documentation in lay society in Norman-Angevin England.[11] From the eleventh to the fourteenth centuries, he argues, the very meaning of the word "record" shifted from denoting oral testimony of living witnesses to the authority of a written document. Written "records" replaced oral testimony in a variety of official situations. Previously witnesses were charged with hearing the utterance of a last will and testament; now they were charged merely with "witnessing" a signature. In general, a proliferation of royal document making engendered a growth of literacy and, more important, a reliance on documents by gentry and peasantry alike. When Magna Carta was granted, for example, the barons insisted that copies of the charter be kept in various locations throughout the kingdom. Control of collective memory was being achieved by means of control of a written text.

Yet alongside this developing trust of the written word persisted reliance on hearing and speaking. Clanchy argues that most English knights could read and write, but did not need literacy in order to master the vast majority of their life skills or to carry out their usual activities. During the period he examines, writing remained an arduous and uncommon physical task, and reading, in practice, still meant being read to; even though information might come from a (trusted) written piece, it was absorbed by hearing and not by sight. Moreover, documents themselves were often used in ways that might surprise historians of the present, who gratefully pounce on written evidence for the words that are captured there. The actual words inscribed on a parchment—say, on a title to land—may have been less important than the symbolic value of the object itself; the beautifully crafted parchment to which a large wax seal was affixed was exchanged as a symbol of ownership—functioning exactly as had early medieval tokens of ownership, Clanchy explains, and not as written words per se.

Reliance on living as well as written witness persists among

11. M. T. Clanchy, *From Memory to Written Record: England, 1066–1307* (Cambridge, 1979).

French nobles in the sixteenth century. Consider, for example, a letter of complaint written to Catherine de Médicis in 1567 by René de Mailly, an old Picard warrior distantly related to Eléonore de Roye. He is concerned about the "short notice" he has received of the start of a royal project to review and reform local customary laws. After listing various rights and privileges that his family has enjoyed in the *prévôté* of Péronne "since time immemorial," he reminds the Queen that "thrice in my own time I have had my home at Mailly burned in your service during the wars . . . exactly as my home at Boullencourt was seized and pillaged by the English and Burgundians when they crossed your river Somme and took the town of Montdidier." And so, he concludes, "my remaining titles that had been saved were lost . . . which is what makes me turn to you now and ask you most humbly to send letters safeguarding my rights to your deputies at Péronne."[12] This fascinating letter is filled with tensions between reliance on and independence of written texts. Although written documentation was clearly necessary to the procedures of the official reformation of customary law, and Mailly accepts this necessity, he nevertheless believes that the Queen should and will rely on his memory of what his family's privileges have been "from time immemorial" for the purposes of reaffirming the rights in written form. His own living memory and his living relationship with Catherine are enough, in his mind, to establish these facts. More interesting still is the way Mailly connects events in the distant past with more recent ones. Events of the Hundred Years' War are recounted as though they were located in Mailly's own memory, as though they had happened to himself and to the present monarch. He does not know the past abstractly; it is not arrayed in his mind in chronological and causal sequence, or separately from himself—ways of regarding the past which are the result of objectifying and distancing it by means of texts.[13]

It was possible, then, for noblemen readily to make use of writing and of written texts and yet to remain bound by some of the habits

12. BN, MS fr. 20434, fol. 99, René de Mailly to Catherine de Médicis, 24 May 1567, Montreuil.

13. Elizabeth Eisenstein, *The Printing Press as an Agent of Change* (Cambridge, 1980), pp. 67–68, 191–92. Mailly's present-centered memory also seems to reflect the circular sense of time, in which the living are in permanent contact with dead relations, described by Natalie Davis: "Ghosts, Kin and Progeny: Some Features of Family Life in Early Modern France," *Daedalus* 6 (1977): 92–96.

of communication and modes of knowing typical of oral culture. Even the "written thought" of their letters appears to have been largely oral thought, weighted with the formulaic constructions necessary when words cannot be preserved. Of course, many of these letters were literally oral compositions in that they were composed orally, dictated to a scribe. And in practice they were not separated wholly from face-to-face messages. Some letters were intended merely to be introductions for the bearers, who were charged with speaking the senders' actual messages; others mention an item or two of news before commending the recipient to the "sufficiency" of the bearer. The survival of such missives reminds us that these written pieces actually existed within a context of oral messages. Many of the most important messages between particularly intimate noble correspondents may have been wholly oral, wholly dependent on face-to-face encounters that left no documentary residue. The characteristics of the composition of their letters reflect the habits of dictating, of listening, and of trusting personally conveyed information—and also the habit of structuring information in ways that dependence on those means demands. As we explore the nature of nobles' reliance on literacy, then, let us simultaneously analyze some of the conceptual and social implications of both their oral and their literate communication.[14]

14. It must be noted that discussing oral and literate modes of communication with regard to the nobility is not the same thing as discussing their education per se. We know that most nobles' education at mid-century included "apprenticeship" in military skills (during the period of nourriture, which was an apprenticeship in a general sense), as well as some formal instruction from a tutor. Occasionally this instruction may have been followed by a year or so at a college in Paris. Yet even if we knew more about nobles' education—if we were able to know, for example, precisely how many nobles had extensive education—we would still need to analyze its impact on nobles' uses of literacy and of learning. Most discussions of education equate literacy with learning: they do not distinguish among the possible ways of making use of literacy skills and book learning, nor do they note the values and interests this learning is supposed to impart. On formal education as socialization in certain skills and behaviors rather than as access to "knowledge," see Jerome Karabel and A. H. Halsey, eds., *Power and Ideology in Education* (New York, 1977). The best work on nobles' education is John David Nordhaus, "Arma et Litterae: The Education of the *Noblesse de Race* in Sixteenth-Century France" (Ph.D. dissertation, Columbia University, 1974). See also Jean-Marie Constant, *Nobles et paysans en Beauce aux XVIe et XVIIe siècles* (Lille, 1981), pp. 474–79. For the older view, see J. H. Hexter, "The Education of the Aristocracy in the Renaissance," in *Reappraisals in History* (Evanston, Ill., 1961), pp. 56–79.

II

Perhaps the most salient characteristic of nobles' relationship with and use of words is their sensitivity to the spoken word. This sensitivity went much deeper than—and in large measure accounts for—their obvious comfort with orally conveyed information. We have already noted the potency of their words in the example of the prince de Condé's defiant letter to the duc de Montpensier in 1568. On the run with his forces in western France, Condé relied on a threatening reference to the power of his personal honor as a form of self-defense. The same kind of power of words can be found in Condé's experience some years earlier. After Condé's exoneration following the Amboise affair, the crown attempted to effect a formal reconciliation between his family and the Lorraine family, of course in order to ease tensions for its own purposes. François de Lorraine, duc de Guise, made a formal apology to resolve some of the animosity between the families arising from the Lorraine role in Condé's arrest. Guise's words, recorded at the time, betray the power he felt they had. He had first apologized or, more precisely, "given satisfaction" to Condé's brother Antoine, and then extended the apology to Condé as well. Because, Guise said, "I will make no difficulty in saying to the Prince what I have said to the King of Navarre, . . . I pray him to be content with what the King of Navarre has contented himself with."[15] The implication is clear: words are not said lightly. In fact, Guise did not actually speak the crucial words to the Prince. He guarded himself very carefully, it seems, despite the pressure from the crown. He managed to smooth over hostilities with a mere statement of willingness to say the words again, and thereby surrendered less of his own power in the exchange. This reliance on verbal force was made possible by the inherent forcefulness of the spoken word in the nobles' experience. The nobles retained a sensitivity to *words as sounds*, and to the special power with which words, thus experienced, are laden.

Walter Ong has synthesized a large body of research on contemporary and past societies concerning the implications of words as sounds, as experienced by various nonliterate peoples. Persons whose principal experience of language is oral, Ong argues, do not

15. BN, Colbert 27, fol. 341, minutes.

envision words as objects that can occupy space and later be reclaimed by sight. Literates such as ourselves in contemporary Western culture have a deeply rooted experience of words as objects in a visual field; words are in books, on signs, on labels—all of which are themselves objects and part of the inanimate environment around us. In oral cultures, in contrast, words are not things at all, but rather events. They exist only momentarily, while they are being uttered—that is, while they are "happening." And because the source and receiver of a sounded word is always a living person, word events tend to be experienced as acts that one person is performing on another. Spoken words also exist in literate cultures, of course, but their especial power in nonliterate or face-to-face cultures comes from the general oral experience of words. Sounded words in a predominantly oral culture have power because they cannot be conceived as things that can somehow exist in a neutral space between persons; they are not separated from human animateness. Indeed, words necessarily have power precisely because they do not stand alone in such cultures. Words are always accompanied by gesture, facial expression, movement. Cultures with a primarily oral experience of language have been described as "verbomotor" because they attend not simply to words but to words in conjunction with actions.[16]

Hearing alone could mobilize a French nobleman in the sixteenth century. It was an active and instrumental, not a passive or incidental, experience. In their letters to one another and to the crown, nobles reveal the power that hearing embodied for them; knowing of an event, learning a fact, receiving a command are routinely described in terms of hearing of the event, hearing the fact, hearing the command.[17] More important, the act of hearing always has an effect; knowing, learning, and receiving commit a noble to re-

<hr />

16. Ong, *Orality and Literacy*, especially chap. 3. The term "verbomotor" was originated by Marcel Jousse, *Le Style oral rhythmique et mnémotechnique chez les Verbomoteurs* (Paris, 1925). I have found very useful the discussion of this concept by Rhys Isaac, "Dramatizing the Ideology of Revolution: Popular Mobilization in Virginia, 1774 to 1776," *William and Mary Quarterly*, 3d ser., 33 (July 1976): 358–61.

17. See, for example, BN, MS fr. 20394, fol. 8, Charles, cardinal de Vendôme, to François de Lorraine, duc d'Aumale, n.d., n.p.; BN, MS fr. 4717, fol. 91, Philippe d'Humières to Jacques d'Humières, 2 April 1577, Maineville; BN, Colbert 27, fol. 78, Paule de Termes to François de Lorraine, duc de Guise, 20 October 1560, Poitiers.

sponse. The sire de Morvilliers reveals as much when he writes to the crown of the disturbances around Boulogne. He closes his letter, "[I want] to hear from your majesties how I should conduct myself amidst this unrest . . . which I have charged the present bearer more fully to describe for you if it pleases you to listen to him so as to remedy the problem [sy ainsy le vous plaist entendre pour y remedier]."[18] One could command others, therefore, or could be commanded, simply *to hear* a given message. Consider, for example, the command recorded in the deliberations of a "council" of Huguenot noblemen gathered to secure and defend La Fère for Condé's son in 1580. Regarding the management of the stores of food and munitions, it was recorded that "a esté commandé au controlleur du magazin *d'entendre* et obeyir au commissaires dudict magazin."[19]

We can see in their letters further evidence of their word–action attentiveness and some indications of its significance. We can note that some features of their letters reflect the problems inherent in making a written text achieve the same results as face-to-face action. It is interesting to note, for example, that the vocabulary used in letters to describe their requests and promises to one another is heavily weighted with words that convey or cause action, if only in anticipation of reaction in their recipients. Rather than "ask," nobles "pray," "enjoin," "persuade"; rather than "tell," they "warn," "give order to," "send to know," or "make heard." The prince de Condé writes to the sire d'Humières, governor of Péronne, in 1567, ". . . I wanted to write to you this [letter] and by means of it [et par icelluy] pray you kindly to give the order to [provision my company of men-at-arms at Péronne]."[20] Condé seeks to mobilize Humières, to engage him in emotional and physical action. One month earlier, a Condé very anxious over provincial unrest had written to Humières somewhat more imperiously concerning his seeming failure to keep the peace: "[I trust that] following the contents of this [suivant le contenu d'icelluy] you will set to work as I would hope to do it

18. BN, MS fr. 15543, fol. 16, Morvilliers to Catherine de Médicis, 30 September 1567, Boulogne.

19. BN, MS fr. 4047, fol. 95, "Registre des expeditions du conseil estably à La Fère par Msgr. le prince de Condé," 28 May 1580, La Fère.

20. BN, MS fr. 3187, fol. 79, Louis de Bourbon, prince de Condé, to Jacques d'Humières, 23 May 1567, Paris.

[vous vous soiez mis en devoir comme j'estime de le faire]."[21] "You will set to work as I would hope to do it." Note the interactive nature of Condé's command. The task's goal is not objective but reflexive: "Do it as I would wish it done." This way of structuring requests and commands is incessant in nobles' correspondence: maintain the peace so well that no inhabitant will complain; serve the king so well that he will know the affection you bear him.[22] In short, envision all your actions as *interactions* with others.

In general, the nobles had only limited means with which to characterize political activity except by concrete references to action. They rarely—virtually never—use the abstract terms that historians have applied to them, such as "client" and "supporter." Rather, they use concrete words that never stray far from their lived experience. They speak, for instance, not of being "followers" but rather of "following." And they use the word literally, not figuratively; the physical act of following is always being described. One letter depicts a young noble as having just "returned home from following the prince de Condé," that is, having accompanied the Prince's household as it moved from place to place in the provinces.[23] The memoirist Claude Haton uses similar language when he describes the retreat of the duc de Guise from court after the death of the young François II. Guise was clearly trying to stage a menacing withdrawal that would demonstrate continued strength despite the King's death. There were more than five hundred men-at-arms, Haton reports, "to follow him and to put hand to arms in his favor."[24] The possibility of supporting the Duke is expressed here by the description of two concrete acts—that of following and that of putting hand to weapon.

Insofar as nobles did describe states of being rather than performance of action, it was with a small number of terms that delimited relationships according to a few select criteria. The word "enemy" always refers to an active affront—an enemy is in arms and in the

21. Ibid., Condé to Humières, 1 April 1567, Anizy.

22. BN, MS fr. 20645, fol. 48r, Louis d'Ongnies, sire de Chaulnes, to Guise, 28 February 1557, Paris; BN, MS fr. 3188, fol. 5, Condé to Antoine de Croy, prince de Porcien, May 1563.

23. BN, MS fr. 3196, fol. 14, Eléonore de Roye, princesse de Condé, to Porcien, 25 May 1563, St-Germain-en-Laye.

24. Claude Haton, *Mémoires*, 2 vols. (Paris, 1857), 1:117.

field against you, or he is an opponent in a personal feud; he is someone who threatens honor. Somewhat more abstract is the term *serviteur*. Nobles describe themselves as "servants" (serviteurs) of fellow nobles, or of the crown. They often close letters with the phrase "your humble and obedient serviteur" before their signatures. The phrase serves as a formula by which a relatively humble noble acknowledges the greater honor of the recipient of the letter. Relative equals describe themselves to each other with a different set of terms: "I am your good friend and cousin" or "I am your good friend and relative" or some minor variant.[25] These formulaic word clusters do little but refer to relative stature, usually including the important distinction of kinship relation. But these are the terms in which "political" obligation or loyalty is discussed, when it is discussed abstractly at all: "If you do such-and-such a favor for me, I will be as good a friend to you as any that you have," or as an old familiar promises the prince de Porcien, "I will be as good a servant to you as I was to your father."[26] Relationships in theory are discussed in terms of relationships in practice, and the only fixed distinctions in practice are basic distinctions of stature.

But, one might protest, surely these kinds of descriptions do not comprise everything nobles truly knew about their relationships with each other. Surely, for example, Porcien would know just how good a servant that fellow had been to his father. The answer to this protest is yes, relationships did have a known content in the sense that each relationship had accumulated weight. The more strands of family tie and past action that linked two nobles, the more significant and resilient their relationship could be. Our young "follower" of the prince de Condé, for example, was linked to the Prince by marriage ties and also by past cooperation in rebellion against the crown as well as by continuing contact—such as his sporadic appearances in Condé's household. But this weight could not be measured or converted automatically into a known quantity of loyalty or obligation, as the term "client" implies, because literally dozens of other relationships existed side by side with the one in question.

25. See, for example, BN, MS fr. 3006, fol. 45, Antoine de Bourbon, King of Navarre, to Anne de Montmorency, 20 November 155?, Paris; BN, MS fr. 3128, fol. 95, François de Châtillon, sire d'Andelot, to Jean d'Humières, 14 October 1556, Abbeville.
26. BN, MS fr. 3192, fol. 24, ? to Porcien, 16 June 1563, Paris.

Our young nobleman must have had many other important reference points, particularly in other members of his family, to claim his attention. More important for the moment is the fact that abstract states—alliance, opposition, support, resistance—existed in any case only when and only how they were defined in moments of action. The young nobleman was a "follower" of Condé only at the time he was following and only in the sense that he was present in Condé's entourage—where, perhaps, further action could happen. His presence there would certainly have buttressed Condé's stature. But, as it happens, it does not appear that he was called upon to put hand to arms during that stay. If we could ask the prince de Porcien, "How good a servant *was* that fellow to your father?" he would probably answer not "He was a trustworthy client" or "He was a consistent ally" but rather with references to action: "He was beside my father at St-Quentin and picked him up when his horse fell."

We know, in fact, that noblemen did reflect on their relationships in these terms. The Champenois nobleman Jean de Mergey, we have seen, wrote of his past relationship with the comte de La Rochefoucauld in precisely this way; he conveyed the content of their relationship in his memoirs by describing a long series of incidents in which they both had been involved. He illustrated his distinguished service to La Rochefoucauld, as we have seen, by relating that he had cleverly pretended not to recognize the Count when both were captured at St-Quentin, in order to help the Count avoid being saddled with a large ransom. The Count, he relates, acknowledged his efforts but told him not to bother, as his identity had already been discovered.[27] Mergey continued to describe his career in general, and his tie with La Rochefoucauld in particular, by relating such personal experiences in great detail. His depiction of his career is thus a disjointed narrative; it is comprised of a series of incidents such as the following one, which occurred on the eve of a battle:

[I was sent to the Count] et estant en la chambre dudict sieur comte qui estoit toute ouverte et où chacun entroit attendant le dernier soupir

27. Jean de Mergey, *Mémoires du sieur Jean de Mergey, gentilhomme champenois*, Collection universelle des mémoires particuliers relatifs à l'histoire de France (n.p., 1785–90), 40 (1788): 33–34.

dudict sieur comte, je me mis avec les autres gentilhommes qui es-
toient en la chambre à le regarder et luy moy attentivement et assez
longuement, enfin il appella tout bas son chirurgien Bastien qui estoit
au chevet de son lict luy demandant "n'est-ce pas là Mergey," qui lui
dict que "ouy"; "a-t-il esté malade car je le trouve tous desfaict,"
"non," luy respondit Bastien: alors il me fit signe de la main que
j'alasse à luy, ce que je fis: il me demanda, mais fort bas, car il ne
pouvoit quasi parler "si j'avois esté malade," je luy dis "que non," "je
vous trouve fort desfaict," je luy respondis en soubzriant "que c'estoit
à cause que je ne beuvois pas mon soul de vin" . . .[28]

[I was sent to the Count] and being in the bedchamber of the said
Count, which was completely open and where each man entered
awaiting the last breath of the said Count, I placed myself amidst the
other gentlemen who were in the bedchamber to watch him, and he
looked at me long and hard and finally he called in a low voice to his
doctor, who was at the head of his bed, asking him, "Isn't that Mergey over there?" and he told him yes. "Has he been ill, because I find
him not looking well [all undone]." "No," the surgeon told him.
Then he made a sign to me that I should approach him, which I did.
He asked me, in a very low voice, because he could barely talk, if I had
been ill, and I told him no. "[But] I find you not looking well." I
responded, smiling, that it was because I had not been drinking my
usual measure of wine.

Mergey concludes this story by announcing that following his little
joke, the Count's spirits began to lift and his health to improve.

Important here is not merely the fact that Mergey constructs his
overall relationship with La Rochefoucauld as a series of incidents,
but also the way he constructs those incidents. The scene in the
bedchamber is described as it was lived: Mergey enters the room,
notices others gathered there, and stands among them; the Count
looks at Mergey and speaks to his physician, standing by the bed; he
motions to Mergey, who approaches the bed, where the Count
speaks to him. This is a narration of movement, of gestures and of
speech events, described sequentially as they were experienced by
the author. Mergey does not present a diagrammatic schema of

28. Ibid., pp. 73–74.

what he encounters. The doctor's presence at the head of the bed is noted, for example, only when he becomes a bit player in the drama—only when the Count turns to speak with him. Other examples of these characteristics of narrative construction appear in the various documents produced by noblemen. In the deliberations of the assembled noble defenders of La Fère in 1580, for example, is the following resolution:

> Sera faicte recherche des chevaulx inutilles pour estre pris de ceulx qui n'en doibvent avoir, leur en faisant honneste paiement, et seront delivrés au Gros cappitaine du charroy pour les employer suivant qu'il sera commandé.[29]

> A search for unused horses will be made, to be taken from those who have no right to have them, a just payment being made to them, and they will be delivered to Gros, captain of the cartage, to be used as he will be commanded.

The search for horses is described as it would occur; surplus horses are to be taken from those who have no right to them, an honest payment being made in return, and the horses will be delivered to the commander of the cartage (transport) in the town, where they will be put to use according to the orders he will be given. We follow the proposed action each step of the way.

III

What a nobleman "knew," then, about his relationships with others or about his own stature was profoundly shaped by this verbomotor sensibility— by the importance of dramaturgic expression of and creation of meaning. Narrative, and not diagram or analysis, was his system for organizing knowledge.[30] Our ability to make

---

29. BN, MS fr. 4047, fol. 95, "Registre des expeditions du conseil . . .," 28 May 1580, La Fère.

30. I am grateful to Rhys Isaac for bringing the issue of dramaturgy to my attention, and for many fruitful discussions of its implications. See Isaac, "Dramatizing the Ideology of Revolution" and *The Transformation of Virginia* (Chapel Hill, N.C., 1982), especially pp. 323–57.

sense of nobles' behavior depends, in turn, on our sensitivity to this event-centeredness. In other words, we must enlarge and recast our definition of what constitutes a historical event in light of the nobles' own criteria of significance; their political life must be interpreted with the aid of dramaturgic definitions both of public events and of personal ties. Sustenance of honor, for example, had to be acted out in order to be efficacious. When the sire d'Humières was named to the King's order of St-Michel, the *collier* of office was not simply sent to him from court. It was conferred on him in person by the sire de Senarpont, lieutenant general of the province, acting for the King; he wrote to the honoree and arranged a visit (which required them both to travel to a town situated between their principal command posts) for the purpose.[31] In our efforts to understand nobles' behavior, the potential importance of even minor incidents—such as Mergey's intimacies with La Rochefoucauld at the Count's bedside—cannot be overlooked. Contemporary observers account for loyalties and jealousies in the light of such previous "events." The memoirist Haton, for example, offers two explanations for the behavior of the connêtable de Montmorency at one point in 1556, when Montmorency was hoping to dispatch his rival, Guise, to command in Italy. The first explanation, that Montmorency would then have "no one who would dare say or attempt anything against him in the household of the king or to the king himself" ("plus personne . . . qui osast dire ni attenter contre luy en la maison et personne du roy") would have the ring of modern political calculation were it not for the precise terms Haton uses to describe Montmorency's strategizing: with the elimination of Guise, there will be no one who will dare "*dire ni attenter contre luy* en la maison et personne du roy." This, once again, is a concrete description of political activity; the potential challenge to Montmorency is described as potential action—the acts of speaking and of physical interference. The second explanation Haton offers, moreover, sounds petty and arbitrary to modern ears—that "the Constable had been envious of Guise since the battle of Renty" ("il avoit une jalouise couverte du connetable envers ledict Guise depuis la bataille de Renty"). It seems arbitrary, however, merely because it is event-

---

31. BN, MS fr. 3244, fol. 130, Jean de Monchy, sire de Senarpont, to Jacques d'Humières, 22 October 1560, Senarpont.

centered.[32] We are not privy to the specific offense Montmorency felt as a result of Guise's conduct in that battle (although it is interesting that Haton expects his readers to know the meaning of the event). In any case, out of all the preceding months and years of competition between them for the King's favor, why is this incident singled out to explain current behavior? We cannot answer that question without being privy to Montmorency's remembrance of the event and its effect on his honor.

We have better evidence regarding Condé's memory of an event in his own life. Condé's remembrance of his disastrous loss of face in October 1560 drove him to seek to reverse its meaning. We have noted that he lost honor, and therefore his legitimacy, because no fellow noble defended his honor when it was challenged in the King's presence. The incident reveals to us thus both the power of the currency of honor and the power of the community to recognize and sustain it. We can now also see that sensitivity to performance as a source of meaning was a crucial component of the significance of such an incident; and it helps to explain Condé's subsequent preoccupation with reversing its meaning by means of similarly constructed events. The "map" of historic events surrounding this incident conventionally includes the uprising at Amboise, Condé's contribution to that uprising (in whatever form it took), the fact of Condé's arrest and trial, and the role of the rival Lorraine family in bringing both about. We might adjust our analysis of the events to include and to emphasize the *very moment* of the accusation and arrest of Condé in the presence of the King. It may have been this moment that effectively dishonored and almost annihilated the Prince. In other words, the important thing was not a belief on the part of some of his peers that Condé was guilty of a treasonous act, but rather that this possibility took shape because it was acted out.[33]

We do know that in the months following the timely death of François II, Condé worked to exonerate himself by means of further events of this kind. He began to orchestrate these events from his prison at Orléans. At first he refused to budge from his quarters there—refusing the offer of freedom on his brother's recog-

---

32. Haton, *Mémoires*, 1:29.

33. See the discussion of a parallel case of action causing belief (and not vice versa) in peasant society: Sabean, *Power in the Blood*, chap. 6.

nizance—until he had been declared innocent of the charges against him by the royal council. Meanwhile, he wrote to the Queen Mother and to his brother Antoine, asking them, among other things, to send the Guises away from court while the case was being considered.[34] "I wish to face my accusers," he wrote, "I will show them that they are evil and traitorous, and if they do not leave [the court], so much the worse for them!"[35] He tried to manage a face-to-face encounter with the Lorraine brothers in the weeks that followed, while they tried to avoid such an event. He finally decided to leave Orléans in late December. But rather than proceed to the family's estate at La Fère (where Antoine and the Queen, hoping to prevent further volatile confrontations, wanted to send him), he tried to reach the court and had to be turned back by his brother, the Constable, and an escort of armed retainers. They delayed his approach long enough to enable the Lorraine brothers, traveling from the court to Notre Dame de Cléry, to avoid encountering him.[36] Apparently this show of force persuaded Condé to retire to La Fère until the council had ended its deliberations.

Upon Condé's return to court in early March, one of his first acts was to threaten to challenge Guise to a duel. The Queen Mother, desperate to prevent disruption of the equilibrium at court, continued to work, with Antoine and the Constable as her intermediaries, to defuse the situation. On March 13 the council officially declared Condé's innocence, and Guise and Condé at last came face to face. But they did so in an encounter that was carefully staged and delimited by these intermediaries. Guise delivered to Condé the measured and barely apologetic statement we examined earlier; it was designed to assuage Condé's demands at as little cost to himself as possible. Not surprisingly, this encounter, though filled with tension, did not produce the dramatic satisfaction Condé was searching for. The English ambassador reveals the unresolved tensions in a letter dated the following day: "There have lately been some jars between the great parties in the Prince of Condé's matter,

34. *Recueil des choses mémorables faites et passés pour le faict de la religion et estat de ce royaume (Mémoires de Condé)*, 3 vols. (London, 1748), 1:755–58.

35. Cited in Lucien Romier, *Catholiques et Huguenots à la cour de Charles IX* (Paris, 1924), p. 35.

36. Alphonse de Ruble, *Antoine de Bourbon et Jeanne d'Albret*, 4 vols. (Paris, 1881-86), vol. 3, chap. 11.

though all were made friends again to outward show. In most men's opinions, some great matter will follow shortly hereupon one side or the other, or else one of them must leave the court, which is not thought meet for the greatest to do, and the other are not minded to do."[37] And shortly thereafter Condé did leave the court, though armed with an honorable premise for doing so. He announced that he was dissatisfied with the pronouncement of his innocence by the council and that he now demanded a full investigation and complete exoneration by the Parlement of Paris. Such was only his right as a Prince of the Blood, he maintained. In fact, his original trial should have been conducted there. On March 17 he left Fontainebleau for the capital.[38]

Particularly interesting in these efforts to cleanse his sullied honor are Condé's attempts to come face to face with Guise. He wants his accusers to declare themselves to him, he taunts, still in prison. He will find them at court, he will challenge them to a duel. The most effective way to reestablish his honor was to force his challenger to witness a demonstration of it. Of course, in the Prince's position he needed to be insistent and uncompromising. He had nearly been executed; he needed to recover his credit and begin to put it to use at court. The new king, Charles IX, was indisputably a minor, and the possibilities for wielding influence at court were as great as they were ever likely to be. Nevertheless, Condé seems to have favored a more belligerent course of action than other nobles counseled him to take. One observer, for example, relates that "one day [while in prison] as some of his friends . . . were advising him to an honorable method of being reconciled with the family of Guise . . . he answered in a great passion that there was no way of doing it but by the sword . . . [and that] he could not forbear this and other threats."[39] But if his words and actions were particularly inflammatory, then and in the months to come, they were certainly within the bounds of possibility. Aware of the potential impact of his actions, the Queen Mother tried to block the very events Condé was trying to stage, or, as in the eventual encounter of March 13, at least

37. *Calendar of State Papers, Foreign Series, Elizabeth I, 1560–61* (London, 1865), no. 28, Nicholas Throckmorton to William Cecil, 14 March 1561.

38. Ruble, *Antoine de Bourbon*, 3:61.

39. Michel de Castelnau, *Memoirs of the Reign of Francis II and Charles IX* (London, 1924), p. 90.

to provide a safer script for them. Perhaps we hear in his friends' counsel to the princely prisoner a similar attempt at stage managing; would it not be in their interests to avoid an explosive confrontation between two such powerful courtiers? In any case, Condé's seemingly exaggerated posturing was not meaningless or ridiculous; it was dangerous. They, like the Queen, wanted to stave off an "event" that would further Condé's interests alone.

All of Condé's efforts during these months reflect a need to place himself at the center of a staged scene in order to empower himself. At first he refuses to leave his prison cell at Orléans unless his terms are agreed to. Later he attempts to seize the ground on which he can establish his honor by riding to find Guise at court. Later still, when Catherine has succeeded in staging the events at court to her satisfaction and not his, the Prince exits the stage and leaves for Paris. The ritualized exchange of courtesy in all nobles' letters effectively sustained their honor precisely because it, too, was couched in terms of dramatic encounter. Their letters were designed not merely to convey esteem or to display status but to do so by means of the dramatic power for which the writers felt a need. It is significant that courtesy was both the first and the last thing communicated in a letter. It could function in this way as a scene-setting device: it set a scene appropriate for the "action" of the letter. It was communicated with a choice of salutations—"Monsieur," "Monsieur mon compagnon" (between equals), "Monseigneur" (to one of much higher status)—and especially with the careful use of closing words, such as those we have already noted: "your friend and cousin," for example, or "your humble and obedient servant." The effect of these statements could be amplified in the body of the letter, as in one we have examined from the very young prince de Condé requesting the honor of a military command from the more powerful Guise. Preceding the formulaic closing of the letter, Condé concludes his actual request with "and assuring you that if you do me this good turn and pleasure as you have done in the past, you will further oblige me to obey you." And a postscript further reinforces his deference; he adds in his own hand that he doesn't want to importune Guise, but he nonetheless begs him "to do me the favor of letting me know what it pleases you that I should do and to give me the means to serve the King and you" ("me faire tant de bien ce que de me mander se quy vous plest que je fasse et me donner le moien de fere service au Roy et à vous").[40] The request is made circuitously and rather effusively, to our sensibilities, by references to the pleasure the result would bring Condé and to Guise's pleasure in ordering what he wills; Condé thus couches his request in terms that emphasize Guise's power and thus make it more desirable for Guise to do what Condé asks.

What distinguishes these kinds of scene settings from what might have occurred in a face-to-face encounter is, in part, their dramatic rigidity. In face-to-face encounters, particularly between nobles who knew each other well, and especially when others were present to enrich the dramatic possibilities, any of the available strands of the two nobles' relationship might easily be called to the surface. Condé was an aspiring young warrior struggling to survive honorably, eager for Guise's largesse. But he was also Guise's first cousin, and he was the youngest member of a family whose other members were the familiars of Guise and his family. The Prince was also a potential thorn in Guise's side, since he had just become a relative by marriage of Guise's great rival Montmorency. Letters containing specific requests often required a noble to commit himself to one version of the relationship for the purpose of the request. He had to select and insist on one definition of status and relationship and carry it through the entire written "encounter." This selection of one facet of a relationship to set the required tone of a letter is often most evident in letters between relative equals. Fellow commanders in neighboring fortresses could write to each other with a minimum of fuss, routinely sharing information about supplies and troop movements. When one of them wanted to presume upon the other, however, he might choose a more deferential form of address; he could sign the letter, "your friend and servant," rather than with the more presumptuous "your friend and companion," for example. In this way he put himself in a position to make a request of the other (such as hoarding available manpower in his own sector of the war effort) without having to obligate himself to return the favor. Similarly, the duc de Guise could, by signing letters to supplicants as "your friend," deny the status of dependent to them, and hence deny their requests without loss of esteem.[41] The basic distinctions of status

40. BN, MS fr. 20470, fol. 51, Condé to Guise, 7 July 1551(?), n.p.
41. My attention was called to the possible function of these modulations of greetings by the discussion of Judith T. Irvine, "Status Manipulation in the Wolof

and relationship which formed their political vocabulary were manipulated, in moments of action, to produce results. These results constituted what nobles "knew" about their relationships with each other. Of course, results were not predictable—would Guise decide to grant Condé the command he had requested?—despite the dramatic force of the letter that was designed to bring about the desired outcome.

We can glimpse in their letters, in short, their sensitivity not only to exchange but also to the *individual instances* of exchange between people. We have noted that they often seem to measure their mutual loyalty and reliability in terms of other relationships: the bishop of Amiens writes to the young heiress of Louis de Lannoy, sire de Morvilliers, offering her advice on how to manage her affairs, and concluding with the promise that "wherever I have the means you will find me as good a relative and friend as you have in this world" ("là où j'auray moyen vous me trouverez aultant bon parent et amy que vous aies en se monde").[42] She can rely on him *as much as* she can rely on any other "relative and friend." In other cases, a noble will describe a relationship by referring to the past of that relationship: the amiral de Coligny writes to the sire d'Humières, "You will find me always as much your friend as I have been before this" ("aultant votre amy que j'ay esté par cy devant").[43] But noble correspondents also very deliberately measure relationships with reference to action being performed at that moment, in terms of the gift then being exchanged or the office then being solicited. Writing on behalf of a lesser nobleman to the duc de Guise (then the duc

Greeting," in *Explorations*, ed. Bauman and Sherzer, pp. 167–91. Jean-Marie Constant has noted the omnipresence of the terms "ami" and "serviteur" in nobles' descriptions of their relationships but is unable fully to account for the variability in the meanings of these terms: *Nobles et paysans en Beauce*, pp. 239–52. See also the attempt to distinguish formula and meaning in the language of conjugal relations by Muchembled, "Famille, amour et mariage: Mentalités et comportements des nobles artésiens à l'époque de Philippe II," *Revue d'histoire moderne et contemporaine* 22 (1975): 245. A useful discussion of greeting formulas is found in Dale Kent, *The Rise of the Medici: Faction in Florence, 1426–1434* (Oxford, 1978), pp. 84–87. Kent does not acknowledge the flexibility of formulas but does regard them as distinctly meaningful and purposeful, and worthy of historians' interpretive attention.

42. BN, MS fr. 3208, fol. 125, Antoine, cardinal de Créquy, to Marie de Lannoy, damoiselle de Morvilliers, 21 August 1569, n.p.

43. BN, MS fr. 3128, fol. 53, Gaspard de Châtillon, amiral de Coligny, to Jean d'Humières, 24 May 1553, Paris.

d'Aumale), the duc de Montpensier asks him "pour l'amour de moy avoir ledict sire de La Chappelle et les affaires il a à la court ou il s'en va pour recommendés de sorte qu'il puisse cognoistre la presente luy ayt vallu de quelque bonne chose envers vous."[44] Montpensier wants Guise's affection for him to be at least strong enough to give La Chappelle evidence that Montpensier's letter had some good effect ("quelque bonne chose"). A final and very striking example is contained in the letter of the old family familiar to the prince de Porcien. The writer reminds Porcien that because he had been "tres affectionné serviteur de feu monsieur votre pere," he will "me consacrer le votre," and, he continues, "vous obeyir et servir en tout ce qu'il vous plaira me comander *d'aussi* bonne et prompte volunté *que* je vous voys tres humblement mercier des deux pistoles que m'avez envoyez."[45] First the writer refers to a previous relationship. Then he attaches his promise of service to the Prince to a concrete event in the present—the receipt of two guns. The letter has become the stage on which this action is performed.

Nobles' relationships, then, were composed of events, and all of their letters embody a tension between the expected spontaneity of such personal interaction and the closed and defined format of a document. Letters were both more precise than face-to-face communication, in that only one strand of a relationship found expression, and less precise, in that no possibility of action existed. Nobles' language about relationships in their letters thus reflected a vision of relationships as tied to moments of action, and discussed relationships in terms that kept them alive with possibilities that only action could realize. But the vague formulas available to them were less well suited to the precision required of letters than to the face-to-face world from which the formulas came. The seeming awkwardness and effusiveness of Condé's request to Guise, for example, stems from the relative poverty of communicative resources available for confining such an insistent message to writing.

Nobles' personal interaction thus appears more static and the results more inevitable than was in fact the case. Condé seems to be dependent on Guise because his relationship with the Duke is de-

---

44. BN, Clair. 341, fol. 183, Louis de Bourbon, duc de Montpensier, to François de Lorraine, duc d'Aumale, 25 February 1548, Paris.

45. BN, MS fr. 3192, fol. 24,? to Porcien, 16 June 1563, Paris; my emphasis.

fined in terms of the action then taking place. Our interpretive difficulty lies both in the fact that their relationships are depicted only in writing and in our own habits of relating to writing. We tend to envision their relationship in terms of the structure we see embodied in the document before us. Condé, in contrast, would not have mentally confined the relationship in such diagrammatic terms. The documents we have before us thus should not be "read" as we read, but rather should be approached as written texts embedded in and reflecting many of the needs and habits of face-to-face communication. Thus the formal characteristics of nobles' letters—salutations, closings, patterns of language use—cannot be read in isolation or as automatically meaning what they seem to mean to us—either genuine dependence, for example, of Condé on Guise, or mere formulaic bowing. Thus our awareness of some of the modes of thought and expression characteristic of oral cultures helps to illuminate the meaning of nobles' behavior—both the meaning it had for them and the meaning it has for us.

— 5 —

The Ties of Territory: The Bourbons as Provincial Landholders and Feudal Lords

W E MUST now consider the sources of the bonds between nobles, such as they were, in the context of provincial political
life. The efforts to develop a theory of clientage to describe relationships between nobles, and between nobles and the crown, have in
large measure been attempts to understand the ways in which landholding shaped these relationships. All the notions of clientage that
historians of the sixteenth century have posited share the assumption that the power of warrior nobles continued to be based on
territory—that land created power and also gave power its regionalized character. Vassalage ties, some historians have argued, remained an important structuring force for nobles' relationships, and
were supplemented by the new material links of patronage distribution. Even for Robert Harding, who has emphasized new ties at the
expense of old ones, territoriality remains a salient feature of clientage organization. Appointed by the crown as governors in the
regions of their feudal and seigneurial authority, greater nobles were
simultaneously important landholders and dispensers of provincial
offices and commands. Whole segments of royal governing apparatus, particularly its military facets, became "their private spoils system," Harding has argued.[1]

But the reality behind these assumptions has proved very elusive.
Certainly there was, in the revealingly vague words of Harding, "a

---

1. Robert R. Harding, *Anatomy of a Power Elite: The Provincial Governors of Early
Modern France* (New Haven and London, 1978), p. 30.

liaison between land and power."[2] There is much disagreement, however, over the nature of this "system" of power. Was land merely revenue, a resource to be distributed by the wealthy, exactly like other sources of revenue, such as offices, pensions, and commands? Was the territorial nature of power merely an organizational feature of a large patronage system? Or was land itself somehow the source of bonds? While the regional character of greater nobles' power in the sixteenth century seems to be beyond dispute, its actual mechanisms remain unclear, in part because we do not know what lord–vassal relationships meant to these warriors. Further, the connection between relationships fostered in this way and those sustained by the deliberate distribution of commands and offices to provincial nobles must be more fully explored.

Here we will consider such questions about landholding anew, primarily by means of the example of the Bourbon princes and their authority in Picardy, and in light of the preceding conclusions concerning the flexibility and action-centeredness of all relationships among nobles. Vassalage ties, we will find, were important to such relationships only insofar as they coincided with or reflected other ties that ensured physical proximity: geographical proximity of major estates and residences, military service in the same companies, and, above all, daily living within the household of a great noble. The household was in many ways the most important structuring force in nobles' relationships, in the limited sense that geographical proximity mattered to their relationships and in the richer sense that household life reflected the *kinds* of bonds that could obtain among nobles at any time and in any place. It is highly significant that the former can be diagrammed, whereas the latter can be better understood dramaturgically.

I. Landholding and Vassalage

1.

Lucien Romier assumes, but does not explore the assumption, that land created loyalties when he explains the presence of Picard followers among Condé's entourage at the outbreak of civil war: "a

2. Ibid., p. 44.

portion of the Picard nobility was, in fact, vassals or relations of the Bourbons."[3] J. Russell Major tries more effectively to test the importance of vassalage ties. He argues for their continued importance after examining the attention that nobles paid to feudal obligations: the regularity with which they rendered homage, the care with which they sought their lord's permission to render homage by procuration when necessary or to dispose of their lands in ways that required the lord's permission. He argues further for the primacy of feudal ties when he notes that the households of the ducs de Nevers "were made up largely of their vassals, who were also to be found among those who commanded their towns and chateaux." Vassalage relationships were natural ones, or at least they still felt in some way natural to these noblemen. Indeed, the new bonds that were forming between nobles—patron–client bonds—were modeled on older vassalage ties. Patron–client bonds, Major argues, were contractual in a meaningful sense. The amount of land a noble held did not, in the end, limit his power, Major argues further, since "neither fiefs nor specific payments were required [in these new relationships]"; rather, "the number of clients a lord had was limited only by his prestige, influence and the popularity of his cause."[4] But these new bonds were characterized by mutuality, often formally expressed in loyalty oaths that mimicked the practice of giving homage. He goes on to argue that the two systems blended in such a way that a great noble's lands could be used as a source of patronage. But fundamental characteristics of vassal relations still obtained; there was an expectation of mutuality, as well as an expectation that ties through land were felt to be distinctive by the nobles involved. Indeed, land did not merely provide the structure for patronage, it was still the source of meaningful ties in its own right.

Major's error lies in making use of a classic definition of feudalism in ways that overlook the larger context of noble life in the sixteenth century. An extreme example of this equation of lands with loyalties is the following account by one nineteenth-century archivist and editor, Victor de Beauvillé. He accounted for the presence of the sire de Morvilliers alongside Condé in the civil wars in the following terms:

3. Lucien Romier, "Les Protestants à la veille des guerres civiles," *Revue historique* 124 (1917): 2–3.

4. J. Russell Major, "Crown and Aristocracy in Renaissance France," *American Historical Review* 69 (1964): 635, 637.

[The] Prince de Condé had become, following his marriage to Eléonore de Roye, seigneur of Ailly-sur-Noye, of Broyes and of Sourdon. On the thirteenth of December, 1561, [Antoine de Bourbon] had
acquired . . . the lands of Raineval, Thory and Louvrechy. Thus en-
circled, and encouraged by his Huguenot wife, Louis de Lannoy [sire
de Morvilliers] embarked on the dark path and became a zealous
partisan of the Prince de Condé.[5]

As we will see, this analysis is flawed on many counts. It is almost
absurdly mechanical in its analysis of the relationship between land
and loyalty. This historian would have us believe that Morvilliers
suddenly opted for Condé's camp (the "dark path") in 1562 because,
a scant three months earlier, a land purchase by Condé's estranged
brother had completed a kind of territorial choker around him;
Beauvillé does not inquire of what these lands consisted that they
might have either intimidated or obligated Morvilliers to respond
with support. In fact, in the case of Condé's lands of Ailly-sur-
Noye, Broyes, and Sourdon, the answer is: very little. These were
Condé's three small seigneuries in the Amienois, located at some
distance from other Bourbon holdings. None of the three included a
residence that Condé would visit in his lifetime. And neither
through these lands nor through Antoine's new acquisition of Raineval did Morvilliers become a vassal to the Bourbons. Beauvillé's
assertions are useful in one sense: they raise questions about the
importance of physical proximity. Did proximity of two nobles'
lands matter for reasons of strategic power or for reasons of personal
contact? Such concrete factors must be weighed in an effort to assess
the importance of vassalage and other territorial connections between nobles.

For Harding, the link between land and personal ties is more
circumstantial. In a sense, he sidesteps the issue when he depicts the
greater nobles not principally as landholders but as patrons. Important to Harding are the various means by which great-noble governors linked lesser nobles to themselves by dispensing jobs, plain and
simple. He distinguishes three kinds of employment that the governor controlled to a greater or lesser degree within each province: for
lesser nobles, appointment to the governor's large household; for

5. Victor de Beauvillé, ed., *Recueil de documents inédits concernant la Picardie*, 4 vols.
(1860–82), 4:630.

somewhat more prominent warriors, positions in the royal companies of *hommes d'armes*; for nonwarriors, primarily, the many royal offices in the provinces. He does not detail the precise connection between service in a governor's provincial household and territorial connections of some other kind, beyond presuming that a connection between provincial residence and localized service existed. Harding notes that governors' companies of gendarmerie were made up almost exclusively of men native to their governments. He sidesteps the issue of the source of these relationships by affixing them with the conglomerate label of "indigenous patron–client networks." He does assert that the character of the tie between the great-noble patron and the client in the gendarmerie resembled lord–vassal relationships in that the "loyalties that knit the gendarmerie together were obviously personal and reciprocal."[6]

The evidence of the coincidence of the Bourbon family's landholdings and the personal ties they cultivated in Picardy reveals that both Harding's and Major's position have some merit in general terms. Landed wealth, as Harding argues, was merely one of the ways in which great nobles rewarded associates and worked to nurture their attachments to themselves; Antoine de Bourbon and his brother used their positions as governors of the province and as commanders of companies of men-at-arms together with positions within their households or on their lands to reward and support a vast coterie of noblemen. But vassalage ties did not play precisely the role Major has suggested. Some of these men were vassals of the Bourbons to begin with, or became vassals in consequence of service to them—but vassalage was not, by itself, enough to establish a close, working tie between a nobleman and one of the Bourbons. In a great many instances, vassalage appears as an economic and administrative tie—political in the sense that proper administration was a source of power for the lord, but not in the sense that meaningful personal ties necessarily were nurtured by these businesslike relationships.

In order to examine these relationships by means of the example of the Bourbon princes, we must begin by noting the location and the extent of their Picard lands. The holdings of the family in northeastern France extended from the Ile-de-France northward and eastward through Picardy, Artois, and Flanders. Northernmost were a

---

6. Harding, *Anatomy of a Power Elite*, p. 25.

number of seigneuries in Imperial territory, including the county of Enghien. St-Pol and its dependencies were north of Amiens, today contained within the Department of Pas-de-Calais but then not under the control of the French crown. East and south of Amiens lay a cluster of lands that were the real heart of the family's holdings, beginning with François de Bourbon (d. 1495) and his wife, Marie de Luxembourg. These lands included the seigneurie of La Fère and its dependencies, scattered for the most part to the north, along the river Oise, as well as the chatellenies of Ham, Bohain, Beaurevoir, and Marle, respectively to the west, north, and east of La Fère, and their dependencies. These lands formed a kind of semicircle, ranging from the southwest to the northeast of the town of St-Quentin. La Fère itself, on the Oise, was about halfway between St-Quentin and Laon, to the southwest (today in the Department of Aisne).

Marie and François and their heirs appear to have considered these properties in certain geographical terms as well—not with reference to their location near towns (necessary for orienting modern map readers), but rather as distinct clusters of estates. The estates of St-Pol and those to the north and several minor seigneuries in the Amienois were settled on the younger sons of succeeding generations, while La Fère, together with Ham, Bohain, Beaurevoir, and Marle and François's inheritance of Vendôme passed to Marie and François's eldest son, Charles, duc de Vendôme, Condé's father. They then passed intact to Condé's eldest brother, Antoine, and then to Antoine's son Henri de Bourbon (Henri IV). Like many of their contemporaries, Marie and François chose to emphasize one estate as their primary residence among the many that they held. They chose La Fère, and remodeled the château extensively and sumptuously. Marie, widowed in 1495, passed most of the rest of her long life there, until her death in 1546.[7] La Fère was both the residential and the administrative heart of the family's holdings in Picardy. The Chambre du Conseil et des Comptes de La Fère oversaw the accounts for all of the family's holdings.

Historians' references to extensive Bourbon holdings in Picardy

7. P. Poissonier, "Marie de Luxembourg, dame de La Fère," *Société académique de Chauny, Bulletin* 6 (1900): 38–43; P. Héliot, *Les Demeures seigneuriales dans la région picarde au moyen age: Châteaux ou manoirs? Recueil des travaux offert à M. Clovis Brunel,* extrait (Paris, 1955), pp. 574–83. As noted above, pp. 80–81, it had been stipulated in Marie's marriage contract that her inheritance of the comté of St-Pol would pass intact to her second son.

are not wide of the mark. This was an impressive collection of seigneuries; they comprised the inheritance of old, prestigious families. Each included a fortified residence; some of the fortifications were quite elaborate. The remodeled residence at La Fère consisted of some twenty-three rooms.[8] The income these estates generated for the Bourbons was impressive as well. Only a very small fraction of La Fère's accounts have survived, but it is enough to offer a rough gauge of the worth of these lands and to permit a comparison of the Bourbon fortune with those of other families. In 1548–49, the only year for which full accounts survive, the chatellenies of La Fère, Ham, Marle, and the other seigneuries in the vicinity, together with the remaining family estates far to the north (that is, all of the estates in the region except those of St-Pol, which now belonged to the cadet line), brought in 71,154 livres tournois (l.t.).[9] This total is somewhat smaller than the truly extraordinary levels of income generated by the Albret lands in the south, acquired by the Bourbon family by means of the marriage in that year of Antoine de Bourbon with Jeanne d'Albret. Accounts from Albret seigneuries a few years later reveal a staggering income of over 127,315 l.t. from the combined revenues of the kingdom of Navarre, the counties of Foix and Armagnac, the viscounty of Béarn, and other estates in the region.[10] Nor, by itself, did the income from the Picard territories equal the total income of another ducal family at that time, that of the duc de Nevers, Antoine's and Condé's brother-in-law. The income

8. A description of the château and an inventory of some of its furnishings were compiled by Poissonier, "Marie de Luxembourg," before La Fère's archives were destroyed in World War I.

9. AN, KK278, "Recettes des terres du duc de Vendôme en Picardie et dans les Pays-Bas, 1548–49," especially fols. 24r and 59r. A partial inventory of the accounts since destroyed has survived: AN, PP100³, no. 3. The income generated by these lands in that year was actually significantly higher than the total of annual receipts of the various seigneuries, owing to the sale of one holding in the Low Countries which brought in 156,505 l.t. Reliable figures concerning estate receipts are often hard to come by, as accounts do not always clearly distinguish between extraordinary income and ordinary revenue. Accounting practices can also make revenue appear to be larger or smaller than it actually was. See J. Russell Major's discussion of the Albret records, "Noble Income, Inflation, and the Wars of Religion in France," *American Historical Review* 86 (1981): 25. This estimate of Bourbon income for 1548 thus should be used with some caution and for rough comparative purposes only—particularly, of course, as expenditures (and hence the meaning of nobles' income) are even more difficult to assess.

10. Major, "Noble Income," p. 32.

from Nevers's many scattered estates was about 115,000 l.t. at this time.[11] Nevertheless, the roughly 71,000 livres of annual revenue from these Picard lands would have been sufficient by itself to differentiate the Bourbons from all but a very few of the greatest families in the realm.

In the period 1589–1624, the fortunes of the greatest princely families in the realm averaged 1,465,500 livres, which, according to contemporary formulas, would have represented about 73,000 l.t. in yearly revenue. The families of dukes and peers unrelated to the royal house averaged about one half of these levels of total wealth and annual income.[12] At the same time, according to Jonathan Dewald, the provincial elite—those families that dominated provincial political life—typically enjoyed a landed income of about 10,000 to 15,000 livres a year.[13] Plainly, the Bourbon family resources in and north of Picardy were very great; the income these lands provided Antoine de Bourbon in 1548 was on par with the incomes produced by the greatest fortunes in the land.

The youngest son of his generation, Louis, soon to be prince de Condé, would be well provided for from this family patrimony, and without the need to break up the principal cluster of the family's estates. Before his marriage, as was customary, he was supported by pensions drawn from the family's landed revenues. When he married for the first time at the age of twenty-one, in 1551, a number of lands from among the more scattered of the family holdings in the region were settled on him. They included three seigneuries in Brie, three small seigneuries south of Amiens, and two from the family's holdings to the north, in the Low Countries. Easily the most substantial of these seigneuries, in terms of both the revenues they generated and the residences they offered, were two of those in Brie: La Ferté-sous-Jouarre and Condé-en-Brie. These two seigneuries together produced about half of the total income from the lands settled on him at his marriage: approximately 6,000 livres out of a

---

11. Le comte de Soultrait, *Inventaires des titres de Nevers* (Nevers, 1873), p. 528.

12. Jean-Pierre Labatut, *Les Ducs et pairs de France au XVIIe siècle: Etude sociale* (Paris, 1972), pp. 248–49.

13. Jonathan Dewald, *The Formation of a Provincial Nobility: The Magistrates of the Parlement of Rouen, 1499–1610* (Princeton, 1980), p. 124. I have relied on the formulas that Dewald uses to gauge the approximate annual revenue from a given capital value of a family's fortune. See especially p. 116, n. 5.

total of approximately 10,000 livres tournois in annual income.[14] Each boasted a residence that Condé would routinely frequent in his adult life. The château of Condé was situated southeast of Château-Thierry on the Surmelin, a tributary of the Marne; La Ferté lay approximately twenty miles to the west, on the Marne. The château of Condé had been enlarged some years before the Prince's tenure by his uncle the cardinal de Bourbon (d. 1557). The cardinal supposedly enjoyed it as a *grand rendez-vous de chasse*, but the evidence of its sixteenth-century dimensions which survives indicates that it was more than a mere hunting lodge; it seems to have been fortified by walls and by some defensive earthworks.[15] Of the château of La Ferté, nothing at all has survived, although it is possible to appreciate the strategic location it occupied at the confluence of the Marne and the Petit Morin.

The selection of these holdings for the establishment of the family's youngest male heir was undoubtedly made on the grounds that they were among the more dispensable portions of the family inheritance. The seigneuries of Condé and La Ferté and the rights comprising the third of the Brie seigneuries, the vicomté de Meaux, had been acquired by Condé's grandfather François de Bourbon from the Rohan family in exchange for lands in Brittany and Anjou. The three had then been transferred to Condé's uncle the cardinal by an official division of the family's holdings among the three sons of François some years after his death. By the terms of the division, the three holdings that eventually came to Condé were granted to the

14. MC, Titres A₅, "Contrat de marriage entre Louis de Bourbon et Eléonore de Roye," 22 June 1551, Anizy-le-château, copy; ibid., "Etat des biens paternels et maternels de Mons. Henri de Bourbon, prince de Condé," June 1570, n.p. This document was intended as a kind of inventory of the Prince's holdings after his death. The annual revenues from each holding are approximated only. However, comparisons with the precise revenues recorded in 1548–49 (for those Bourbon lands included in both documents) confirm the reliability of these approximations.

15. Xavier de Sade, the current owner of the château of Condé, kindly supplied me with information concerning the former appearance of the château, supplementing that in his article "Le Château de Condé-en-Brie," *Vieilles maisons françaises*, no. 53 (July 1972), pp. 16–23. The château today bears little resemblance to its sixteenth-century self, but, unlike many other châteaux in the northeast, Condé owes its transformation to deliberate renovation over the centuries, not to neglect and modern warfare. Ironically, whereas nineteenth-century sketches and photographs suggest the sixteenth-century dimensions of many châteaux that are now in ruins, we must remain relatively ignorant of the sixteenth-century state of the château de Condé.

cardinal in return for forfeiture of all future claims on the remainder of the family's properties.[16] The recent arrival of these holdings into the family and the path they took through the family—bypassing the two elder sons in the next generation—suggest their insignificance in relation to other family holdings and their suitability for the support of the youngest and least significant heir. These and the other estates settled on the young prince were geographically marginal as well. Condé, La Ferté, and Meaux lay ninety miles to the southeast of the nearest of the cluster of family estates around La Fère. Ailly-sur-Noye, Sourdon, and Broyes, the Prince's estates close to Amiens, were situated about seventy miles to the west of La Fère. The remaining estates in the Low Countries were, obviously, far to the north, and were under the control of hostile Imperial forces at this point.

The young prince de Condé would eventually gain control of further family estates following the death of his elder brother Jean—the only remaining brother in lay life after Antoine—at the battle of St-Quentin. Most important among these estates was the county of Enghien in the Low Countries, which was worth about 7,500 l.t. in annual revenue, or about 1.25 times the combined revenues of La Ferté and Condé.[17] From his original position of obscurity as the youngest of five living sons, Condé eventually rose to a position of great prominence within the family, and his control of family estates naturally reflected this change in status. But the Prince's family had carefully enhanced his landed wealth at small cost to the patrimony years before the (obviously) unexpected death of Jean by the best means available: a strategically brilliant marriage. Both of Eléonore de Roye's parents, Charles de Roye and Madeleine de Mailly, were

16. BN, MS fr. 4643, fols. 250–59v, "Partage faict par Marie de Luxembourg, duchesse douairière de Vendômois, comtesse de St-Pol, entre ses trois fils Charles de Bourbon, duc de Vendômois, François de Bourbon, comte de St-Pol, et Louis, cardinal de Bourbon, évesque de Laon," 1 February 1518, La Fère, copy. The copy states that the act dated from the time of the marriage of Charles. This certainly seems possible, since formal allotment of the patrimony after François's death in 1495 would only then have become necessary. Charles de Bourbon was married on May 18, 1513.

17. AN, KK278, "Recettes des terres . . ., 1548–49," fol. 40; MC, Titres A$_5$, "Etat des biens paternels et maternels . . .," June 1570. The revenue for Enghien in 1548–49 is listed as 7,346 l.t., 15s, 5d; in 1570, it is estimated at 7,600 l.t. The Prince also gained the family's share of the county of Soissons at this point.

the last surviving representatives of old Picard families, and Eléonore was the elder of their two daughters. She eventually brought to the marriage lands worth about 687,000 l.t. in total capital value.[18]

The marriage contract stipulated only that the bride would bring 6,000 l.t. in *rentes* annually to the marriage as long as her parents were still living, and twice that amount after their deaths. The provision of rentes was a very common arrangement in marriage contracts. And this dowry was precisely the average size of dowry enjoyed by members of the aristocratic elite, the nobles who were provincial governors, according to the calculations of Robert Harding.[19] Thus Condé had realized his best possible expectations with this marriage. Yet the union promised even more. When the tie was contracted, Charles de Roye and Madeleine de Mailly were still hoping for a male heir, and the marriage contract for their daughter included the conventional renunciation of further claims on her parents' estate should their hope be realized. But the hope must always have been a rather faint one—Madeleine was now almost forty years old and it had been years since the birth of her last child—and the members of both families who arranged the marriage must surely have known that it was unlikely to be fulfilled. Indeed, Charles died six months later, in January 1552, and Eléonore and her new husband became the principal beneficiaries of the Roye-Mailly inheritance.

Beginning in 1553, Madeleine de Mailly (who would live until 1567) began to transfer control of various family seigneuries to Elé-

---

18. Ibid. See above, n. 13, concerning estimating capital values of landholdings.
19. MC, Titres A₅, "Contrat de marriage," 22 June 1551, Anizy-le-château, copy. Following the formulas used by Dewald, I have estimated a capital value for Eléonore's dowry by multiplying the annual income from the rentes by 10. This estimate places the dowry near (in fact slightly above) the average dowry of about 100,000 livres which Harding has calculated for all governors' marriages before 1560. Harding has capitalized all dowries in rentes according to a different formula, but as he has found relatively few dowries comprised of rentes, we may still use his figures for comparison. See Harding, *Anatomy of a Power Elite,* pp. 111–15, especially p. 113, n. 11. The marriage strategies of the warrior nobility as a whole have received scant attention. Such evidence as we have of dowry size suggests that there may have been a good deal of variation in a single family's strategy from marriage to marriage, as well as variation among families of comparable status. An "average" dowry size might therefore be of limited usefulness in our efforts to understand the significance of a particular dowry.

onore and her husband. First came the transfer to Condé of the barony of Conty, south of Amiens. Then, in 1558, four groups of seigneuries located in the *bailliages* of Hesdin, Amiens, Montdidier, and Vermandois were given to Eléonore by her mother. In 1561, most of the remaining Roye patrimony was officially divided between Eléonore and her younger sister, Charlotte; their husbands agreed with Madeleine de Mailly on a division: Condé accepted the seigneurie of Muret, south of Soissons, with its dependencies, together with several other, scattered holdings, and Charlotte's husband, the comte de La Rochefoucauld, took principally the county of Roucy and the seigneuries of Nizy-le-comte, both east of Laon. At the time of this division, Madeleine retained for her own use until her death a number of estates that later appear in a 1570 inventory of Bourbon-Condé holdings. These remaining holdings included Bretheuil, Francastel, and Villers-le-vicomte, situated close together between Beauvais and Amiens, and Plessis-de-Roye, to the east of these holdings, near Noyon; records of any special conditions accompanying their eventual transfer to Condé, Eléonore, or their children have not survived.[20]

The total worth of these lands—estimated at approximately 687,500 l.t. on the basis of the 1570 inventory of revenue—meant that Condé had, in effect, received a dowry larger than that of most other noblemen in a single marriage. The 1558 donation of lands included, in addition, an outright gift consisting mostly of jewelry—a common provision that had not been included in the couple's original marriage contract. Of course, the couple did not immediately enjoy income from all of these lands. As was commonly the case, Madeleine reserved usufruct of most of the lands for her lifetime. Yet, insofar as the surviving documents can inform us, it seems clear that these family lands were deliberately put to use on behalf of Condé and his wife in succeeding years. Here the question of what these holdings "meant" to Condé begins to gain concrete dimensions. The barony of Conty was donated directly to the Prince in 1553, subject to Madeleine's usufruct. The act stipulated that

20. MC, Titres GE$_5$, "Donation de Conti . . . et de Rot . . . à Louis de Bourbon . . .," 21 July 1553, n.p.; and the following documents in Titres A$_5$: "Donation faicte par Mme de Mailly à Eléonore de Roye . . . ," 28 May 1558, n.p.; "Partage de la succession de Charles de Roye," 10 October 1561, n.p.; "Etat des biens paternels et maternels . . . ," June 1570.

Condé could pass the land to children of a future marriage, if he so chose; Madeleine had thereby in effect separated the holding from the Mailly inheritance. She was responding, she declared, to the Prince's "dissatisfaction" with the original marriage contract. Those provisions, the grant claims, had been neither in accord with Madeleine's true wishes nor appropriate to the "grandeur and excellence" of the Prince.

Most interesting are the circumstances in which, nine years later, Madeleine renounced her right of usufruct and granted the Prince full possession of this barony, together with a smaller seigneurie nearby. She chose the months of April and May 1562, as rebel troops gathered at Orléans around Condé's banner, to carry out the final transfers of rights.[21] The 1,100 livres of annual revenue from these lands was a paltry sum by comparison with the costs of warfare and with the sums later raised by others—including Madeleine herself—on the rebels' behalf. Thus a more immediate goal may have been to provide encouragement and symbolic support, visible to Condé and to other members of his family. Earlier that spring, Madeleine had alienated the revenues of one of the seigneuries given to Eléonore in 1558 (of which she still retained usufruct), also on the Prince's behalf. Together with the fruits of two of Condé's minor seigneuries, Madeleine offered hers in order to secure a substantial loan of 30,000 livres from a merchant at Antwerp.[22] This transaction was in addition to later negotiations she undertook for the rebel cause at Strasbourg and elsewhere during the months to come.

In the absence of estate accounts from Condé and of further records detailing grants from Madeleine to the young couple, the income the two enjoyed from Roye-Mailly lands before Madeleine's death in 1567 cannot be known with any precision. A very rough estimate might be 6,600 l.t., the combined revenues (as calculated in 1570) from Conty and Muret, which were the only two holdings definitively in the hands of the Prince and Princess before Madeleine's death. This amount would have brought their income to above 23,000 l.t. as of 1561. But whatever the income that found

21. MC, Titres GE₅, "Donation de Conty . . . ," 3 April 1562, n.p.; ibid., "Donation de Rot . . . ," 9 May 1562, n.p.

22. Ibid., "Reconnaissance de debt . . . ," 7 February 1572, n.p. Many surviving pieces, documenting transactions from the 1550s and 1560s, actually date from later years and identify earlier transactions as they provide a history of a current situation. This 1572 record documents the fact that the debt had not yet been paid.

its way into Condé's personal accounts, the lands from his wife's family were put to use on their behalf. Tenure of an estate was precisely delineated but did not directly reflect the actual uses and applications of its resources; use of the Mailly-Roye inheritance depended on cooperation and negotiation between Madeleine and her children.

In addition to income, these estates offered residences, and here, too, there was no clear distinction in practice between those the couple held and certain of those belonging to members of the family of either the Prince or the Princess. Three of the holdings from the Roye-Mailly inheritance included impressive residences. At Conty, south of Amiens, was a fortified château that had been extensively rebuilt in the fifteenth century by one of Madeleine de Mailly's ancestors. It was situated on a hill overlooking the town of the same name on the Selle, which flows north to join the Somme at Amiens. Plessis-de-Roye—transferred to the young couple at some unknown later date—and Muret, from the Roye patrimony, included châteaux that supposedly had been Charles de Roye's favorite residences.[23] But the Prince and the Princess, together and separately, often sojourned at estates belonging to other members of their families—particularly at La Fère, belonging to Antoine; at Anizy, belonging to Condé's brother the cardinal de Bourbon; and at Roucy, which belonged to Eléonore's sister.[24]

The manner in which the prince de Condé made use of another

23. M. A. Gabriel Rembault, "Eglise, château et seigneurie de Conty," in *Eglises, châteaux, beffrois et hôtels de villes les plus remarquables de la Picardie et de l'Artois*, ed. H. Duseval et al., 2 vols. (Amiens, 1846–49), 2:43–58; MC, Titres GE_5, "Procès-verbal pour la visitation des officers de la seigneurie de Plessis-de-Roye," 5 November 1597, n.p., copy. La Falaise, one of the small seigneuries that remained in Madeleine's hands until her death, may also have included a small château. See "Declaration des pairries, fiefs, terres et seigneuries tenues et mouvans de la baronnye de Boves," 1610, n.p., in Beauvillé, *Recueil de documents*, 4:412–14. As Beauvillé notes, many seigneuries such as La Falaise have been "lost"; their physical remains have disappeared, making impossible any precise knowledge of their extent or their features.

24. The couple's visits to these various residences have been calculated primarily from the provenance of their letters. The seigneurie of Anizy-le-château, west of Laon, should not be confused with Nizy-le-comte, east of Laon, which was part of the Roye-Mailly inheritance of Charlotte de Roye, Eléonore's sister. Anizy was probably held by Charles, cardinal de Bourbon, who was responsible for some renovations made there. See L. Hautecoeur, *Historie de l'architecture classique en France*, vol. 1, *La Formation de l'idéale classique* (Paris, 1965), pt. 1, *La Première Renaissance*, pp. 43, n. 3, and 284, and pt. 2, *La Renaissance des humanistes*, p. 211.

holding that he later gained further illustrates that a calculation of income does not reflect the full usefulness of a holding to a nobleman. This holding was Valléry. Valléry was located west of Sens, south of Paris, on a tributary of the Loing. It had been presented to him by the widowed maréchale de St-André shortly after he himself became a widower at Eléonore's death in July 1564, perhaps as part of an attempt to woo the Prince into a second marriage. It was certainly a most generous gift; the château had been extensively remodeled in the latest Renaissance style during the maréchal de St-André's life, and was frequently cited by contemporaries as evidence of the vast wealth St-André had managed to accumulate in his years as a favored courtier. Surviving descriptions of the buildings and the reputation of the château in its own time suggest that it was the most sumptuous and the most outwardly impressive of all of Condé's residences. Immediately after Condé received the gift he began to use the château as frequently as he did his other dwellings, perhaps more frequently, though it was located at some distance from his other holdings and was in no way hallowed by family association.[25]

When we attempt to account for this behavior, an important interpretive issue emerges. Residence at Valléry would not merely have been pleasant for the Prince, it would also have been a source of prestige for him. When Valléry was transferred to his control in the years between the first two civil wars, Condé was engaged in a variety of maneuvers to secure his power at court. His brother and rival was dead, and a relatively favorable peace treaty had been extracted from the crown; Condé could concentrate on further buttressing his preeminent position. He cast about for another marriage partner, and tried to temper his relationship with the cardinal de Lorraine in order to reduce the now seemingly unnecessary hostility

25. AN, Y105, fols. 183–84, "Donation à Louis de Bourbon par Marguerite de Lustrac, veuve de Jacques d'Albon, mareschal de France," 11 July 1564, Valléry. The AN inventory incorrectly identifies Henri, Louis's son, as the recipient of this gift. A marriage between Henri and Marguerite's daughter had been considered, but any union had been prevented by the daughter's death. The affection between the two families resulting from the planned marriage was made the pretext for Marguerite's extravagant gift to Louis de Bourbon. For descriptions of the château, see A. Challe, "Valléry," in Extrait de l'annuaire de l'Yonne (1842), pp. 145–85, and L. Hautecoeur, Histoire de l'architecture classique, vol. 1, La Formation de l'idéale classique, pt. 2, La Renaissance des humanistes, pp. 278–79.

between them. His splendid new acquisition of Valléry would symbolize and therefore amplify his preeminence. He thus may have used Valléry in ways that had little to do with its possible use as a source of material support for his followers. In other words, the value of a landholding to Condé could include its symbolic value.

2

This sketch of some of the uses of property in the Bourbon family has made clear that landed property had many possible uses and significances for the nobility. It must be remembered that seigneuries were not actually chunks of territory but rather conglomerations of rights. They were flexible sources of revenue, in that one could use these rights in a variety of ways, as Madeleine de Mailly did. Property rights could be assigned or alienated in various ways; any property could be collateral for a loan or the means of constituting rentes.[26] It could be bought, sold, exchanged. But seigneuries, and seigneurial residences, were also a means to display power, prestige, and identity, and were a constituent of family identity over time.[27]

Given the plural meanings of landholding, how did ties of vassalage connect lesser provincial noblemen to members of the Bourbon family? A good way to begin to answer this question is to compare other evidence of nobles' association with the Bourbons—presence in their households, guard of their scattered estates, enrollment in their companies of the royal gendarmerie—with records of the identity of their vassals. The various records in which such information might be found have survived very randomly. Much of

26. *Rentes constituées* amounted to loans, with a noble's lands as collateral. A nobleman "sold" a rente when he obtained a payment of capital (which, we would say, he was borrowing) from another party in return for an annual fee (the *arrérages*—in our terms, a loan payment). Many regulations hedged this practice in order to keep it from technically equaling lending money at interest. For example, the fiction that this was not repayment for a loan was maintained by a regulation that the buyer (lender) could never demand back the purchase price (principal). Occasionally noble families went deeply into debt when too high a percentage of their income went to keeping up with payments of arrérages. See Bernard Schnapper, *Les Rentes au XVIe siècle: Histoire d'un instrument de crédit* (Paris, 1957).

27. See the discussion of the nature of the seigneurie in Dewald, *Formation of a Provincial Nobility*, 163–83.

the discussion to follow draws on evidence of Antoine de Bourbon's associates rather than those of his brother the prince de Condé. Several muster rolls naming the men enrolled in each brother's company of the gendarmerie have survived. However, household accounts that identify men formally associated with the household and inventories of dependent fiefs and fiefholders survive only for Antoine, and there are certain limitations to this evidence. We have only one household account, from 1548–49; muster rolls from then until his death in 1562; and one inventory of fiefs dependent on the Picard lands, from 1585. Fortunately, the recent history of many fiefs is recounted and previous fiefholders are often identified in this 1585 document compiled for Antoine's son Henri (Henri IV). Thus we can identify noblemen who were both vassals of Antoine and householders or hommes d'armes. We find that only a few of the men steadily associated with Antoine were also among his vassals.

This somewhat surprising finding does not necessarily mean that such ties as did exist were without significance. Rather, it reflects the complex conditions that impinged on the meaning of vassalage ties. These conditions included the wider context of property relations that obtained between nobles. The limited significance of vassalage ties for noble relationships lies in part in the very fluidity of landed wealth: very little personal obligation was felt to ride on the vassalage tie and, conversely, the connection could be defined by the actual proprietary interests in each case. Further, in this arena as in others, no part of a noble's public life was disconnected from the rest; the wider context of two nobles' relationship impinged on any particular interaction over a given seigneurie and the obligations attached to it. Hence vassalage, like any other facet of a relationship, reflected the impact of other features of two nobles' relationship, such as kinship, familiarity, stature.

Indeed, although strong ties between nobles did not automatically arise in the specific lord–vassal link, that link could *reflect* a tie. That is, some noblemen became vassals of Antoine or of Condé in the course of years of service to them because they were rewarded with seigneuries alienated from the Bourbon patrimony. An occasional noble to whom a Bourbon was indebted would be repaid by a gift of land or seigneurial revenue. The very flexibility of the seigneurie—the many possible ways in which the rights and revenues could be alienated—made it an ideal tool for rewarding an associate in terms that potentially could serve to express a personal link as well. Vassalage, in one sense, was merely one of the ways in which property relations reflected ties between nobles.

It must be noted further that one reason that many nobles—particularly many of the most prominent ones—otherwise associated with Antoine were not also his vassals is in some ways a technical question of historic political geography. Picardy, as we have seen, developed a prosperous economy that supported a relatively large number of prosperous noble families, no one of which succeeded in imposing its authority over others during the Middle Ages. The pattern of infeudation that developed reflected this division of authority: Picardy abounded in relatively modest fiefs that were held directly from the crown.[28] Thus even such relatively vast holdings as those of the Bourbon family did not occasion suzerainty over a large number of substantial fiefs. The web of lord–vassal ties which nominally did exist often linked many of the more prominent noblemen of the province in mutual dependence; the minor fiefs of one family could be dependencies of a major seigneurie of a fellow. Several of the small holdings in the bailliage of Hesdin which Condé gained through Eléonore, for example, were held of Louis d'Ailly, sire de Picquigny, one of the most powerful men in the province. Several others in the bailliage of Amiens were held of Antoine de Créquy—also one of the provincial elite—because of his major holding of Dommart-en-Ponthieu.[29] Still others of Condé's very minor tenures were held of more modest nobles.

The majority of Antoine's vassals, then, were relatively modest provincial noblemen. The significance of their vassalage tie to the Bourbons varied according to the differing circumstances of their stature and their past association with their feudal lord. The case of one of Antoine's householders, Jean de Pipemont, illustrates one possible experience of vassalage. Pipemont served as *maréchal des logis,* or quartermaster, in Antoine's household.[30] By 1580 either he or (more likely) his heirs came to hold two fiefs from the Bourbons. The first was merely a section of woodland; the second boasted at

---

28. Robert Fossier, *Histoire de la Picardie* (Toulouse, 1974), pp. 102–209 passim, and *La Terre et les hommes en Picardie,* 2 vols. (Paris and Louvain, 1968), 1:732–34.

29. MC, Titre A₅, "Donation faite par Mme de Mailly à Eléonore de Roye," 28 May 1558, Paris.

30. AN, KK278, "Recettes des terres . . . ," fol. 99.

least a modest dwelling. Interestingly, this second holding, Courainval, had earlier been raised to the status of fief by Marie de Luxembourg. By the same date the family had also acquired two other holdings in the Laonnois. One was a small seigneurie dependent on the bishopric of Laon. The other, northeast of Laon, had been elevated to a barony by 1665. Jean de Pipemont's great-grandson was baron de Couvron.[31] The Pipemonts thus built up their holdings successfully over three or four generations from a very modest start. Their holding of Courainval was clearly a very modest one, if we may judge by the extant description of it in 1585. There is no mention of fortifications or enclosures of any kind, or of gardens, vineyards, meadows, or woods, or of income from *censives* or *rentes*; it was listed simply as a "maison et terres labourables," a farm now held as a fief.[32]

Another family acquired dependent fiefs from the Bourbons by a somewhat different process. Pierre de La Vieuville, a member of the household, also served as an officer in Antoine's company of men-at-arms.[33] He was one of the few men in Antoine's company who would later rise to command his own company of gendarmerie.[34] The family held at least one seigneurie south of Laon in the preceding generation, and by the time of Pierre's active career in Antoine's entourage, had added a second one nearby.[35] The family did not become vassals of Antoine until later, at some point before the 1585 records of the Bourbon fiefs were compiled. What the La Vieuvilles acquired was a cluster of six small fiefs near the confluence of the Serre and the Peron, between La Fère and Marle, to the north of their original seigneuries near Laon. All six fiefs had previously

31. M. Melleville, *Dictionnaire historique, généalogique, biographique et agricole du département de l'Aisne*, 2 vols. (Laon, 1857), 1:28–29.

32. AN, Q¹*10², "Déclaration des fiefs, terres et seigneuries tenus et mouvans des Roye et Royne de Navarre," 26 November 1585, La Fère, fol. 200v.

33. AN, KK278, "Recettes des terres . . . ," fol. 98v; BN, Clair. 257, p. 1503, "Revue . . . de 100 hommes d'armes . . . de Monseigneur le duc de Vendômois," 21 January 1555, Sens; BN, Clair. 258, p. 1541, "Rolle . . . de 97 hommes d'armes . . . de Monseigneur le duc de Vendômois," 22 April 1557, Sens; BN, MS fr. 21524, p. 1703, "Revue . . . de 97 hommes d'armes . . . de Monseigneur le roi de Navarre," 15 November 1558, Chartres, and p. 1739, "Revue . . . de 100 homme d'armes . . . de Monseigneur le roi de Navarre," 6 August 1561, Agen.

34. Fleury-Vindry, *Dictionnaire de l'état-major français au XVIᵉ siècle*, pt. 1, *Gendarmerie* (Bergerac, 1901), p. 261.

35. Melleville, *Dictionnaire historique*, 2:173.

belonged to another family—a family in some financial difficulties, it appears, since the dwellings included were in dilapidated condition.[36] The La Vieuvilles became vassals of the Bourbons, then, as they added to their landholdings over the course of years.

The Pipemonts and the La Vieuvilles represent two different phases of family aggrandizement. The Pipemonts rose to the status of fiefholders by means of their service to the Bourbons. It is unclear whether Courainval was raised to a fief expressly for a member of this family, but at the very least, the family was able to purchase these and later lands as a result of their service in the Bourbon household. The La Vieuvilles enjoyed more resources; they had amassed land earlier. Pierre de La Vieuville exercised by far the more numerous and more prestigious charges within and without the household. After years in the army and other commands, he and his heirs were able to purchase more lands—not, from the appearance of the lands, to live on, but solely for additional income.

But in the case of both families, vassalage was less a cause than a consequence of their relationship with the Bourbons. Whatever familiarity and obligation existed between them and their eventual lord had been built on foundations of past household and military service. Indeed, the most obvious and immediate consequence of their acquisitions of these lands was the aggrandizement of their stature as substantial landholders. The more precise significance of vassalage, per se, is harder to discern. Each aspect of the two families' circumstances contributed to the character of whatever relationship they had with the Bourbons as vassals. How many and how substantial were any other lands the La Vieuvilles may have acquired, for example? How did the revenues from their new fiefs compare with those of their old ones? Such questions are difficult to answer for most modest nobles, and in any case we can establish the significance of the answers only by placing them in a broader context.

Some of the meaning of vassalage can be gleaned from Picard nobles' transactions in land and from evidence of their fulfillment or neglect of their own vassalage obligations and lordly prerogatives. The 1585 record of Bourbon-Navarre fiefs and similar records of other major seigneuries suggest that lord–vassal relationships were

36. AN, Q^{1}*10^{2}, "Déclaration des fiefs," 26 November 1585, fol. 227r–v.

not immemorial personal relationships to be taken for granted but rather, to a significant degree, economic and political relationships continuously to be negotiated. The 1585 list was the result of extensive investigation into the status of fiefs and the identity of their holders. It was intended to remedy the accumulated confusion and irregularities of the years since 1552, when such an investigation had last been carried out. In a number of instances, the agents acting for Henri de Navarre, heir to his father, Antoine de Bourbon, were unable to identify the holder of a particular fief, or even to verify the existence of certain small fiefs. The officers were forced to conduct a search for one fief that, "it was said," was located between two villages near La Ferté-Chevresis. Eventually they discovered the heir of the previous holder living in a house (which presumably constituted the fief) "close to the church and cemetery" of one of the villages. But the man they found, one Guillaume Moreau, said that he recognized the bishop of Laon as his lord, and that he had carried out all his obligations to the bishop. The perplexed officers decided, in the end, to search the archives at La Fère for a title that would document the Bourbon claim before attempting to seize the fief.[37]

Some of their master's other vassals, however, were found clearly to be delinquent in fulfillment of their obligations. These obligations included doing homage, submitting a written version of the homage (an *aveu*), paying a fee (a *relief*), and furnishing a description of the fief to the lord (a *dénombrement*) when the fief changed hands. Both the young comte de Chaulnes and Henri, the second prince de Condé, were Henri de Navarre's vassals for minor fiefs, and both had been delinquent. Next to the entry for Chaulnes's small fief, consisting of arable land, fields, and a willow grove, it was noted that Chaulnes had paid the relief but had failed to furnish the required dénombrement. A fief held by the young Condé, consisting of rents from a small parcel of land near Laon, had already been seized by Navarre's agents.[38] Seizures of fiefs for such delinquency are noted in many similar documents. Between 1536 and 1538, Antoine d'Ailly, sire de Picquigny, systematically seized the delinquent fiefs—fourteen in all—of his seigneurie of Raineval (the holding that Antoine de Bourbon later bought from his son Louis, the

37. Ibid., fols. 223v–34r.
38. Ibid., fols. 205r–v, 228.

next sire de Picquigny). Among the fourteen was the fief of Bacon-val, which belonged to Charles de Roye. One Saturday morning in November 1538, Ailly's agents seized it. It was a minuscule fief, consisting primarily of a small amount of woodland and pasture, leased out for fourteen livres a year. Minuscule or not, Charles de Roye furnished Ailly with the missing dénombrement the following spring in order to reclaim his property.[39]

Some of the significance of such careful inquiries and pursuits of rights is suggested by the circumstances surrounding another investigation by the agents of Bourbon-Navarre. The status of another small fief held by the young Condé of his cousin was carefully scrutinized by Navarre's officials in 1585. This fief was situated east of Laon near Nizy-le-comte and was one of the fiefs that Navarre's officers had initially been unable to identify. An entry further on in the 1585 record reveals that they eventually came into additional information about the "missing" fief. They learned that, years earlier, officials acting for the first prince de Condé had attempted to strike a deal with his brother Antoine concerning the status of this dependency. Condé's officials had informed agents of his late brother that Antoine in fact held a few small fiefs, scattered here and there, from Condé, which were in delinquent status; the Prince would fulfill his duties for the fief at Nizy-le-comte, they had said, if Antoine would fulfill his own duties to Condé for the fiefs held from the Prince.[40]

In this interaction between brothers, the nominal lord–vassal relationship clearly bears the imprint of the larger relationship between the two men. The precise significance of this proposed exchange of recognition and feudal duties is not altogether clear because some of the pertinent facts about the seigneuries and their holders are not known. It is unclear (since the investigators could not even identify it) exactly of what Condé's fief at Nizy consisted. Whether such an exchange of information would have been markedly in Condé's favor in strict economic terms is thus unclear. Perhaps Condé was pressed financially and, seeking to exploit every possible source of revenue, prevailed upon his sibling to resolve the status of this

39. "Saisie féodale des fiefs tenus de Raineval," 1536–38, in Beauvillé, *Recueil de documents*, 4:280–83.
40. AN, Q¹*10² , fol. 235.

holding. More likely, in view of the insignificance of the fief, would be a less urgent desire to regularize its status. Regularizing the status of this fief was most likely one of many routine, periodic management efforts of this kind—such as those by Antoine d'Ailly to bring into compliance all of his vassals of Raineval. In this case, however, the officials acting for Condé could make use of a family relationship to make the results of that effort as advantageous to their master as possible.

Similarly Charles de Roye, a prominent noble in his own right, would hardly have been threatened or even disconcerted by the seizure of his tiny fief of Baconval by his provincial neighbor and peer Antoine d'Ailly. A lesser noble whose few small holdings were each more vital to him might have found such seizures more ominous. Accounts such as those recording the work of Ailly's officials suggest, however, that a lesser noble might not have faced disastrous loss of income as frequently as might be supposed. Seizure of a fief in most cases appears to have been simply a step in a process to ensure compliance with routine practices. In some cases, the lord returned control of a seized fief to his vassal in anticipation of due receipt of a dénombrement for the property within, say, three months' time.[41] There would, in any case, also have been informal leeway—the months between the time the fief was seized and the time the income of the fief (if it consisted primarily of ground rents) would be paid into the fiefholder's lord's pocket and not his own.

Still, there is no question that petty nobles were disadvantaged in relation to great nobles when property rights were in dispute. Antoine d'Ailly paid notaries as well as men of his own a total of approximately twenty livres to seize the various delinquent fiefs of Raineval and to obtain the proper authorization from the nearby officer of the royal *prévôté* of Montdidier.[42] If the status of a fief were in dispute, the costs required to resolve the dispute could be a much greater burden to a very modest noble than to his superior. Such a dispute could easily arise, as we have seen, when many years had elapsed since the lord had last attempted to determine and regularize the status of the dependencies. The case of Guillaume Moreau of

41. Ailly's agents provided this leeway when they seized several Raineval fiefs.
42. "Saisie des fiefs . . . de Raineval."

Laon becomes instructive here. By taking care of his feudal duties, he forestalled the claim by Navarre's agents. It would seem to be to the advantage of a petty noble, then, to carry out his formal obligations; the consequences for the family of an ambiguous situation vis-à-vis the lord might be very costly. A vigorous investigation at the hands of well-paid officials, such as those at work in 1585, was to be avoided.

It would be more difficult for a very modest noble than for his lord to keep written records of, say, the reliefs he had paid. An inventory of Ailly papers stored at their principal château of Picquigny lists many written pieces formally and informally verifying that *hommages* had been rendered and reliefs paid by the sires de Picquigny over the years. They kept records of the obligations due them as well as of many of the obligations they had themselves performed.[43] The records kept are more sporadic than systematic and they appear to have been organized rather haphazardly—no doubt a reflection of contemporary practices in regard to written texts. But however haphazardly they were kept by our standards, the existence of such texts depended on the expense and expertise necessary to house, catalogue, and make use of them. A prominent noble such as Ailly was in a much better position to defend his claims than were his vassals, not only because he could make better use of written documentation but also because he could support the expense of a lengthy investigation. It also would have been easier for him, in view of his generally greater resources, to mobilize oral resources: to identify and gather witnesses who would support his claims when an investigation was conducted.[44]

The expression of vassalage relations found in the scrupulous carrying out of formal obligations, such as the rendering of homage, was thus, in part at least, an expression of business and political acumen in the nobles' own self-interest. It reflected, among other things, the need to defend one's property interests against one's

43. AN, R⁴774*, "Inventaire des titres de la chambre des comptes de La Fère," n.d.; "Inventaires des terres, titres, dénombrements et enseignemens appartenans à . . . Charles d'Ailly, vidame d'Amiens, baron de Picquigny . . . ," 2 August 1515, in Beauvillé, *Recueil de documents*, 3:258–97.

44. See the importance of oral testimony to the inquiry over a sale of two holdings by Charles d'Ailly: "Enquête concernant la vente à réméré des terres de Thory et de Louvrechy . . . ," p. 1507, in Beauvillé, *Recueil de documents*, 4:186–264.

lord. Whether or not it also may have been an expression of loyalty to the lord in some other sense, it was in this respect a transaction over the issue of *power*. Attention to the formal requirements of feudal ties could thus be described as simply business as usual. Moreover, the meaning of these formal behaviors in each case varied with the relative power of the lord and vassal; the business of rectifying claims between Condé and his brother was a transaction between relative equals, but such was hardly the case in a transaction between either of them and a lesser vassal. The example of Condé and his brother also suggests that other ties between noblemen— familiarity and a commitment to some kind of cooperation arising from kinship or long interaction—became the context that gave meaning to the dual lord–vassal relationship that also existed between them. Their "business" relationship as expressed in lord– vassal relationships was simultaneously one facet of and one arena for the expression of their larger relationships.

It is when agents seem most zealously to be performing their duties on the lord's behalf that we can see the distinct facets of the vassalage relationship: its businesslike dimension with its ingredients of power and conflict, its symbolic value as an expression of the bonds linking two men, and the connection of these possibilities to the larger relationship between the two nobles involved. In a letter to a prominent noble (not of Picard origin) a vassal reports his dissatisfaction with the way he is being treated by his lord's agents. "I am very upset," he says, "to have to complain about your officers, who have refused to deliver control of my lands to me, despite the homage I have performed to you for them." As the letter goes on, we learn that he has sent to these agents a copy of the homage he had performed in person when both noblemen were at Blois. He is therefore being meticulous in the performance of his obligations. He is also aware that things of this sort can cause tensions between men, because he then states his fear that the agents' actions will "sow doubts between you and me" ("mectre question entre vous et moy"). He insists that he does have just claim to the lands in question (it seems that the agents were denying his claim, not simply taking their time in turning the lands over to him). But then he says—and here we see the larger relationship between the two men coming into play—"but even if I have no right to them, it doesn't matter, because you will want to give them to me" ("je pense que me la vouldrez bien donner").

He then closes his letter by touching on the two other aspects of vassalage which interest us: its businesslike nature and its symbolic nature. He again alludes to the potential problems that might arise out of this situation, in terms that are commonplace ones of exchange between nobles. "Before your departure," he asks, "kindly put an end to this, and all my life I will feel myself drawn to you." He concludes, however, by invoking the vassalage tie in a markedly ritualized and formalized manner: "I assure you that you have no vassal on this earth who more desires to do you service with the aid of Him who gives all power and to whom I pray on your behalf."[45] It is important to note that the mention of vassalage in this way (as opposed to businesslike ways) was very rare in nobles' correspondence. The power in this statement—the conviction—resides not in the actual vassalage relationship per se but rather in all of the trust and familiarity that clearly marks their relationship generally. Full understanding of vassalage relations, then, requires us to consider other elements of nobles' relationship, including their understanding of their other bonds.

When vassalage ties are considered in the light of other property relations, their complexity becomes even more obvious. Property relations were themselves complex. Financial gain, political power, and personal ties could all be represented in them and affected by them simultaneously. Indeed, most striking is how nonfeudal transactions in land or goods reflected and affected personal ties. In 1571, for example, Jeanne d'Albret wrote to Françoise de Warty, widow of the sire de Picquigny, expressing her relief that a difference that had arisen between their two families over the past sale of the seigneurie of Raineval to Antoine de Bourbon, her late husband, was being resolved. (Ironically, this is the seigneurie that, one historian alleged, drew the sire de Picquigny into the Bourbon orbit.) Louis d'Ailly, sire de Picquigny, Françoise's late brother-in-law, had sold Raineval and its dependencies to Antoine in 1561 for 50,000 livres: 2,000 in cash and 48,000 designated to be paid over the next three years to redeem rentes in that amount which the sire de Picquigny owed. Difficulties arose after the sale when Antoine and, later, Jeanne failed to redeem a portion of the rentes as stipulated in the contract. Françoise de Warty then contested the sale. When the negotiations to work out the difficulties over the sale seemed to be

---

45. AN, 90 AP 8, Jean de [illegible] to Nicolas d'Anjou, n.d., Amboise.

bearing fruit, Jeanne wrote to Françoise that she was happy to learn of Françoise's desire to know

> how I would like to resolve the contract made by my late husband and the late vidame d'Amiens [Françoise's brother-in-law]; I will send my instructions to my council in Paris, and I am sure you will be willing to accept them, and by this means you will be free of the pain and annoyance that this problem has caused, and I will be too, as I would rather have had you by my side during these last troubles than anyone else I know, because of your piety and virtue, and because of the affections that you bear me.[46]

While the difficulties do not seem to have diminished Jeanne's regard for Françoise, they do seem to have constrained Françoise's support for Jeanne, who had hoped to have Françoise with her during the recent civil war.

This example is a particularly weighty one in view of the sum of money at stake. There is evidence to suggest, however, that a constant ebb and flow of loans, gifts, purchases, and sales of land and of rentes linked noble families to each other, and that the Raineval transaction was exceptional only in size. The surviving estate accounts for 1548–49, for example, reveal that Antoine was able that year to reimburse a number of creditors for various loans they had made or rentes they had purchased in previous years. The variety of these transactions is striking. Antoine redeemed a rente that had been sold to the sire de Créquy; he reimbursed another prominent nobleman for two loans totaling 3,375 livres—one made to assist in the fortification of La Fère and another made as a contribution toward the expenses of Antoine's marriage the previous year.[47] This nobleman was governor of the county of Marle for Antoine and his assistance with building at La Fère and with Antoine's marriage is a reflection of some intimacy between them. Indeed, sales of rentes and land between and within families in certain instances reflected both financial need and confidence in a familial tie. In 1560, Eléonore de Roye prevailed on her great-uncle the connêtable de

---

46. Jeanne d'Albret to Françoise de Warty, 25 November 1571, La Rochelle, in Beauvillé, *Recueil de documents*, 3:544.
47. AN, KK278, "Recettes des terres . . . ," fols. 71v, 72r–v, 78v.

Montmorency to buy one of her seigneuries to enable her to meet pressing financial obligations while Condé was imprisoned after the Amboise affair. The Constable agreed to buy the seigneurie in question and resell it to her within one year at the original price, thus enabling a very desperate Eléonore to retrieve jewels and household furnishings she had mortgaged.[48]

Vassalage relations and other property relations were thus intertwined with all of the components of which nobles' relationships were constructed: the relative power of the nobles involved and the ties of kinship, service, and familiarity which connected them. Each sale of land, each seizure of a fief was both a context in which other aspects of the relationship could be expressed and itself a component of the relationship. In the case of significant conflict, such as that between Françoise de Warty and Jeanne d'Albret, strained property relations might temporarily eclipse long and affectionate familiarity. In some instances the performance of vassalage obligations, such as the rendering of homage, could be a means of symbolizing two men's familiarity and connection.[49] The evidence examined here, however, does not sustain the presumption that vassalage by itself constructed or sustained significant bonds between noblemen.

II. Lands and Households

I

Though vassalage did not by itself produce a tie of significance between nobles, it cannot be inferred that landholding did not shape nobles' relationships in significant ways. Whatever else they represented, seigneuries were also estates. They were places to gather

48. MC, Titres GE$_5$, 15 January 1561 and 22 January 1562.
49. J. Russell Major has recently argued that lord–vassal obligations had become simply administrative procedures by the seventeenth century. Specifically, the performance of homage through the gestures of kissing and kneeling had waned, in part because mores with regard to such humbling and intimate gestures had changed. See "'Bastard Feudalism' and the Kiss: Changing Social Mores in Late Medieval and Early Modern France," *Journal of Interdisciplinary History* 17 (1987): 509–35. Further study of noble practices in this regard may reveal whether, if performance had waned, vassalage had lost all power as a symbol to represent bonds between them. In this article Major slightly modifies his earlier arguments concerning vassalage. The importance of vassalage itself had diminished, he now stresses, but the contractual patron–client ties that replaced it mimicked vassalage ties.

with others, to eat, and to sleep; they were sources of foodstuffs, supplies of wine, and game to hunt; they were places where the task of supervising all of the property rights of the lord was undertaken by officials who resided there. Hence we must also examine great nobles' lands as the settings for human communities. What did it mean to be one of the noblemen who frequented such a community? What, in short, did it mean to be a member of the provincial household of a great nobleman such as Antoine de Bourbon or his brother the prince de Condé? As the examples of Pipemont and La Vieuville suggest, association with the household of a great noble did represent a significant tie to him, and potentially to other members of his family. The great noble's household played a central role in defining the relationships between him and the lesser nobles who served him in varying capacities there. Such households created material interdependence of the great and more modest noblemen within it. And to the community of the household as well as to outsiders—nobles who might be guests there or who might otherwise observe it—households were small theaters in which dramas of honor and deference could be acted out. But they were not only microcosms of the wider noble society; rather, they were the origin point for some of the most important constituents of nobles' relationships.

2

This analysis draws mainly on documents produced by two great noble households. One is Antoine de Bourbon's household, documented in the 1548–49 summary account for all of Antoine's lands in Picardy—one of the few such documents concerning the Bourbon lands to survive. These accounts record the receipts from every Bourbon seigneurie in the region for that year, as well as one-time receipts from sales of land, loans, and other transactions. It also records many expenditures. It is in these accounts that we can note Antoine's younger brothers and sisters receiving stipends, and other noblemen being reimbursed for loans. Most useful are the records of payments to other noblemen reimbursing them for outlays of various sorts, which reveal their activity on behalf of the household. These records also include the annual list of *gages* (stipends) for members of the household—from cooks, secretaries, and stable boys to the most prominent of the provincial nobles to have a formal place in the household. The survival of these accounts enables us to identify such household members as Pipemont and La Vieuville when they appear in other associations with Antoine, as his vassal or as a member of his cavalry company.

A more extensive series of documents produced by another noble household permits us to view much more of the daily life of such a community and to understand what roles the men and women named on a list of household members actually played. These documents are monthly records of the daily maintenance of the household of Nicolas d'Anjou, marquis de Mezières (d. 1570), and those of his daughter Renée (d. 1574) and son-in-law, François de Bourbon-Montpensier (d. 1592). These accounts, unlike the one surviving register from the Bourbon family, were completely distinct from seigneurial accounts and did not record revenue. The only receipts listed are small amounts of cash actually provided by Anjou or his wife, Gabrielle de Mareuil, to meet daily expenses; the origin of this cash is not recorded. Expenditures listed are of two kinds. "Extraordinary" expenses are one-time outlays, such as those that appear in the extant accounts of Antoine's household. By comparison with the expenses of this kind listed in the 1548–49 Bourbon accounts, these day-by-day records are highly detailed and enormously rich in the data they provide about life in the household and the activities of its members. Here journeys of household members on the lord's business are recorded upon their return, when they claim reimbursement for their meals and lodgings en route. The costs of making routine repairs inside the château are noted down to the last nail—literally. Equally valuable are the records of "ordinary" expenditures, detailing the daily outlays for food, drink, and other household necessities and listing precisely what was consumed every day. From them we can gauge not only what noblemen ate but also, among other things, the size of the assembled company, the importance of meals in the life of the community, and the constant comings and goings of noble guests.[50]

50. Monthly accounts from the Anjou-Mareuil households survive in considerable numbers, but with many gaps, from the years 1541 through 1570. Accounts from the household of their daughter, Renée d'Anjou, survive for the early 1570s, as do accounts from that of her husband, François de Bourbon-Montpensier, throughout the 1570s: AN, 90 AP 21–24. These accounts are part of the very rich remains of the archives of the seigneurie of St-Fargeau. This seigneurie and most of the family's

A great noble's household in fact consisted of men and women of all social ranks, from nobles of considerable stature to craftspeople and laborers. Household members made and repaired the lord's clothing; helped him to dress and undress; prepared and served his food; guarded his wardrobe, weapons, and furnishings; groomed and fed his horses and mule teams; maintained his carts and coaches and drove them from place to place when he traveled; fed his hunting dogs and coddled his precious falcons; wrote his letters and kept his accounts; said mass or preached; dispersed cash and distributed alms. At a minimum, a household included five to ten noble attendants at most times and some thirty to forty commoners, all salaried members of the official "maison" of the great nobleman in question. Antoine's official household in Picardy was somewhat larger than the household of Nicolas d'Anjou or that of his son-in-law François de Bourbon-Montpensier. It included about forty noblemen and seventy other dependents, ranging from well-paid secretaries to stable hands and dog tenders. The fragmentary evidence of daily accounts which survives suggests that daily maintenance of this retinue could cost up to 90 livres a day, compared with the 20 to 50 livres usually required in the Anjou and Montpensier establishments.[51]

The actual household, however—all the people who were fed and housed together on a daily basis—varied in size, and at any one time could be significantly larger than the official list reflects. Nobles associated with the household came and went on their own or the lord's business. But the household could grow temporarily to include local employees of the nobleman, such as a gardener or a gatekeeper. These employees always lived in a given château and hence were part of their employer's household when he was in residence there. Also included were such local artisans as bakers,

---

holdings were located south of Paris, in what is now the Department of the Yonne. Numerous titles and legal papers and much correspondence also survive from the sixteenth century. Most of the data that follow are drawn from the surviving accounts of the Anjou-Mareuil household. Sources will be cited only when data are drawn from other places—either from the smaller number of Anjou-Montpensier documents or from other sources entirely.

51. M. Matton, *Inventaire sommaire des archives départementales antérieures à 1790, Aisne*, II, *Archives civiles*, Série B (suite)—F (Laon, 1878), p. 1. Cf. figures from other households in Sharon Kettering, *Patrons, Clients, and Brokers* (Oxford, 1986), p. 215.

pastry makers, and blacksmiths. Records of extraordinary expenses reveal that when a nobleman traveled, the services of such artisans were procured locally. Every migration of the household of Nicolas d'Anjou left a wake of blacksmiths' and harness makers' bills, for example. But traveling also brought into the household people who were not needed otherwise. Extra carters, mule drivers, and guides were hired for traveling, and they needed housing along the route and food for themselves and their mounts. Though the company to be maintained on the road was usually smaller than the normal household, a day's travel could easily cost more than an average day in residence at one's own château. A seamstress or a bootmaker might receive room and board at the château for several days while working there, in addition to the piece rates paid for the articles she or he made. Extra launderers and chambermaids, beyond any permanently employed, were also part of the household when a nobleman was in residence in a château. At any one time a great nobleman's household might thus include about twice as many attendants and workers as the official list of his household officials reflected. François de Bourbon, heir to the duchy of Montpensier, routinely fed 75 to 100 people in 1570 and 1571, although his regular salaried officials numbered only 45; and this larger figure does not include the many honored guests who came and went daily.[52]

The effort to keep track of all of these temporary residents in the household is readily visible in household accounts. The secretaries who recorded daily expenses of all sorts tried to keep track of the number of mouths being fed. Those who kept François de Bourbon-Montpensier's accounts, for example, from time to time tried to draw up lists of the people who were authorized to be included in the "ordinaire de Monsieur"—that is, in the "ordinary" living expenses of the household.[53] More routinely, secretaries to the Anjou family tried to make note of visitors to a château as they recorded the amount and the cost of a given day's provisions. The presence of

---

52. AN, 90 AP 24, Dossier 1, "Liste de personnes desfraiées à l'ordinaire de Monseigneur," n.d., n.p.; and the following documents from Dossier 2: "Dépense extraordinaire du prince dauphin [François de Bourbon-Montpensier]," June 1571, Champigny; "Dépense ordinaire du Monseigneur le prince Dauphin," September 1571, n.p.; "Dépense ordinaire du Monseigneur et son train et cheveaux," May 1572, n.p.

53. Ibid., Dossier 2, "Dépense ordinaire du Monseigneur et son train."

local or short-term workers is revealed in records of payment for them; a secretary records in the accounts precisely how much it cost to feed the carters and muleteers each day on the road, or how many meals a local mason enjoyed while repairing the château. Secretaries also tried to note the noble visitors who were present each day. In the margins of each day's list of provisions are notations such as "Monsieur de X et son fils à diner" and "Madamoiselles X et Y et leur train toute la journée," identifying individual guests, the size of their party, and the number of meals they took in the household. Also named occasionally were prominent nobles of the household who joined and left the entourage as a matter of course—sometimes traveling on the lord's business, sometimes journeying to their own nearby estates.

One goal of these careful notations of expenses was to permit the secretary to document the outflow of funds. No running balance was kept of money available or amounts spent; rather, the secretary's employers would from time to time give him small sums of cash. Meanwhile, he kept track of expenses and at the end of the month totted up credits and debits. Invariably he had disbursed more than he had been given in cash over the course of the month. Thus accurate records were important to him to justify expenditures and to ensure reimbursement at the end of the month. But in these records we can also see more than just the needs of the secretary. The way the secretary chose to justify his expenditures must have reflected what his employers thought important. The attempt to keep track of precisely who was fed and housed reflected the weight the lord and lady of the house attached to this issue. In these records we can glean something of the significance for human relationships of the exchange of food and services and of the outright gifts of food recorded here.

The desire to keep track of mouths fed (both human and animal) reveals that these expenses were deliberate and discretionary. Some, it is true, do seem virtually automatic. Guides and carters are paid off routinely along a journey, and obviously have been fed along the route as a matter of course. Noblemen in the household come and go continually on various business; they journey to inspect and perhaps to buy new horses or hunting birds. The accounts of the household record that each man is reimbursed for his food and feed for these journeys. Clearly, then, there must have been an understanding concerning whose expenses and what sorts of expenses were routinely authorized. This assumption is further borne out by the fact that noblemen of the household themselves often took charge of dispersing funds and authorizing payments for food. Many of the Anjou expenditures, however, were individually considered and authorized by Nicolas d'Anjou or his wife, Gabrielle de Mareuil. In the section of the monthly accounts reserved for one-time payments for goods and services, these decisions of the lord and lady are interspersed with the seemingly automatic expenses. New shoes are purchased for a page, a doctor's bill is reimbursed for a valet who falls ill on a journey, the expenses of feeding a particular guest's horse (an issue when the household was on the road and paying cash for feeding its own animals) are assumed—each, the secretary records, by "command" of Monsieur or Madame. What is important here is not precisely which expenses were individually authorized but the fact that the resources of the noble household were neither randomly nor casually given away. Great nobles' liberality was real, it seems, but it was also self-conscious and purposeful.

In order to understand the effects and significance of this liberality, let us examine the outlays for food in particular more closely. Food and drink represented by far the greatest expense of the noble household. Indeed, food expenses assumed the same proportion of total expenses in the Anjou and Montpensier households as they did in a small peasant household—well over 50 percent of expenditures, and usually 65 to 75 percent. The percentage is hard to gauge exactly because the household accounts record not whole budgets, just the flow of cash through the hands of the secretary, month by month. Yet these records also reveal that the actual resources devoted to food were consistently greater than the large cash total recorded every month. The household routinely used—and the records note—foodstuffs from the lord's own lands: meat slaughtered on the estate, game that the household members had hunted, wine and produce from the lord's tenants.[54] However its value is calculated, it seems clear that food was the single most important kind of suste-

---

54. Cf. Major, "Noble Income," pp. 36–39. Major's estimate of the amount spent on food in the Albret household *appears* to be somewhat lower, but he does not analyze such records for the Albrets in detail. He concludes, however, that "food was a very small part of their total expenses" (p. 36). While this conclusion may be warranted (depending, of course, on how broadly one construes "total expenses"), it underestimates the amount of "ordinary" expenditure devoted to food.

nance that a nobleman could supply his dependents and guests. Reimbursement for food and drink on a journey was essential to a lesser nobleman; reimbursement for fodder was a rare and privileged gift to a noble intimate.

The material value of food reinforced its symbolic value. Food and meals were ritual means by which distinctions of rank and dependence on the lord were represented. Hierarchical distinctions appear to have been acted out at the meals shared by household members and guests. Not that their meals were highly elaborate or deliberately wasteful; food was plentiful but not wastefully abundant. Meat had to be eaten soon after slaughtering; at times there are daily purchases of meat to supply the household. Leftover meats in the Anjou household are often served the next day in meat pies. Nor were the dishes served necessarily elaborate. The daily fare included red meat and poultry (or several kinds of fish during Lent), onions, cabbage, or lettuce, cheeses and eggs (particularly during Lent). Small amounts of fruits and nuts found their way into the dishes as well; occasionally the accounts record a pound or two of almonds or of cherries. Much greater variety of foods did appear at times, particularly when members of the noble family were staying in Paris and were frequenting the court. Fruits and vegetables, particularly, were added to the menu at these times; oranges, peas, and artichokes are common additions.[55] Even when the household's cuisine was at its simplest, however, distinctions of rank could be acted out by means of staple foodstuffs. Every meal included the two staples of bread and wine. From five to ten dozen small loaves of bread were consumed in the Anjou household every day. Always the bread was of two kinds, white for the gentlemen and ladies and bread of lower quality for the commoners. A threefold distinction was made in the kinds of wine served at meals. One kind of wine was reserved for "la table de Monsieur" and for the guests who sat with him there, a second kind for the "gentilhommes," and a third for the "commun."

These distinctions may also have been echoed by distinctions in other foodstuffs served to the various members of the household. The small amounts of fruits that are noted among routine purchases

---

55. A single day's expenses might be high but would thus not necessarily signal wastefulness. Cf. Mack P. Holt, *The Duke of Anjou and the Politique Struggle during the Wars of Religion* (Cambridge, 1986), p. 174.

may have been reserved for "la table de Monsieur." In any case, the unvarying distinctions among kinds of wines and bread were clearly visible to everyone at every meal. So were the distinctions represented by the seating arrangement at meals. Monsieur and Madame kept a separate table; there, we know, wine of the highest quality was served, and perhaps special dishes as well. It is certain that in the Anjou household, "la table de Monsieur" was covered with a cloth chosen especially for it, distinguished in records of purchase from other lengths of cloth. It is also likely that Monsieur and Madame's small collection of ornate tableware—enameled and vermeil serving platters and drinking goblets—was reserved for use here. Tableware of precious metals was always included among such a family's belongings. These pieces often were part of the marriage settlement, along with jewels and clothing, and might also be purchased outright by great nobles who could afford to add to their collections.[56] The symbolic value of these pieces lay in part in the labor power they represented; like fine tapestries, they were beautifully worked. Their value as symbols of power also lay in the preciousness of the materials themselves. They represented power because they were part of a noble's wealth—wealth that he could put to use to serve his interests. There are countless references in all sorts of documents to the pawning or sale of these pieces, along with precious jewels, to meet both routine debts and the extraordinary exigencies of warmaking. (For purposes of sale or pawn, their value was assessed by the weight of precious metals in them.)[57] The fact that such tableware often constituted noteworthy gifts between nobles also testi-

56. Passing references to such objects appear in the Anjou-Mareuil accounts. The papers of François de Bourbon-Montpensier include records of expenditure for silver and vermeil platters, basins, and goblets at a total cost of more than 500 livres: AN, 90 AP 24, "Mise extraordinaire," September 1572, n.p. Many household inventories and inventories after death mention such pieces among the belongings of prominent noblemen. See, for example, ANMin C XIX-111, "Inventaire après décès d'Anne de Boulogne, vicomtesse de Turenne," 18 March 1531, Paris. Evidence from these accounts and inventories bears out Braudel's assumptions concerning the presence of such articles: Fernand Braudel, *Civilisation materielle, économie et capitalisme, XVᵉ–XVIIIᵉ siècles,* vol. 1, *Les Structures du quotidien: Le Possible et l'impossible* (Paris, 1979), pp. 264–65.

57. See, for example, an inventory of the twenty pieces pawned by the last sire de Genlis before his death: "Inventaire de l'argenterie mise en gage par Jean de Hangest, seigneur de Genlis," 5 January 1573, n.p., in Beauvillé, *Recueil de documents,* 3:546–48. Eléonore de Roye, as we have seen, pawned some of her belongings in 1560: BN, MS fr. 3260, fol. 81, Eléonore de Roye to Anne, duc de Montmorency, 29 September 1560, Anizy.

fies to its symbolic possibilities. Henri II, for example, bestowed valuable goblets on certain particularly favored nobles in celebration of the 1559 peace treaty.[58] Their usefulness as symbols of favor, in such a case, also seems to rest on the value that was attached to a dish or goblet per se—that is, to the power of the symbol of eating and drinking, and to the meaning with which such activities might be charged.

The rankings of honor were displayed in other facets of daily life within the household as well. A great nobleman displayed his stature in all of the furnishings of his person and of his dwelling. François de Bourbon-Montpensier had more than a dozen doublets and pairs of hose and at least a dozen capes and cloaks stored for safekeeping at one residence while he journeyed elsewhere. The richness of the garments is more striking than their number. They were fashioned in black, purple, yellow, orange, and scarlet velvet and satin. Some were worked in damask, edged in silver or gold thread. Sleeves, linings, fasteners, hoods, and collars were of contrasting colors or of fur.[59] Such clothing, like food, could be a gift bestowed by a great nobleman on a lesser nobleman in the household. It was quite routine for the lord and lady of the household to furnish clothing for young pages.[60] A pair of shoes or a shirt for a page is a common item among "extraordinary" expenses. This furnishing of basic needs was paralleled by outright gifts of some of their own elegant pieces of clothing to adult noblemen of the household. Three pieces of clothing, for example, including an elegant tunic with gold fastenings to be worn with armor, were bestowed by François de Bourbon-Montpensier on the noble governor of his in-laws' most important château (where, significantly, most of this clothing was stored).[61]

58. BN, MS fr. 3187, fols. 88–99v, "Estats des dons et presens envoiez par le Roy à monsieur de Humières . . . pour estre distribués aux personnes cy apres nommées . . .," n.d., n.p.

59. AN, 90 AP 24, Dossier 1, "Inventaire des accoustremens et aultres hardes de Monseigneur le prince daulphin . . . baillés en garde . . . [au] gouverneur [de St-Fargeau]," 26 September 1576, St-Fargeau.

60. Clothing for pages is frequently mentioned in the Anjou-Mareuil accounts. In more modest noble establishments, common servants and their families also enjoyed this benefit. See AN, 292 AP 1, "Livre de raison d'un seigneur provençal, 1562–79," n.p.

61. AN, 90 AP 23, Dossier 2, "Inventaire des accoustremens . . . de Monseigneur," 26 July 1595, St-Fargeau, verified copy.

The household's furniture also simultaneously displayed rank and constituted another form of largesse. Furniture in these residences consisted in the main of trestle tables and benches, mattresses and bedframes with varying kinds of coverings and hangings, wall hangings (tapestries), and coffers and chests for storing linens and displaying dishes. The only actual chairs in the household of Nicolas d'Anjou were for his use alone. When he traveled from his principal château to a less well-appointed residence or to court, the chairs (which folded rather like director's chairs) went with him. He also took with him screens that partitioned his chamber in the château. Both in the château and on the road, the lord and lady enjoyed the comfort of wall hangings and abundant bed hangings and coverings. Indeed, as one reads inventories of the contents of rooms in various noble residences, it becomes evident that bed furnishings and other hangings and coverings, such as wall hangings and tablecloths, were among the most obvious means to display luxury and signal rank. All tables, including the small trestle tables that might stand near beds, had their coverings—and when these coverings were threadbare or meager, an inventory noted their condition. Inventories also noted the precise quality of bed furnishings.[62] Beds were scattered everywhere in a noble's large residence. The lord and lady might have separate grand beds in their individual chambers, but their rooms would also be supplied with smaller beds for relatives or for pages. Antechambers had small pallet beds and camp beds of various sorts. Most rooms, sometimes even the "grande salle," were multipurpose rooms and contained more or less the same kinds of furnishings: a table or two, a coffer or two, some candlesticks, hangings, and two or three beds. The careful inventories of these furnishings make it clear that the hangings and coverings, mattresses and pillows on the lord's and lady's beds were by far the most luxurious in the château. Thus with beds, as with clothes and food, the great noble's household provided basic comforts and necessities for many people, while at the same time symbolically reinforcing that noble's control of all of this bounty.

---

62. "Inventaire fait au château de Folleville," 5–6 May 1571, Folleville, in Beauvillé, *Recueil de documents*, 4:324–36; and the following documents in AN, 90 AP 23: "Inventaire des meubles au chastel de St-Fargeau," 26 March 1565, St-Fargeau; "Inventaire des meubles au chastelet de St-Fargeau," 19 May 1567; "Inventaire des meubles estans à St-Fargeau," 1 November 1570.

This bounty was a primary constituent of a great noble's power, not simply because of the sheer wealth it reflected but also because of the significance of that wealth in human terms. It was not incidental to the nature of a great noble's preeminence, but rather essential to it, that it was built on control of the necessities of life: food, clothing, and shelter. This power had two dimensions: the power to be the source of these necessities for others, and the additional power to create not mere sufficiency but real abundance around one's own person. The lord and lady maintained an illusion of control over the physical environment.

This comfort and this control were all the more powerful precisely because they were acted out in the context of human relationships. A great noble's wealth entitled him to command the attention and the labor of dozens of other human beings. Members of the household saw the power of the lord reflected not merely in objects but in themselves. The household was a group of people that existed for the purpose of serving him. Vast amounts of human labor were required to meet the needs of any household in preindustrial Europe. The level of physical comfort and the amount of leisure time these nobles enjoyed thus depended on even greater contributions of human labor. Some of the comfort enjoyed by a great nobleman depended on the visible wealth he could invest in fur-lined cloaks, thick tapestries, and satisfying food. Most of his comforts, however, as well as his freedom to travel and to protect himself, depended on the work of people who lived with him.

This labor is everywhere apparent in household account books. As we have seen, a constant stream of workers of all sorts passed through the Anjou household: seamstresses, launderers, masons, blacksmiths. When Anjou, his wife, and their daughter traveled, they relied on carters of all sorts, on ferrymen and guides. Always attached to his household would be a cook, bread-store keepers, and a sommelier, each with assistants; stablehands, grooms, and falconers; laundresses and furriers; secretaries and clerks. The gentlemen of such a household were not idle, either. They met with and approved payments for workers at the château; they often supervised purchases of food and supplies, including supplies of cloth for tablecloths and other household linen. Above all, they traveled. They journeyed great distances to buy and sell horses, dogs, and hunting birds; they accompanied Monsieur on his journeys, sometimes traveling ahead of the main party to locate an inn or to inform the guard of another family château of Monsieur or Madame's impending arrival. The fragmentary Bourbon records reveal, for example, a very important and rather costly journey made by one gentleman of the household, Pierre de Chepoy, north into Imperial territory; there he personally recovered the receipts of the family's holding of Enghien, in Imperial hands. His journey lasted thirty-seven days, and he was reimbursed almost 200 livres for his expenses on his return. Two months later, he again journeyed north, this time to Bruges, to oversee the sale of another property. On other occasions he traveled to Brussels and to Cateau-Cambrésis, starting sometimes from La Fère, sometimes from his own nearby estates. All the while, messengers ran between him—at home or on the road—and La Fère.[63] Gentlemen and young noble pages also guarded their lord's belongings. Both on the road and in residence in a family château, noble retainers were given explicit charge of costly clothes, furs, and arms. They also guarded his person. Young noble dependents in particular might sleep in the same room as their master. The murder of the comte de Chasteauvillain, discussed in Chapter 4, was accomplished only because of a successful ruse for inducing the Count to make a visit unattended by his familiars. In telling his story of the encounter at La Rochefoucauld's sickbed, the sire de Mergey made special note that the chamber was "completely open" and anyone was able to enter; easy access to the person of the Count was evidently unusual.

Thus, although great nobles enjoyed more leisure and luxury than other members of the society, it would be a mistake to characterize their daily lives as pampered or their attitude toward physical security as casual. Luxury of certain sorts was taken for granted, but even the most rudimentary physical and material security was not. Competent servants and retainers were a must. The mother of the prince de Porcien at one point delayed a pressing journey to Paris (where she needed to pursue a legal matter) because her son had sent no one trustworthy to guard the château during her absence. She begged her son to attend to this matter, since "this is for the preservation of *your* goods [biens]"; she needed someone to take charge of the château and the nearby woods, where there had recently been

63. AN, KK278, "Recettes des terres . . . ," fols. 84, 76r–v, 93v–94.

some "goings-on."[64] When Nicolas d'Anjou left his principal château for a journey of several months and a sojourn in the capital, he left behind a very precise inventory of all its furnishings, down to the last cauldron for laundry and the last broken andiron, so that he could later judge the efforts of the château's noble guardian in his absence.[65] Within the château, all the coffers of linen were kept locked at all times. The laundress slept on the floor in front of the door to the chamber where they were stored. Every repair or job of work recorded in the accounts was itemized down to the smallest detail. The number of nails used to hang a tapestry in Madame's chamber is carefully noted when the worker is paid. On one level, such notations may represent merely a kind of literalness in the making of a written record which reflects particular habits of writing and recording. But on another level, because of their literalness, they help to reveal how both objects and labor were valued. The records also indicate that Monsieur and Madame were involved in and aware of all types of decisions and transactions concerning these matters.

This weighting of every piece of work and of every piece of goods helps us to interpret the significance of the activities of gentlemen in the household. Their work, like that of the laundress, was most often immediate, small-scale, and practical. When Monsieur expresses interest in acquiring a certain horse, a noble in the household is dispatched to look it over, perhaps to lead it back to the estate if it is purchased. When workmen come to repair the well in the courtyard in Monsieur and Madame's absence, the noble guardian on the scene tells them what to do and keeps an eye on their progress. When Monsieur's traveling party runs low on provisions, a noble of the household rides to the nearest town to buy a cask of wine with his own money, only later to receive reimbursement. The significance of these activities—as of the daily lives within the household—lies in their rootedness in the ordinary. Relationships within the noble household were grounded in and shaped by the thoroughly ordinary business of simply living. Simply living meant

64. BN, MS fr. 3632, fol. 139r, Françoise d'Amboise to Antoine de Croy, prince de Porcien, 31 March n.y., Renel.

65. AN, 90 AP 23, "Inventaires des meubles qui sont demourés au chastel de St-Fargeau au partement de messeigneur et dame qu'ils auroyent faict pour aller à Paris . . . ," 26 March 1565, St-Fargeau.

sustaining life in such a way as to sustain the power of the head of the household. It meant maintaining the physical apparatus of that power, from fortress walls to precious silver plate, and it meant witnessing that power by eating his food, accepting his gifts, and sleeping near his person. It is in the household that we see the blending of public and private personae which was at the heart of noble life. Public life had a private, even intimate face, and private life had a public face. The occasions of contact with other nobles of all ranks within the household setting are intimate, domestic occasions and the service rendered by lesser noblemen is concerned above all with immediate physical and material needs. Simultaneously, the most ordinary activities—eating, drinking, sleeping—are charged with symbolic power and display honor and authority.

3

The forty noblemen officially included in Antoine's household ranged in stature from unknown men of obscure origins to those of marked prominence within the province. Indeed, the most prestigious nobles in the household—including, for example, the man who undertook such demanding journeys for Antoine—are barely distinguishable from the most elite families of the province, such as the Lannoy-Morvilliers, Senarpont, and Humières families. Some details of the careers of these men and their family members help us to understand more fully the significance of their ties to the household.

Claude de Bourbon-Vendôme, sire de Ligny, eldest son of a bastard line descended from Antoine and Condé's great-grandfather, was a chamberlain in Antoine's household at a salary of 200 livres a year.[66] Approximately Antoine's contemporary, he was married in 1542 to the heiress of an established family of the second rank, Antoinette de Bours, who brought seigneuries west of Abbeville in the Vimeu to the marriage. No legitimate children survived the couple. Claude's brother André, sire de Rubempré, enjoyed a very successful career, beginning with the sponsorship of his Bourbon cousins and other kin by marriage. His military commands began

---

66. AN, KK278, "Recettes des terres . . . ," fol. 97v.

with the lieutenancy of the company of the comte d'Enghien, Antoine's brother. After the battle of St-Quentin (and Enghien's death), he assumed the lieutenancy of another company, that of his brother-in-law, who happened to be the eminent Jean d'Estrées. In 1562, as we have seen, he fought briefly alongside his kinsman Condé. He was made captain of his own company in 1563 and, in the 1570s, commanded in Abbeville with the heightened authority of governor and lieutenant general of the town. His lands were southwest of Abbeville, in the Vimeu, and in the Norman-Picard borderland of Bray; his first marriage had been to an heiress from that region, his second to a daughter of the Roncherolles family of the Norman provincial elite.[67]

A somewhat less prestigious family was represented in Antoine's household by Pierre de Chepoy, sire de Villette, near Chauny. Chepoy was a relatively mature man when he undertook his journeys to the Low Countries in 1548. In 1528 he had married the widowed mother of Claude and André de Bourbon-Vendôme. Pierre served as an officer in Antoine's company of men-at-arms during the 1540s and later as governor of Ham, the Bourbon fortress west of La Fère, on the Somme. His daughter and sole heir, Antoinette, eventually brought his estates (near Chauny and La Fère) to a very fortunate second marriage with Louis de Lannoy, sire de Morvilliers. Interestingly, she had first married another member of Antoine's household. The Chepoy family died out with Antoinette's generation. Pierre de Chepoy's nephew, her cousin and the last of the line, earned a number of honorable commands in association with various Picard nobles. From 1561 to 1563, Robert de Chepoy was an officer in the company of Antoinette's husband, Louis de Lannoy-Morvilliers; he then rose to the rank of lieutenant in the company of François, sire de Crèvecoeur. He married one of the daughters of Louis d'Ongnies, comte de Chaulnes, and served as governor of St-Quentin after his father-in-law. He also acquired membership in the Ordre de St-Michel and inclusion in the royal

---

67. Père Anselme, *Histoire généalogique de la maison royale de France*, 9 vols. (Paris, 1733), 1:378–80. Some of the lands both brothers gained in marriage are identified in "Arrière-ban d'Amiens," October–November 1557, in Beauvillé, *Recueil de documents*, 3:387, 412–13. Rubempré's commands of a company of *hommes d'armes* are catalogued in Fleury-Vindry, *L'Etat-major*, p. 39, whose data vary in some respects from Anselme's.

household as *gentilhomme de chambre*, honors that by then had become routine.[68]

Also among the most prominent of Antoine's householders was Henri de Roucy-Sissonne. Henri, a maître d'hotel to Antoine in 1548, was the eldest of three sons; the other two were Joachim (d. 1576) and Charles (d. 1585), who later served as governor and bishop, respectively, of Soissons.[69] Undoubtedly they were recommended for their charges in Soissons by Antoine, or by one of the two cardinals de Bourbon, uncle (d. 1557) or nephew. Henri held the principal family seigneurie of Sissonne, east of Laon, which included a small but strategically valuable fortified château. Like other gentlemen of the household, Henri apparently carried out various management tasks for Antoine.[70]

Most of the forty or so nobles in Antoine's household were like the Roucy-Sissonnes, in that they or members of their families discharged various offices and commands around the province; the careers of most of them reflect the somewhat more modest stature of their families. One of the less distinguished was Jacques de Renty. A chamberlain in Antoine's household who carried out some management tasks, Renty also served as lesser officer and eventually as lieutenant in Antoine's company of the royal gendarmerie until Antoine's death in 1562. By 1560, Renty had also been named to the post of captain of the town of La Fère for the king—doubtless at Antoine's recommendation. Later he also served briefly as governor of Antoine's château at Ham. He was eventually named *chevalier de l'ordre du roi*, as this honor became more common. He never achieved the rank of governor of a major town, however, or of a company of men-at-arms.[71]

68. Fleury-Vindry, *L'Etat-major*, pp. 70–73, 224–27; Père Anselme, *Histoire généalogique*, 7:739; and the following documents in Beauvillé, *Recueil de documents*: "Arrière-ban d'Amiens," 1557, 4:398; "Château et seigneurs de Folleville," 4:628–30; "Dépense de bouche faite à Villette par Louis de Lannoy, sire de Morvilliers," February 1566, 4:316–17; "Quittance de Robert de Sepoy," 16 August 1571, 3:345.

69. M. de Callay, "Charles de Roucy-Sissonne et Soissons," *Bulletin de la société archéologique, historique et scientifique de Soissons* 10 (1900): 167–86; Melleville, *Dictionnaire historique*, 2:89, 127, 203–4.

70. AN, KK278, "Recettes des terres . . .," fol. 3v.

71. Fleury-Vindry, *L'Etat-major*, pp. 70–73; Achille Palant, "Jacques de Renty, gouverneur de La Fère," *Bulletin de la société académique de Chauny* 6 (1900): 98–105, and "M. de Renty, son château et son tombeau," *Annales de la société historique et archéologique de Château-Thierry* (1889), pp. 79–94.

Much like Renty was another chamberlain, Antoine de Dompierre, sire de Joncquières. In the 1550s he appears as an homme d'armes in Antoine's company. Later he secured a place in the household of Antoine's son Henri de Navarre. The honor of inclusion in the household helped to nurture a complex of action that would continue for about ten years. Joncquières was often in personal attendance on Navarre; in fact, he was one of only a handful of associates to remain with him after the St. Bartholomew's Day massacre (1572), when Henri was under virtual house arrest at court. Later he returned to Picardy and governed two of Navarre's châteaux—Bohain and Beaurevoir, north of La Fère.[72]

Subordinate to such men as Renty and Dompierre in the household were still more humble men. One Jehan Disgne was honored as a *gentilhomme de la falconnerie* at an annual stipend not inferior to the amounts paid to far more prominent men, such as Roucy-Sissonne. There was also a maître d'hôtel with the intriguingly foreign name of Carlos de Bazon: perhaps a Spaniard from the kingdom of Navarre, or a soldier who had joined Antoine's suite in the field? Both men also served in Antoine's company as hommes d'armes. Unlike some of their more elevated fellow householders, Bazon and Disgne would never hold positions of command within the company; those positions went to the more prominent men, such as Renty, who were more likely to exercise outside commands or governorships as well.[73]

A number of the somewhat more modest nobles in the household appear in later years in a similar relationship to the prince de Condé. As we have noted, Antoine de Dompierre, sire de Joncquières, can be traced in close association with Antoine and his son during the civil wars. During the 1560s he served in Condé's company of men-at-arms. After Condé's death in 1569, he joined Navarre's entourage, but in 1580 again served a Condé when he left his post as governor of Navarre's châteaux of Bohain and Beaurevoir to help seize and hold the town of La Fère against the crown for the young

---

72. BN, Clair. 257, p. 1503, "Revue . . . de cent lances des ordonnances . . . de M. le duc de Vendômois," 21 January 1555, Sens; BN, Clair. 258, p. 1541, "Rolle . . . de cent lances . . . des ordonnances . . . de M. le duc de Vendômois," 22 April 1557, Sens.
73. AN, KK278, "Recettes des terres . . . ," fols. 98v–99, 110v–11.

prince, Louis de Bourbon's son.[74] Another man, Hercule d'Ailly, sire d'Ausquerque, was a representative of an obscure branch of the distinguished Picard family; he was a gentleman in Antoine's household, governor of Ham for a short period, and in the 1560s an homme d'armes in Condé's company of the royal gendarmerie.[75] Nicolas de Bours, sire de Gennes, another member of Antoine's household, appeared to fight with Condé in the first civil war, and his son appeared in 1580 to help Condé's son defend La Fère.[76] No records of the composition of Condé's household have survived, but it can be assumed that some of these men, or members of their families, enjoyed that formal association with the Prince. Like that of his brother, Condé's household no doubt reflected the social composition of his company of the gendarmerie, which included men of quite prominent families, middling nobles such as Ailly-Ausquerque, and unknowns such as Carlos de Bazon.[77] Indeed, Condé's company in the 1560s included a number of foreigners, primarily Scotsmen. These Scotsmen may have been part of the retinue brought to France by Mary Stuart when she married François II (d. 1560). Scots are mentioned among French combatants in the northeast during the Imperial Wars, some in battles in which Condé also participated.[78]

Antoine's and Condé's households thus included noblemen of a variety of ranks, ranging from men of considerable stature to what might be called common soldiers. The nobles of greater stature

74. BN, Clair. 261, p. 1753, "Rolle . . . de cent lances . . . des ordonnances . . . de M. le prince de Condé," 5 October 1565, Péronne; BN, Clair. 266, p. 1859, "Rolle . . . de cinquante lances . . . des ordonnances . . . de M. le prince de Condé," 2 June 1567, Péronne; BN, MS fr. 4047, fols. 93ff., "Registre des expeditions du conseil estably à La Fère par Msgr. le prince de Condé," 1580, La Fère.

75. Ailly appears on the muster rolls of Antoine's and Condé's companies. See nn. 70 and 72. See also Matton, *Inventaire sommaire*, p. 3.

76. "Arrière-ban d'Amyens levé aux moys d'octobre et novembre, 1557," in Beauvillé, *Recueil de documents*, 4:398.

77. Random references to noblemen in various kinds of documentation sustain this impression. One example from 1573 was a donation of woodland by Condé's son Henri to two merchants (undoubtedly for the purposes of paying off debts), supervised by a man identified as one of his maîtres d'hôtel, who also appears in muster lists of Henri's company in 1574.

78. BN, Clair. 263, p. 1859, "Rolle . . . de cinquante lances . . . des ordonnances . . . de M. le prince de Condé," 2 June 1567, Péronne; Jacques-Auguste De Thou, *Histoire universelle*, 16 vols. (London, 1734), 3:174.

might also serve as officers in Antoine's company and hold positions of particular honor and responsibility within the household. Lesser nobles also served under Antoine's or Condé's command, or guarded other estates, and they often owed some of their own landholdings to Bourbon generosity. It seems that the close association between Bourbon family members and these more modest nobles was likely to endure over many years and more than one generation. Such was the case with members of Antoine's household who served his brother Condé as well, or who went on to serve one of their sons.

Common to all noblemen in Antoine's household was a territorial connection of another sort. While few were actually his vassals and only the less prominent were likely to have been granted property by him, virtually all of them lived close by, even when they were on their own estates. In other words, the most dramatic way in which land itself seemed to structure or determine these relationships was simply in terms of physical proximity. With the significant exception of his kinsman Claude de Vendôme, most of the noblemen in Antoine's household, whether his vassals or not, held lands in the eastern reaches of Picardy, in the area around La Fère. The sire de Chepoy's residence was on his estate of La Villette, between Chauny and La Fère. Henri de Roucy-Sissonne held lands to the east of La Fère. The Vieuvilles began with land in this region, and later purchased other holdings by which they became vassals to the Bourbons. The pattern is repeated with family after family. As we have seen, household accounts reveal them traveling back and forth from their own estates to the great noble's household. The sire de Chepoy, for example, often went home to his estates at La Villette. From there he left for his voyages to the Low Countries for Antoine. Antoine paid for messengers to travel back and forth from La Fère to La Villette when he needed to communicate with Chepoy about his concerns.

Although we lack documents that would enable us precisely to identify members of Condé's household, similar patterns of landholding and residency may be detected among some of his hommes d'armes. Among them were Antoine de Dompierre, sire de Joncquières, who served in Antoine's company as well, and members of the Bayancourt-Bouchavannes family, who are found also in Antoine's household. Some of these men held lands near La Fère, others closer to one of Condé's own estates, such as Muret, near Soissons, or Condé-en-Brie itself. The muster lists of the royal companies dating from 1567 and after are particularly useful in efforts to identify their members, as from that date the domicile of each man enrolled was listed, in order to cut down on fraudulent double enrollments.

Particularly noteworthy in these notations of domiciles is the fact that a number of noblemen list one of Condé's estates as their domiciles of the moment, although they also identify themselves as "sire de" some holding or other. Such men were living there temporarily, no doubt as guardians or commanders on Condé's behalf. Still others identify their town or holding of origin but then go on to name "la suite de Monsieur le prince" as their domicile.[79] Such identification was not reserved for modest noblemen alone, or even for official household members. The prince de Porcien and the baron de Plancy were described by others or described themselves in these same terms at various junctures. Though very prominent noblemen might be in the "suite" only intermittently, and lesser nobles and other household members more regularly, in all cases this kind of connection existed as a matter of course. The household of a great noble such as Antoine or Condé is therefore not merely a convenient unit to consider if one wishes to glimpse the provincial noblemen regularly associated with him or most dependent on him; it also represents a form of association that marked all these relationships. It did not simply parallel other connections, whether landholding, military service, or kinship, but helped to constitute all of them.

It is therefore not surprising that noble men and women negotiated some of the terms of their association with a prestigious household. The terms of all forms of association between nobles were negotiable. An unusual letter that reveals such negotiations under way is very illuminating in this regard and deserves some scrutiny. It concerns the household of the young prince de Porcien. Once again, his mother, Françoise d'Amboise, is writing to exhort him to pay better attention to his affairs, in particular to his household.

79. BN, Clair. 263, p. 1859, "Rolle . . . de cinquante lances," 2 June 1567, Péronne.

Since details of this kind are not common in nobles' correspondence, it seems we have Porcien's irresponsibility to thank for the information his mother has unwittingly left us. She writes:

> . . . [le] sire de Ronchères . . . m'avoit dict que l'avez retenu des vostres et qu'il estoit en deliberation de se remployer à vostre service de bien bon afection, mais qu'il falloit que sa femme fut aussi avec ma fille, ce que je trouve bon.[80]

> . . . the sire de Ronchères has told me that you have retained him among your men, and that he was deliberating returning with all good will to your service, but that his wife would also have to be with my daughter[-in-law], which I think is good.

Françoise goes on to explain that she has heard that Ronchères's wife is "fort honneste," "de bonne maison," and "bien nourrie." She specifically recommends that this young noblewoman be given the place in her daughter-in-law's entourage now taken by a certain woman who, Françoise recounts, "is not worthy [digne] to serve in the position [l'estat] in which she serves, as I will explain to you in person very soon." Then she reveals that she has had rather detailed discussions with the sire de Ronchères about precisely what sort of position he will enjoy in the household. Although she reports that "he told me that he would be happy with whatever pleases you," she counsels her son to "give him a position that you two decide on together." Do not lose this opportunity, she warns, if you want to do youself some good.

In this report of negotiations we note the anxiety of greater nobles to be well served by worthy, well-esteemed subordinates. This specific concern stands out over and above Françoise's more general concern that her son is not paying adequate attention to any of these matters. We also notice that the sire de Ronchères is himself making choices about whom to serve and on what terms to do so. We learn

---

80. BN, MS fr. 3196, fol. 64r–v, Françoise d'Amboise to Antoine de Croy, prince de Porcien, 9 July 1564, Paris. Antoine de Bourbon's accounts reveal that he, too, had at least one married couple in his household, though only the husband was named on the official list of household officers.

at the outset that he is considering rejoining Porcien's entourage, and this time he wants his wife with him.

We do not know why this man left Porcien's household earlier or why he was now ready to return, although the clear implication is that Porcien is lucky that he is willing to consider doing so. We do have a description of one such separation by Jean de Mergey. At one point he pauses to inform the reader that at a certain juncture (in 1569) he was no longer with the comte de La Rochefoucauld, but instead was in the service of another nobleman. "I left the Count's presence, not out of feeling or choice," he relates, "but because Madame his wife [had] seized certain lands that belonged to me . . . and [La Rochefoucauld] did not dare, for regard for her, to show me the affection he bore me." He concludes: "That is why, during this trip, I placed myself with monsieur de Bonneval." (We may note in passing the concreteness of his terms: "je *me mis* avec monsieur de Bonneval.") Finally, he adds that when he next saw the Count, La Rochefoucauld nevertheless greeted him warmly, with an epigram: "Mergey," the Count supposedly said, "encores que vous ne soyez pas avec moy, vous estes tousjours à moy."[81]

So, just as difficulties over land transactions or vassalage obligation might temporarily enforce distance in a relationship, so withdrawal from a household might be a short-term necessity. Certainly we have only Mergey's self-glorifying account with which to understand that such ties as he had to a noble of La Rochefoucauld's stature could weather competition from his family. But the example of the sire de Ronchères suggests that relationships within the household were flexible and capable of sustaining tension. This quality is illustrated dramatically by entries in Antoine's household accounts regarding members of the Roucy-Sissonne family. While Henri de Roucy-Sissonne was receiving an annual stipend and being reimbursed for outlays he had made for the household, Antoine was involved in legal proceedings against Henri's brother, whose holding Origny-en-Thiérache was a fief of Antoine's châtellenie of Marle.[82]

81. Jean de Mergey, *Mémoires du sieur Jean de Mergey, gentilhomme champenois,* Collection universelle des mémoires particuliers relatifs d' l'histoire de France (n.p., 1788), pp. 72–73.
82. AN, KK278, "Recettes des terres . . .," fols. 89–90.

4

A great nobleman such as Antoine or Condé was surrounded at all times by an entourage of noblemen and commoners. Among the noblemen were kinsmen, local provincial nobles, and others who had become familiars, often through military campaigns. Some of these men were guardians of various châteaux, some were salaried members of an official household and were occasionally present in the actual household, still others were more continuously present and followed their lord to musters and perhaps into war. The way in which these men were connected to Antoine or Condé through landholding reflected what was most important in their relationship with him: the fact that they were familiar to each other, that they were in close proximity, that they could be in each other's company. They might be given property by Antoine, and they might hold a fief in the vicinity already. They might have lands near one of his other seigneuries or be given command of one of Antoine's outlying châteaux. Land was the origin of relationships insofar as it either facilitated or expressed what truly sustained a relationship in sixteenth-century warrior culture: face-to-face familiarity.

This does not mean that the territorial connection between Antoine and the members of his household was an accident, simply that it was a function of a multitude of idiosyncratic, personal connections. The physical proximity of Antoine's associates to him reflects both material and psychological dependence on landholdings. Overall, a nobleman such as Antoine spent the greater part of his time at his various estates. He often maintained residences in nearby towns as well. As we have seen, he needed trusted associates to guard these residences and their surrounds. He stored weapons and provisions in them and he hunted there, and made use daily of other produce from his domains. The image of Nicolas d'Anjou's laundress, asleep in front of a chamber door to guard the household linens, is not precisely a military image, but the comparison is not inappropriate. A residence such as Antoine's château of La Fère or Louis de Lannoy's Folleville was secure enough to hold out against small bodies of troops. Such houses were often used by their owners as refuges, and they might be invested to withstand more determined sieges, as was La Fère in 1580. Most important, estates were not only property, they were also rights and privileges. Landholding was inseparable from lordship; this ruling function was captured in the practice of alienating selected rights to others in return for service. Landed estates, military power, and personal authority were still thoroughly intertwined, and it was in the household that they intersected. In the household, Antoine shared both his goods and his authority; by definition, this practice mandated ties with local provincial noblemen.

If these nobles are envisioned as clients dependent on the lord's landed wealth, however, much of the significance of both the territorial connection and household service is lost. These connections were characterized by their immediacy, their variety, and their flexibility. And connection by means of the household was not limited to the small group of household officials. The lists of salaried official household members which survive are very limited sources precisely because they suggest that the household was a fixed group of individuals. In fact, the actual household was a fluid group; some "official" members were in the lord's company much of the time, others less frequently. Many other nobles and commoners came and went as well: workers, soldiers, guests. The importance of the detailed monthly accounts that have survived from the Anjou household lies in their revelation that the household was neither an entity nor a place but rather a way of living. The term "household" describes the environment in which prominent nobles always lived, surrounded by a group of attendant noblemen and commoners. This environment was thoroughly portable. As correspondence and accounts reveal, a prominent noble traveled incessantly from residence to residence, from residence to command post, from command post to court. Chairs, bedding, linen coffers, writing desks, clothing, weapons, and casks of wine, as well as tents for making camp, were carted on the road. Even during military campaigns the lord was surrounded by valets, pages, and lesser noblemen under his command. Even there he received visits from guests. The size and the composition of the group around him would vary, as might its location from day to day, but the nature of the environment did not. It consisted of people of varying ranks who lived together intermittently but with easy familiarity, providing concrete services for each other. It was an environment in which all of life's activities happened: eating, sleeping, and growing up, talking, fighting, and dying.

All of a noble's relationships, then, must be understood in terms of the kind of human relationships that obtained within the household. All interactions among these people took place within such environments: they were always surrounded by an entourage of some kind, always concerned with immediate physical needs, always on the move. Honor for great nobles at court naturally was associated with comfortable lodgings close to those of the king, and with physical proximity to him during the day. At times great nobles competed for the roles of host and guest. The prince de Condé and the duc de Guise were apparently acting out such a competition in December 1562, after Condé had been captured by Catholic forces at the battle of Dreux in the first civil war. Guise showered his prisoner with courtesies, ate with him at the same table, and offered him the use of the sole available bed on the premises worthy of his rank. Condé, perhaps sensing an opportunity to reclaim some honor, insisted that Guise should have the bed. Sharing the bed then was the only honorable solution.[83]

The importance of this incident lies not merely in the host–guest tension but in the way it was resolved, with the prince de Condé and the duc de Guise asleep side by side. Here we see the simultaneously private and public lifeworld of the nobility in the sixteenth century. We see also that the individuals who inhabited that world had different sensibilities about their relationships with others, literally different boundaries between themselves and others, than obtain today. To such men, service and reward were actual and immediate. They meant clothing, food, and horse fodder as well as lands and offices. The letters with which nobles attempted to bridge distances between them were strained and passionate and awkward. Contact meant face-to-face contact. It meant riding alongside each other on the road, sitting together at table, sleeping together at night. "Loyalty" or "friendship" was acted out in the moments of face-to-face, episodic familiarity which fill the memoirs of the sire de Mergey. All relationships, whether that between Condé and a humble noble of the household or between Condé and an "equal," such as Guise, existed along a single continuum of interdependence and familiarity. Thus the structure of Condé's or Antoine's network of relationships among provincial nobility, although it may identify geography and

83. De Thou, *Histoire universelle*, 4:485.

rank as determinants of relationship, remains external to them. It is not as abstract men of the state that we should think of the noblemen of the mid–sixteenth century, but as men who ate together, slept together, and occasionally murdered each other behind chamber doors.

– 6 –

Conclusion: Noble Men,
Noble Culture, and the State

SCRUTINY of the political organization of the warrior nobility has been in large part an investigation of transition—that of the state and its institutions from something loosely described as feudalism to something else described as absolutism, or, more accurately, the Ancien Régime. Research has revealed that the transition was much more complex than it was once thought to be. At one time the sixteenth century seemed to be a chaotic wasteland. Order was imposed only after 1600, with the introduction of absolutism. The roots of later royal hegemony have now been traced to fifteenth-century monarchs and the conditions under which they ruled. Simultaneously, decentralized administration and representative institutions have been found to persist into the seventeenth century. The role of the warrior nobility in this transition and in the resulting regime has been approached from the perspectives of their participation in the growth of the state, their economic health, and their social cohesion as a group.

I have asked two questions: How accurate is the clientage model as a description of nobles' political organization in the sixteenth century—a question about the degree of nobles' independence of the state. My second question has challenged the first: In what ways is the initial question too narrowly conceived? The consolidation of the state—long at the center of historians' inquiries—occurred at the same time as and was related to profound changes in the nature of individual life and social relations.

We have seen the significance of modes of communication as constituents of perception and behavior. Oral-literate dichotomies in modes of knowing are striking and yet also enormously complex. It will not do merely to create two transhistorical categories of "oral" and "literate" cultures, and to draw on them as explicators of mentalities. Nevertheless, the significance of oral and literate modes of knowing and communicating is undeniable; understanding the shifts that occurred in this realm in the early modern centuries is central to understanding political life, social life, and any of the things we might label "culture." Scholars with interests as diverse as those of Elizabeth Eisenstein and David Sabean have treated these issues, and the parallels in their findings are compelling. Each has argued that this change from the "age of the ear" to the "age of the eye" constituted a change not merely in the content (or quantity) of knowledge but more fundamentally in the mode of its construction. Knowledge, perceptions, and behaviors changed (or failed to change) as "brainwork" changed (or resisted change).[1] Thus this change did not simply entail acquisition of new skills, such as reading and writing, but rather comprised a whole range of perceptual and behavioral habits linked to reliance on particular sources of knowledge. These habits can be described as sensory habits (reliance on sound, smell, and touch rather than sight), as relational habits (reliance on the externalized behavior of oneself and others, rather than on privatized psychological states), and as political practice (a contest over the authoritative source of knowledge).

Eisenstein argues that in some ways the printing revolution did affect what people knew simply in quantitative terms. The greater variety and number of written texts available made accumulation of knowledge more possible. Access to others' past and current research enabled such investigators as Galileo to build on their work and seemingly advance knowledge rapidly as a result.[2] Other effects of newly available knowledge were more complex and more profound in their immediate consequences for human thought. Historicity was fostered by comparison of historical texts and by the shift

---

1. Elizabeth L. Eisenstein, *The Printing Press as an Agent of Change*, 2 vols. (Cambridge, 1979), p. 41; Lucien Febvre, *The Problem of Unbelief in the Sixteenth Century: The Religion of Rabelais*, trans. Beatrice Gottlieb (Cambridge, Mass., 1982), p. 432.

2. Eisenstein, *Printing Press*, chap. 7.

in attention from the retrieval of texts—now no longer necessary—
to the assimilation of them.[3]

But printing altered not merely particular ideas but the way
thoughts were formed. Eisenstein writes, "Scholars concerned with
'modernization' or 'rationalization' might profitably think more
about the new kind of brainwork fostered by silent scanning of
maps, tables, charts, diagrams, dictionaries and grammars."[4] The
suggestive and inconclusive tone of this passage is appropriate to the
complexities of the issue she is addressing. She is pointing toward
the impact of printing on perceptual habits, on the way knowledge
is thereby constructed, and on the way social life is thereby affected.
Reliance on standardized maps, charts, and diagrams placed knowledge of the physical world at a distance from the perceiver. It contributed to a distancing of an objectified world from a human agent
who stood at greater analytical distance from it and less in interaction with it.

Along with distance from the physical world came distance from
other people. Eisenstein suggests that knowledge gained by means
of the eye was knowledge gained silently and privately, not by
means of other people. The nature of knowledge itself was being
redefined, in other words. Knowledge in oral culture was what
people experienced; it was what had happened to them or what
family or neighbors told them of what had happened in other places
at other times.[5] The "new kind of brainwork," in contrast, legitimated anonymous and abstractly organized information. Thinking
itself was a somewhat different activity in the two systems, representing different relationships to human experience and human
agency, and different relationships between the individual and the
community.

David Sabean has attempted to analyze the kind of brainwork
revealed in German village communities in this period; one of his
most interesting examples is an interpretation of events in one village in the eighteenth century.[6] In 1796 some residents of Beutels-
bach (Würtemburg) took it upon themselves to cure an epidemic of

3. Ibid., p. 33.
4. Ibid., p. 88.
5. Walter J. Ong, Orality and Literacy (London and New York, 1982), pp. 49–57.
6. David Warren Sabean, Power in the Blood (Cambridge, 1984), chap. 6.

hoof-and-mouth disease by making a sacrifice: they buried a live bull at a crossroads outside the town. Local authorities afterward tried to determine precisely which villagers had been responsible for what they regarded as a superstitious act. Who had believed that burying the bull would end the epidemic? Who had organized and carried out the burial? Despite many long interrogations of villagers who had witnessed or participated in the burial, however, the authorities were never able to glean the "true" story. They failed, Sabean argues, because the "truth," as the authorities envisioned it, did not exist in the villagers' perceptions and hence could not have informed their actions. The villagers did not decide to bury the bull because of a systematic belief (whether "superstitious" or not) in the efficacy of that method. Nor did they even arrive at a decision at all in the sense that the authorities assumed. The idea was broached at a village council meeting and the villagers discussed it but took no action. At a later meeting a man brought up the idea again, though earlier he had doubted that it would end the epidemic. No formal vote was taken on the proposal. The only "facts" that the investigator could establish with certainty were those of certain actions, not beliefs: a cowherd (there was disagreement as to his identity) had fetched a rope from the town hall to tie the bull; many villagers had been present at the burial, and some had brought stones to kill the bull mercifully as soon as it had been dragged into the pit—even though burial of a *live* bull was reputedly what had stopped the epidemic in other towns.

No single thread of belief or causation which resulted in the burial could ever be drawn out of the villagers, no matter how hard they were pressed individually by the investigators. The investigators, Sabean argues, were interested in the villagers' actions because they wanted to establish guilt. They presumed that actions had to have originated in notions that were weighed and decided upon in the abstract in advance. But the villagers had an alternative sense of what constituted belief, and of the relation of belief to action. The villagers did have ideas—about what might bring an end to their epidemic, for example—but the truth of a particular notion was not something that anyone would or could claim in the abstract. Their knowledge was held not as belief but as opinion and experience: "I've heard that . . . ," "I don't think it will work, but . . ." It was based on the experiences of others and was a launch point for their own experiences.[7] Part of the investigators' difficulty in extracting the "truth" from the villagers thus lay in the fact that the knowledge the villagers had of the event could not be made explicit in the way the investigators wanted. It was inseparable from the process of discussion and action which had actually constituted the event: council members had discussed the possibility of burying the bull; later, someone had fetched a rope, and so on. The villagers' knowledge of the event was also inseparable from its results. These results included the effect of the burial on the epidemic and the later investigation of the burial. As the investigation began to threaten them personally and to expose their village to ridicule, the villagers readily reinterpreted the meaning of the event; they decided that burying the bull had been a bad idea.

Sabean identifies certain elements of this drama which are peculiar to the eighteenth century. One is the authorities' concern with superstition versus "rational" action. In the sixteenth and seventeenth centuries, he argues, authorities' concern over right belief had focused on correct religious doctrine. Consistently through the period, however, authorities were always concerned about the correctness of the beliefs of the villagers over whom they had authority. Their concern for belief stemmed from their presumption that correct action followed upon correct belief. For them, knowledge was not relative, nor was it the subject or result of community discourse—a discourse that included action as a constituent of knowledge, not merely as an expression or consequence of it. Knowledge, from the authorities' point of view, was an abstract system. It was knowledge of the sort that could be contained within the covers of books. Well into the eighteenth century, Sabean demonstrates, popular culture continued to view knowledge as the product of experience and as reflecting or embodying no systematic or abstract view of explanation or causation.[8]

Both knowledge about the world and knowledge about oneself were gleaned by means of interaction with other people, specifically by an individual's interaction with a community and the judgments of that community. The self was a different entity for these villagers

7. Ibid., pp. 195–96.
8. Ibid., chap. 6 and Conclusion.

than it is for us. The people Sabean examines did not have much awareness of themselves as emotional and motivational centers with a personal history as such.[9] Adults could not and would not have been able to look back over their lives and trace their development as persons, or to have a notion about what their personalities were like and how they came to be that way. Rather, the self was defined in the course of its interaction with others. Relationships between neighbors and friends might be close or distant, hot or cold, depending on circumstances—such as whether they were engaged in a property dispute at the moment. Relationships could thus be markedly volatile without the individuals involved thinking of themselves as or in fact being volatile or flighty, in our sense of those words. When pressed for descriptions of themselves, these folk would have resorted to epithetic description. One man might be "contentious." This description would be offered by way of explaining his current behavior, and past behavior would be remembered in accordance with it. Above all, such notions about the self were the result of community description and acknowledgment. A consistent "deeper" reason for someone's behavior—an internal emotional motivation for the acts someone carried out, such as sibling rivalry or jealousy—was not sought or thought about, any more than a consistent, integrated belief was required in order to bury a bull.[10]

This notion of selfhood was in opposition to the deeply internalized and personalized conscience that both post-Tridentine Catholicism and Protestantism were seeking to recognize and develop within each individual. Sabean argues persuasively that it was in the combined interests of church and state in the early modern era to enforce this more "modern" concept of the individual when and where it could.[11] A "modern" individual would have a larger interior space where emotional life would have an objective existence

---

9. Ibid., p. 208.

10. Ibid., chap. 1; Ong, *Orality and Literacy*, pp. 38–39, 43–45.

11. Other recent discussions of early modern religiosity have argued similarly concerning the repressive and controlling characteristics of the reformed Catholic and Protestant churches. See the synthesis by John Bossy, *Christianity in the West, 1400–1700* (Oxford, 1985). A number of historians have also echoed Sabean's cautions about presuming the passivity and vulnerability of popular culture to these changes. See Stuart Clark, "French Historians and Early Modern Popular Culture," *Past and Present*, no. 100 (1982), pp. 63–99.

independent of action. The religious and secular authorities Sabean examines were anxious to prevent conflict from being acted out, by, say, refusal to receive communion. They sought to give the individual the burden of his or her guilt as a private psychological state, and to have him or her turn to the church—not to the community—for psychological care by means of catechism, confession, and so on. They wanted the state and the church, not the community, to control behavior and enforce conformity. Consequently, they needed to foster an alternative sort of individual who would be subject to such control.

Sabean explicitly ties his understanding of these features of popular culture to the habits of oral communication: it is oral communication that unites people in groups, that creates and sustains knowledge about individuals and things by means of public processes accessible to the entire community.[12] In the case of these peasants, however, he identifies the intrusion of the institutions of church and state, not changes in the peasants' oral culture, as the principal motor for change in that society. Scholars of elite cultures—Eisenstein among them—have stressed increased literacy as a crucial component of the historical process that created inward-looking, self-conscious "modern" individuals. The availability of texts encouraged abstract speculation by permitting the distancing of knowledge from lived experience and the juxtaposition and recombination of ideas and data.[13] It encouraged abstract speculation about the self by these means, and also by the very act of reading. Reading is a solitary activity that fosters awareness of the self as an independent cognitive and feeling agent. It permits direct contact with the author of the text—another isolated, self-aware individual.

A well-known sixteenth-century example is Michel de Montaigne, whose detached, skeptical persona has long been associated with the development of modern rationalism. Elizabeth Eisenstein has pointed out that it is all too easy for us to assume that a man such as Montaigne might "naturally" reflect on the events of his time—the extraordinary discoveries, the wars, and so forth. In fact, she argues, neither the seeming irrationality of his contemporary society nor the seemingly exemplary rationality of the observer Montaigne

---

12. Sabean, *Power in the Blood*, chaps. 1 and 3.
13. Ong, *Orality and Literacy*, chap. 4.

adequately accounts for his work. His penchant for reflection was the creation, she argues, of the dissonance and juxtapositions of knowledge made possible by access to printed texts.[14] No way of thinking is natural—it is the product of the available tools for thought. The physical privacy, the mental solitude, the awareness of inner space Montaigne achieved, it might be argued, flowed from the experience of keeping company with books.[15]

Stephen Greenblatt has argued that in this period such individuals as Montaigne were distinguished not only by the interior space they explored within themselves but also by the difficulties this exploration presented for them. In the lack of ease with which such individuals explored their private consciences is reflected some of the conditions that favored or militated against the development of such interior space in their societies. Montaigne was a conscious explorer of his private selfhood. He was aware that he was inhabiting a private space of reflection and conscience which had been his creation.[16] This conscious development of the self in a number of Montaigne's English contemporaries is the subject of Greenblatt's *Renaissance Self-Fashioning*; although he is concerned with elites, he is also, like Sabean, concerned with power claims attached to certain forms of knowledge.[17]

The agent primarily responsible for the inward turning of such individuals as Thomas More (beyond their own creative capacities to find such a solution), Greenblatt argues, is not simply the technical or intellectual capacities of literacy but rather the intrusive state, from which it was necessary to find a refuge. It is not that the state intruded into private life, but rather that the state necessitated the invention of private life. Relying on More's own descriptions, Greenblatt depicts the world of court politics within which More lived and functioned as a world of artifice gone mad. The King, his courtiers, and his servants (such as More) were caught up in the performance of rituals of power now elaborated, according to Greenblatt, to the point of absurdity. Within this world the game of

14. Eisenstein, *Printing Press*, p. 74.
15. See further suggestions about Montaigne in ibid., p. 230. The scholarship on Montaigne includes many studies that explore these issues. See J. Regosin, *The Matter of My Book: Montaigne's "Essais" as the Book of the Self* (Berkeley, 1977).
16. Stephen Greenblatt, *Renaissance Self-Fashioning* (Chicago, 1979), p. 46.
17. The following discussion summarizes material in ibid., chap. 1.

politics was carried out in equally elaborate and complex duplicity; the artificiality of life and the tension between appearance and actuality were unbearably acute. The strain of maintaining the performance in such conditions, for a literate and self-reflective individual such as More, destroyed the integrity of the individual and all but destroyed the individual as well. Greenblatt interprets More's *Utopia* as an idealized solution for this tension. In Utopia, he argues, More created an environment where the individual would have less scope for the kind of private agony that he himself had experienced. The individuals in Utopia bore a remarkable resemblance to the German villagers of Sabean's study: they defined themselves not by private conscience but by public pressure. They regulated behavior by means of public rituals and shaming rather than internal, private mechanisms of conscience and guilt. In his own life, such a solution was not possible, so More was driven to further and further articulation—painful, isolated, self-conscious articulation—of his private individual self.

The state, in general terms, collaborated in the invention of private life, according to both Greenblatt and Sabean. Just as it was more useful for purposes of social stability to have conflict waged internally rather than publicly in village life, so too it was easier to have individuals bear the burden of a psychologically costly court life themselves. In a certain sense, Greenblatt argues, the defiance of the crown which cost More his life was far from being the heroic act of private conscience of a modern individual, but rather was a deliberate effort at nonmodernity; it was an attempt to relink internal conscience and external behavior in a way that More sensed was being lost. It was More's refuge.

Another scholar who has scrutinized simultaneous transformations of individual, social, and political life is Norbert Elias, whose *Civilizing Process* (1939) has found new life in the current climate of historical debate.[18] Elias offers a comprehensive theory of modernization which links social and economic life, the growth of political institutions, and changes in human beings as psychological entities. The historical development of medieval European society (a process

---

18. Norbert Elias, *The Civilizing Process*, 2 vols. (New York, 1978). A useful discussion of Elias is Patrick H. Hutton, "History of Mentalities: The New Map of Cultural History," *History and Theory* 20 (1981): 247–51.

that other societies have since replicated, Elias argues) was characterized by the increasing complexity of economic life and social interaction and by the growth of the state, at all levels, as an arbiter of that interaction and, as of the seventeenth century, as the exclusive arbiter of violence. Human beings as psychosocial entities naturally underwent transformation as the links between them became more complex over the centuries. They brought their affective lives under control, he argues (in anticipation of Sabean). Elias (now anticipating Foucault) focuses on instinctual life as a dimension of affective life; he analyzes the increased invisibility of instinctual life which paralleled that of emotional life.

For Elias, as for other scholars examined here, the early modern centuries were a crucial phase in these processes of change. By the second half of the seventeenth century in France, Elias argues, political and social life was led by an elite that eschewed private violence, that had adopted an elaborate set of courtly behaviors and learned to cultivate emotional privacy and hence political inscrutability. The sixteenth century appears, in his analysis, as a crucial but murky century of transition; etiquette manuals, which anticipated rather than followed real behavioral change in the elite, began to advocate repression of affect in ways closer to seventeenth-century than to fifteenth-century sources. But the details and the mechanisms of the process escape us, if the fact of these changes and their implications do not. Sabean, concerned with popular culture, does not document the profound cultural change that appears in Elias's and Greenblatt's studies of elites. He does chart the responses of village culture to the increased intrusion of church and state. He thereby depicts the early modern centuries as ones characterized by a striking growth of these institutional monopolies on the regulation of society and behavior, and points to the implications of this growth—if still resisted and unrealized—for individuals' private and communal lives.

What is compelling about these various analyses, then, is not that they agree on all factors or even treat precisely the same problems—for they do not—but that they all depict the interdependence of private life, community life, and political life, in early modern society. Scholars who have treated selected facets of these changes, such as the growth of literacy or the printing revolution, have also highlighted the fact of this interdependence; changes in communication, for example, simultaneously changed the nature of the individual, the character of an individual's ties with others, and the nature of his or her relation to public institutions. My investigation of the warrior nobility in the sixteenth century points in these same directions. I have argued that the bonds noble men formed with each other and with the state were complementary; they were flexible, nonexclusive, and episodic. Forming these bonds were individuals who still externalized feelings and displayed their loyalties; in the main, loyalty was more a thing to do than a thing to feel. Or, rather, doing and feeling may have been more equivalent for them than for us.

These scholars' depictions of the role of the state are very useful for historians of the nobility, since they dislodge the state from its position as an unexamined, largely benign organizing principle of public life. As a description of nobles' relationships, the clientage schema was useful primarily in efforts to assess and describe the extent of nobles' attachment to the state. But the difficulties historians have encountered in discerning not only the patterns of nobles' behavior but also the rationale for it have been rooted in a false assumption of familiarity with the world of sixteenth-century "politics" which the schema seemed to describe. Their descriptions have been limited from the outset, since they have judged nobles' behavior according to criteria that were only then, in the sixteenth century, in the process of emerging. This is the same mistake that Febvre identified in scholars who expected Rabelais to embrace the secular thinking that his work seemed to anticipate; historians of the nobility have expected a modern kind of rationalism about political life which only we can perceive, define, or expect. The effort to regard nobles from this perspective has forced historians into awkward descriptions of nobles' motivation and behavior. Data about them continually escape our efforts to systematize them. On the one hand, nobles' behavior was distinguished by "fidélité," yet "infidélité" was not out of the question. Similarly, although certain "cadres" of clients can be distinguished, the system as a whole seems to defy easy categorization; as Robert Harding has recognized, it was "complex and multifaceted."[19]

19. Robert R. Harding, *Anatomy of a Power Elite* (New Haven and London, 1978), p. 21.

I have also questioned the applicability of the expectations of "affection" and "gain" as competing drives of nobles' behavior. The evidence suggests that this, too, is an imposition of contemporary language ill suited to this sixteenth-century culture. The affection-gain dichotomy, as Mousnier and Harding have used it, construes gain in familiar modern terms: as measurable economic gain. (And Mousnier, judging this to be an anachronism, rules out gain as a motive of behavior.) But the problem actually lies in how gain is construed—precisely in the fact that it is construed in particular modern terms, in opposition to affection. The evidence presented here has suggested that the content of these notions was quite different in sixteenth-century warrior culture; they were neither exclusive nor opposing categories of expectation or action.[20] There is no evidence that nobles thought of gain as exclusively material. Certainly, leading nobles tried to defend their property and all nobles had direct, practical experience in matters of this kind. But *gain* was gain in honor. And although honor found expression in and could be enhanced by material advantage—indeed, was impossible without it—it was nevertheless not equivalent to it. As the sire de Mergey's proud stories reflect, the notice and recognition of the great were also things to be gained.

Moreover, we have seen that gain (whether material or otherwise) and personal familiarity and trust were constantly intermingled in nobles' experience. Negotiation of gain and reward was an everyday matter for noblemen of all ranks. One negotiated to have one's horse paid for, to have new clothes, to have adequate supplies for a journey. Simultaneously, one carried out services: one made journeys, bought provisions, guarded belongings. One invited guests to one's residence and hoped to be invited in turn. Material and symbolic gain was not an abstract goal; the quest for it was a process indistinguishable from simply living. Insofar as nobles felt trust in one another, it must have been trust in their familiarity with the people with whom they had long exchanged ordinary goods and services. Not surprisingly, such relationships were often

---

20. I am indebted to William M. Reddy for many useful discussions of these issues. See his *Money and Liberty in Modern Europe: a Critique of Historical Understanding* (Cambridge, 1987).

also hardened in battle, as we have seen; many of Antoine's and Condé's most frequent attendants were also soldiers under their command.

It is a mistake to describe such familiarity, trust, and companionship as "affection," as distinguished from self-interest. Particularly, it is a mistake to see this continual free exchange of service and honor as philanthropic, as Harding does. Noblemen, particularly great noblemen, were free with their goods and attentions in the sense that they valued and practiced liberality. But this was most assuredly not liberality without hope of gain. Gain was the increase in status and power which commanding other people and using their labor conferred. It was the ability to make other people dependent on what you could provide them. Gain meant the power to make a noble of one's own rank accept a gift. And gifts to fellows, not surprisingly, generally took the form of exotic foodstuffs or other costly items associated with food: hunting dogs and birds.

We must also remember that even when there was long-standing familiarity, there was also distance. The sire de Mergey, for years a close associate of La Rochefoucauld, nevertheless measures his distance from the Count by revealing his awareness that their interests do not fully coincide. He leaves La Rochefoucauld's suite when his property interests are threatened, although he is voluble in his continuing respect for the Count. In most cases, lesser noblemen are visible in surviving sources only when they appear in records documenting great nobles' lives: their household accounts, their letters, their plans for battle. But we must imagine these relationships not as they appear in some of these documents—as a list of people "dependent" on the lord—but rather in the ways that certain other documents suggest they were really lived. Some men often frequented the household, but also often resided on their own estates. Periods of close contact were interspersed with periods of physical and thus psychological distance. One might receive charges and honor and simultaneously be the object of a legal action, as were the Roucy-Sissonnes. This is evidence not of capriciousness but of the all-encompassing nature of these relationships. They are public and private, the bonds are material and affective. And therefore neither dependence nor trust is exclusive or total.

Nobles' thinking about and memory of relationships were arranged and constructed as narratives of action; one more scene, yet another encounter could always be grafted onto the story. Their analysis of relationships mirrored—or rather was mirrored by—the various analyses contained in their letters; it was constructed aggregatively, one thing after another. This does not mean that there was no consistency to relationships; trust or hostility could indeed be built up over time. But the way they "knew" this information meant that there was no internal requirement for consistency of the sort we imply when we use such terms as "loyalty" and "disloyalty." If two men who had been associating cooperatively began to behave hostilely, their hostility was not necessarily inconsistent with their previous experience of their relationship. Moreover, the kind of specific, event-centered knowledge they had of relationships carried with it no logical requirement for exclusivity. It would have been impossible for them to think of all of these relationships as competing for space in a single arena, as occupying the same stage.

What they expected of their relationships with others they also expected of themselves. The delimited, episodic way in which relationships were framed was also the way in which an individual such as the prince de Condé might frame his own actions. Despite his apparent "history" of hostility to members of the Lorraine family, for example, he nevertheless chose to cultivate closer ties with them, by means of his brother, after the first civil war. He went so far as to accept an invitation to be a guest at a family château. Other well-known "events," such as the outcome of the Amboise conspiracy, may also be reinterpreted in light of this understanding of motivation and behavior.

Condé's actions that helped to precipitate the first civil war in 1562 may also be reinterpreted in this light. Condé had been formally exonerated for his involvement in the Amboise affair in June 1561, and had participated in the formal reconciliation with Guise arranged by Catherine de Médicis in August. Guise had delivered his carefully worded apology and then, significantly, the two men had been required to embrace. In the months that followed, tensions continued to run high at court. And, as we might expect, these tensions were acted out. Guise, most threatened by the new favor Condé was winning at court and anxious to demonstrate hostility to toleration of the Reformed religion there, periodically staged withdrawals from the court, with all of his retainers in tow—later to return in an impressive display of armed force. Condé, for his part, sought to enhance his stature by other sorts of demonstrations. In October 1561, for example, he made plans to hold a large banquet mockingly to celebrate the first anniversary of his arrest.[21]

The months of February and March 1562 are particularly interesting, as it was during these months that confrontations of this sort finally escaped the confines of the court and were played out by two opposing armies. The great nobles customarily resorted to menacing withdrawals from the court when their interests were ignored. One nobleman who had the least cause to make use of such bold, inflexible maneuvering was Antoine de Bourbon. His status as First Prince of the Blood in the new reign of the minor Charles IX and his increasing disposition to remain a Catholic gave him a great deal of influence with the Queen Mother.[22] Condé's influence, in some ways, was directly diminished by that of his older brother. Condé had long since embraced the Reformed faith and continually pressured Catherine de Médicis officially to tolerate its practice. Having less claim to power than his brother, he had more need to pursue his claims aggressively and to confront his opposition openly.

But an interesting incident happened one night in February. Catherine had declared, and was trying to carry out, a policy of requiring all provincial governors to reside in their governments. By this means she hoped to force the departure of the leading nobles at court and prevent the return of others who had temporarily withdrawn. Witnesses to a discussion with the Queen Mother one evening reported that Condé seemed to favor the plan, as he would receive equal treatment with his rivals, although he vaguely "reserved his rights as a Prince of the Blood." Antoine objected vociferously. It was late in the evening when this altercation broke out, and when Antoine finished speaking, he announced imperiously that he was retiring for the night. Turning to his brother, Antoine commanded Condé to retire with him, "in order to show the Queen that the Prince followed him and not her." Condé, who had been opposing his brother's strategies for months, followed him out of the room.[23]

21. Lucien Romier, *Catholiques et Huguenots à la cour de Charles IX* (Paris, 1924), pp. 240–41, 262.

22. Alphonse de Ruble, *Antoine de Bourbon et Jeanne d'Albret*, 4 vols. (Paris, 1881-86), especially vol. 3, chap. 14.

23. This incident is related in a letter by the Spanish ambassador Chantonnay of 25 February 1562, cited in ibid., 4:70–71.

Catherine's policy failed, and in the months that followed, the hostility among nobles at court quite literally escaped its confines and led almost naturally to civil war. Condé was in Paris with a small group of armed followers when the news of the March 1 massacre at Vassy arrived. This had been a spontaneous massacre of Huguenot worshipers by a group of armed retainers accompanying the duc de Guise. The Prince was still in the capital when Guise himself arrived there from the provinces on March 16, with a large armed "suite."[24] Catherine tried to defuse the situation in Paris by calling Condé to her side at court—at that point, at Montceaux. But Condé chose not to come, perhaps knowing the limits of the authority he would enjoy there. He had to withdraw his inferior force from Paris, however, and he traveled to Meaux, where he then began deliberately to assemble a larger armed force.[25] Soon the decision was made to invest Orléans, and the large rebel force— documented partially in the "Liste des gentilhommes de l'armée protestante"—eventually gathered there.

Much of the behavior exhibited by Condé and his fellow nobles during these months is reminiscent of that of the villagers David Sabean has examined. Why did the civil war break out? (How was it that the bull came to be buried? "Well, Hans fetched a rope"; "Well, there were a lot of people already at the pit when I came.") Condé followed his brother out of the Queen's chamber one February evening, most likely as a way of asserting his special stature as Prince of the Blood. This was certainly a strategically useful thing to do. But it was not a strategy in the sense that it was planned in advance. The answer to the question "How did the war come to break out?" is the same kind of answer the villagers provided about the burial of the bull. Well, he withdrew from court. Well, he had to leave Paris to avoid a confrontation with the duc de Guise, who had superior forces. When Condé's behavior is described in this way, war seems to have been inevitable, not because it was the result of random and disconnected actions (hence "irrational") but because of the nature of those actions. A noble's actions in such instances, like those of the cowherd who fetched the rope, consisted of the ordi-

---

24. The English ambassador, Throckmorton, noted the tension of the situation. See Throckmorton to Elizabeth I, 20 March 1562, in *Calendar of State Papers, Foreign Series, 1561-62* (London, 1866), p. 558.

25. François de La Noue argued that Condé, being outnumbered, was wise to withdraw: F. E. Sutcliffe, ed., *Discours politiques et militaires* (Geneva, 1967), p. 609.

nary possibilities of behavior: traveling about accompanied by armed followers who could put hand to arms for him. In a very real sense, then, the civil wars were inevitable because confrontational behavior and the resort to arms were deeply embedded in nobles' personae and in their lives. More generally, such dichotomies as self-interest/loyalty are inappropriate in respect to nobles' behavior, and so is the very assumption that motivation (of any kind) can be neatly distinguished from action.

An important distinction must now be made. To say that nobles did not have the state as their exclusive or primary frame of reference and that their behavior must be explained in other terms is not to say that noble culture is to be understood in isolation, apart from its relation to the state. Noble culture must not be analyzed in terms of the state or in relation to the state, but rather in its relationship *with* the state. This relationship can be discussed in terms not of dependence and rebellion but of interaction or dialogue. It is in this interaction that historians may be able to see the transformational processes that eventually would bring these warriors into a different sort of relationship with the state.

This awareness may lead us to reinterpret the meaning of contemporary commentaries about noble culture, which often have been viewed as evidence of the cultural emptiness and the self-evident crisis of the nobility. One such work is the well-known *Discours politiques et militaires* (1585) by the Huguenot warrior François de La Noue. A marked cultural distance separated the kind of values that we most easily admire in La Noue—disinterested loyalty, the internalization of gentlemanly values of moderation and learning, the cultivation of a persona in which the public and private are more separated—from the values and practices of the nobility as a group. At the same time that La Noue was criticizing symbolic display and advocating sumptuary laws, great noble men and women were accumulating vast collections of doublets, hose, capes, and coverlets in brilliantly colored and intricately worked satins, velvets, and furs.[26]

Because La Noue's ideas seem distinctly modern and "rational," we may be tempted to accept them not only as accurate evidence of what noble society was like in his day but also as justified criticism

26. Ibid., p. 37.

of that society. In fact, La Noue was engaged in a dialogue with noble culture as I have described it. La Noue's writings were made possible by and reflect a wide-ranging humanist education. We cannot learn from a work such as this what the actual situation of the nobility was, except insofar as we can discern it revealed obliquely by means of the dialogue La Noue is undertaking. La Noue's effort is useful in and of itself, however, precisely because of that dialogue. We cannot take for granted the change that would have been necessary if warriors' values and expectations were to move onto the ground La Noue seemed to be charting. Many scholars have taken it largely for granted, presuming in idealist terms that one set of values and notions would simply replace another.[27] Far closer to the truth is a complex, living relationship between La Noue's literate discussion and the culture he was observing. Carlo Ginzburg might point out, for example, that obliquely expressed in La Noue's humanist terminology are notions long present in the oral culture of warrior society.[28]

Even at such an impressive level, literacy could not have completely reshaped a single man such as La Noue—or Rabelais—so that he was literally ahead of his time. As many scholars of literacy have pointed out, the historical process of change from oral to written communication has been acted out by—and the resulting tension between authorities and behaviors carried by—single individuals in many past and present societies. One obvious example is seen in the many formally educated men and women in Third World countries who routinely cross the "boundary" between their traditional village cultures and Westernized professional lives in urban centers, alternating modes of communication and, it seems, personality types as well.[29] The sire de Gouberville, who wrote in his private journal every day in the mid–sixteenth century, did not use it for self-reflection of any kind; and he never reread his entries.[30] The pace of cultural change for noble society as a whole was slow

27. See, for example, Ellery Schalk, *From Valor to Pedigree* (Princeton, 1986); cf. Mervyn James, "The Concept of Order and the Northern Rising," in *Society, Politics, and Culture* (Cambridge, 1986), pp. 270–308.

28. Carlo Ginzburg, *The Cheese and the Worms* (London, 1980).

29. Clifford Geertz, "'From the Natives' Point of View': On the Nature of Anthropological Understanding," in *Meaning in Anthropology,* ed. Keith H. Basso and Henry A. Selby (Albuquerque, 1976), pp. 230–35.

30. Madeleine Foisil, *Le Sire de Gouberville* (Paris, 1981), pp. 19-26.

and uneven, both across the society and within individuals. And we, who know them primarily through texts, must guard against too ready a sense of familiarity or recognition of rationality in what we think we see on the page.

In any case, if literacy, self-knowledge, and outward behavior were all interrelated, then we undoubtedly should be able to detect hints of a new noble culture not merely in ideas but in behavior. It seems clear that day-to-day language was one of the principal realms in which we should see noble culture acting out change. We have previously discussed their attentiveness to words and the power of words as a reflection of the perceptions of oral culture. We must now acknowledge that the attentiveness to words represented by the duc de Guise's careful apology to Condé in 1561, for example, like the use of language in their letters, reflects a tension between the language of purely oral community life and that of literate communities where words flowed less freely and were not directly translated into action. Thus Guise's apology to Condé represents a successful effort to contain and delimit the possibilities of language, and to make violence a less likely outcome. Modern political life is acted out routinely in the field of words. It seems that the connection between words and actions is beginning to be broken here, for all the power the words still retain.[31]

This increasing weighting of words and self-containment within them naturally carried implications for nobles' honor. Honor was a claim to the privilege of legitimated violence. But in the increased possibility that honor could be sustained by words alone we can see the possibility of an eventual shift in the significance of honor—or, more accurately, in the location of honor. In Condé's threatening posture amidst disaster in 1568 we can hear an echo of François I's supposed declaration upon his humiliating defeat at Pavia (1525): "All is lost save honor." The significance of François's declaration, one scholar has argued, was that it was these words—the insistence on honor, and not the patently humiliating capture itself—that endured as the public memory of the event.[32] The tight relationship

31. Heightened attention to control of the flow of words by some early modern subjects is also pointed out by Sabean, *Power in the Blood*, chap. 3, especially p. 112. It is the principal concern of R. Bauman's study of Quakers: *Let Your Words Be Few: Symbolism of Speaking and Silence among Seventeenth-Century Quakers* (Cambridge, 1982).

32. L. Halkin, "Pour une histoire d'honneur," *Annales: E.S.C.* 4 (1949): 433–44.

between power, defined as the possibility of prevailing in armed conflict, and honor is being loosened here, as it is in Condé's later threatening letter to his cousin Montpensier. The insistence on honor grows more shrill as actual power is reduced and as the consequences of defeat grow. From this point on, honor could lose its ability to exist simultaneously in the public and private realms. It could cease to be the basis for both social order and private identity, and instead become identified solely with private, internalized qualities of individuals. From warriors we would eventually get gentlemen.[33]

But we must be careful not to "recognize" this gentleman too quickly. We must not once again collapse the processes of social and political change into familiar categories. Recent investigations of seventeenth-century society and the state have proceeded along these lines, disrupting the once familiar assumptions about the success of absolutism. These studies have argued that the absolutist state, particularly under Louis XIV, was successful not because it quashed the aristocracy but because it governed in its interests. These interests were guaranteed by a new cooperative relationship with the crown, which without doubt sustained a more centralized control and coordination of political life than had ever existed before. This system was more feudal than modern, however, in that it depended on extraeconomic coercion of the lower classes, represented and defended by legal and economic privilege. Clientage relationships were a form of governing especially effective (even necessary) in this milieu. The aristocracy was more dependent on central government, but personal authority nevertheless persisted as legitimate power. The absolutist state begins to resemble the modern one in its internal coherence, but the nature of political power

33. On honor as order, see James, "Concept of Order," pp. 301–3. Recent studies of this change of self-definition in the nobility point in this direction, suggesting that notions of exalted lineage, "race," and pedigree began to replace expectations that one's capacities ("virtues") would be demonstrated in the public arena and be publicly recognized. The idealist approach of many such treatments must be kept in mind when one uses them to assess the relation of such notions to the actual process of social and political change. For example, it leads to somewhat problematic attempts to discern whether nobles actually *were* more or less virtuous over the course of time. See Schalk, *From Valor to Pedigree*; Arlette Jouanna, *L'Idée de race en France au XVIe et au début du XVIIe siècle*, 3 vols. (Paris, 1976); André Devyver, *Le Sang épuré: Les Préjugés de race chez les gentilhommes français de l'ancien régime, 1560–1720* (Brussels, 1973).

remains quite different.[34] It was simultaneously public bureaucratic power and private patronage power.[35]

Whether clientage schemas are indeed useful ways of describing seventeenth-century practices remains an open question. What is most relevant in these recent descriptions of seventeenth-century conditions is that they rest on a very helpful assumption about the relation of society to the state. They assume that political life resides in the relationship between the two. Further, they provide compelling evidence of the continued importance of warriors as independent political agents through the first half of the seventeenth century.

Courtesy remained important to the warrior-gentleman of the seventeenth century; in fact, now that courtesy constrained violence more effectively, it was even more highly charged. As Orest Ranum has discussed, courtly manners look stultifying and ridiculous at first glance, yet they were a crucial expression and constituent of power for Louis XIV and the elites of his day.[36] The "gentleman" of the late sixteenth and early seventeenth centuries is also defamiliarized in François Billacois's investigation of the practice of dueling in its heyday—the hundred years following the period examined here.[37] On the one hand, the staged violence of a duel could be characterized as a shrill, extreme claim to honor. In their deliberate confrontation with death (and duels did routinely result in death), duelers were behaving much like François I when he claimed honor in defeat at Pavia; honor in both cases was increasingly disconnected from real military power and in fact was a claim advanced deliberately in the face of powerlessness—in the case of the dueler, the annihilation of actual death. On the other hand, dueling also represented the perpetuation of the system of honor described here. It was closely bound in practice to a routine of manners and courtesy by which equals mutually sustained each other's honor. It replicated

34. William Beik, *Absolutism and Society in Seventeenth-Century France* (Cambridge, 1985), especially Introduction.

35. Sharon Kettering argues the case for client networks most forcefully for the early seventeenth century and challenges historians to consider the ways in which private power, such as that represented by patronage and brokerage, is present in all political systems: *Patrons, Brokers, and Clients* (Oxford, 1986).

36. Orest Ranum, "Courtesy, Absolutism, and the Rise of the French State, 1630–1660," *Journal of Modern History* 52 (1980): 426–51.

37. François Billacois, *Le Duel dans la société française des XVIe–XVIIe siècles* (Paris, 1986).

the episodic rhythm of political life we have noted—though with recourse to extreme forms of encounter. The most important function of the duel, Billacois argues (and I would emphasize), was its almost mythic function as a representation of the noble's power of self-definition. The duel was not a form of political opposition in our sense (for that would be ridiculous); it was rather an act that extended beyond the moment to symbolize nobles' willingness to define themselves as distinct from the state that forbade them to engage in it. By its very extremeness, then, it represented the distinctiveness of noble culture. Although nobles had lost much power to the monarchy, at least until the second half of the seventeenth century they persisted in a dialogue with the crown about the nature of their power and their role. The duel was a symbol of a field of power other than the state and independent of it.

Among the other aspects of this gentleman's life which must be explored are his relationships with women of his own class. Robert Muchembled has detected a restriction of roles of noblewomen after the middle of the century among the Artois lesser nobility. Joan Kelly's study of aristocratic women in Renaissance Italy, among others, provides compelling arguments for the premise that male and female culture must be understood in terms of each other and, specifically, that changes in male culture have often occurred by means of changes (usually disadvantageous) in women's lives.[38] We might ask whether the lives of noble women and men slowly ceased to be as equivalent and as intertwined as they seem to have been in the sixteenth century. We also need to ask whether power, honor, and, above all, personhood began to be defined increasingly in terms that reflected a separation of male and female. As Joan Kelly has suggested, the separation of public persona from private persona within single individuals was probably linked to the separation of public and private as social spheres.[39]

Further investigation along any of these lines moves beyond the

38. Robert Muchembled, "Famille, amour et mariage: Mentalités et comportements des nobles artésiens à l'époque de Philippe II," *Revue d'histoire moderne et contemporaine* 22 (1975): 247–55; Joan Kelly, "Did Women Have a Renaissance?" in *Becoming Visible: Women in European History*, ed. R. Bridenthal, C. Koonz, and S. Stuard (Boston, 1987), pp. 137–64, and "The Social Relations of the Sexes: Methodological Implications of Women's History," *Signs: Journal of Women in Culture and Society* 1 (1976): 809–23; Joan W. Scott, "Gender: A Useful Category of Historical Analysis," *American Historical Review* 91 (1986): 1053–75.

39. Kelly, "Did Women Have a Renaissance?"

scope of this book. But it has been my goal to help shift the ground on which noble society in the sixteenth century has stood in historical analysis, and hence to raise such questions. I wish to view politics in the past not as a self-evident practice in terms of a "known" referent—the state—but as cultural practice composed of certain kinds of behaviors and certain constructions of power. It will not be surprising if future analysts find it necessary to consider issues that many scholars still view as marginal to political life: the private lives of men and the daily lives of women. What will emerge from these analyses will be an unfamiliar state—one defined by means of these "Others" within it.

Selected Bibliography

Manuscript Sources

Archives Nationales, Paris

MATERIAL preserved in the Archives Nationales is crucial to any study of prominent noble families; records of landholdings and family papers are scattered throughout the archival collections, and are therefore difficult to describe summarily. Use of the many *fonds* is further complicated by the fact that documents may be grouped chronologically, by feudal jurisdiction, by royal administrative jurisdiction, or by family name in the various series. Documents grouped by family are especially problematic because pieces concerning a particular seigneurie, for example, are usually grouped with the family that held it most recently—usually the last holder before the Revolution. Nevertheless, the collections of the Archives Nationales are of fundamental importance for this study; much of the surviving documentation of Bourbon landholdings in the northeast is preserved here. Records of the principal family lands administered from the household at La Fère are found in series K, P, Q, and R. Series K (the name of which, "Monuments historiques," betrays its disparate contents) also contains a sampling of correspondence, *quittances* (receipts acknowledging payment of pensions and stipends), muster rolls, and marriage and other documents concerning the royal family—that is, in this period, all members of the Valois and Bourbon lines and their descendants. Another series including a variety of documentation is series R, "Papiers des princes" (reflecting later appanage divisions). *Comptes, ban,* and *arrière ban* records, *dénombrements* (lists of the fiefs dependent on a particular landholding), and other documents from a number of Picard families are found here. Scattered documentation of Picard families and their lands is also found in series J ("Trésor des Chartes"), particularly in *cartons* 786–817, which include a variety of pieces ranging from correspondence to records of royal domain lands in Picardy, and in *registres* JJ258–266, which are miscellaneous administrative acts grouped chronologically. Series T, "Papiers séquestrés," is a rich but, for the sixteenth century, very spotty collection of families' papers confiscated in the Revolution. Finally, series Y, which contains records of the Châtelet de Paris, is important for study of Picard nobility, since many prominent nobles from regions close to Paris had legal work done in Paris when they could; wills, gifts, and marriage contracts and other notarial acts are recorded in the *insinuations du Châtelet de Paris*: registres 86–118 correspond to the years covered in this book. Notarial acts themselves are gathered in the Minutier Central; virtually uninventoried for the sixteenth century, they were of limited use for this work. I also used family papers collected in the Archives Privées (series AP in the Archives Nationales); a number of noble families' papers remain in this collection, technically still under the control of the donors.

Bibliothèque Nationale, Paris

I have drawn heavily on correspondence preserved in the various manuscript collections of the Bibliothèque Nationale. Most extensive and richest in sixteenth-century noble and royal correspondence are the Manuscrits français and the Nouvelles acquisitions françaises. As I consulted more than one hundred volumes in these fonds in whole or in part, it would be impractical to enumerate them individually. Interspersed with letters in these volumes is a variety of other documents—originals, copies, and secretaries' drafts (*minutes*); dispatches, instructions to ambassadors, quittances, and other administrative documents, such as reports from various royal agents. Also included—often as copies—are such family papers as marriage contracts, property divisions, and wills. Smaller manuscript collections that contain similar mixtures of documents were also used: the Fonds Dupuy, Fonds Clairambault, and the Cinq Cents Colbert. Quittances are also found in the Pièces originales, and genealogical data—which must be used cautiously—in the Cabinet d'Hozier and the Dossiers bleus. Separate mention must be made of the muster rolls of the companies of the royal gendarmerie, which are also found in both the Manuscrits français and the Fonds Clairambault in large numbers and which I used extensively.

Selected Bibliography

Musée Condé, Chantilly

Despite its name, the Musée Condé is not a rich source of documentation concerning the Bourbon-Condés of the sixteenth century. In that century Chantilly was held by the Montmorency family; the correspondence collected there primarily concerns the members of that family. It is nevertheless abundant, and includes some correspondence of selected Picard nobles. The records in the Cabinet des Titres at Chantilly do include important documentation concerning Louis I de Bourbon, prince de Condé. Series A ("Papiers de famille—Successions") and series GE ("Domaines divers") contain most of the sources I have used concerning Condé's (as opposed to the Bourbon-Vendôme line's) land-holdings.

Archives Départementales de la Somme, Archives
Communales d'Amiens, and Archives Communales de Laon

Most of the historical Picardy is included in the modern departments of the Somme and Aisne. Provincial and communal archives in these and other departments in the northeast suffered greatly in the two World Wars. The very extensive fonds of the Bourbon-Vendôme land-holding records preserved in series B of the Département de l'Aisne (B3436–3456, Chambre du Conseil et des Comptes de La Fère) were destroyed in World War I. Of use in this study were other families' papers preserved in series B and E of the Somme archives and portions of the BB and CC series of Amiens (Somme) and Laon (Aisne), the towns' administrative and financial records, respectively.

Published Sources

Aubigné, A. d'. *Histoire universelle.* Ed. Alphonse de Ruble. 10 vols. Paris, 1886–97.

Barthelémy, Edouard de, ed. *Journal d'un curé ligueur de Paris.* Paris, 1866.

Beauvillé, Victor de, ed. *Recueil de documents inédits concernant la Picardie.* 4 vols. Paris, 1860–82.

Bèze, Théodore de. "Lettres de Théodore de Bèze à divers." *Bulletin de la société de l'histoire du protestantisme français* 25(1875): 312–18.

———. *Histoire écclésiastique des églises reformées au royaume de France.* Ed. G. Baum and E. Cunitz. 3 vols. Paris, 1883–89.

———. *Correspondence de Théodore de Bèze.* Ed. H. Meylan. 9 vols. Geneva, 1960.

Selected Bibliography

Brantôme, Pierre de Bourdeille, seigneur de. *Oeuvres*. Ed. Ludovic Lalanne. 11 vols. Paris, 1864–82.

Calendar of State Papers, Foreign (1547–99). 23 vols. London, 1861-1950.

Castelnau, Michel de. *Memoirs of the Reign of Francis II and Charles IX of France*. London, 1724.

Condé, Louis de Bourbon, prince de. *Mémoires*. London, 1743.

Desjardins, A., ed. *Negotiations diplomatiques de la France avec Toscane*. Paris, 1865.

De Thou, Jacques-Auguste. *Histoire universelle*. 16 vols. London, 1734.

Gaches, Jacques. *Mémoires de Jacques Gaches sur les guerres de religion à Castres et dans le Languedoc*. Ed. Charles Pradel. Paris, 1879.

Haton, Claude. *Mémoires, contenant le récit des événements accomplis de 1553 à 1582 principalement dans la Champagne et la Brie*. Ed. Félix Bourquelot. 2 vols. Paris, 1857.

"Journal de ce qui s'est passé en France durant l'année 1562." *Revue retrospective*, ser. 1, 5 (1834): 81–116, 168–212.

La Morlière, Adrien de. *Recueil de plusieurs nobles et illustres maisons vivantes es esteintes en l'estendue du diocese d'Amiens et à l'environ*. Amiens, 1630.

La Noue, François de. *Discours politiques et militaires*. Ed. F. E. Sutcliffe. Geneva, 1967.

La Place, Pierre. *Commentaire de l'estat de la religion et la république*. Ed. J. A. C. Buchon. Paris, 1836.

Marolles, abbé de, ed. *Inventaire des titres de Nevers*. Ed. J. Soultrait. Nevers, 1873.

Médicis, Catherine de. *Lettres de Catherine de Médicis*. Ed. Hector de La Ferrière. 10 vols. Paris, 1880–1909.

Mergey, Jean de. *Mémoires du sieur Jean de Mergey, gentilhomme champenois*. N.p., 1788.

Pichon, J., ed. "Analyse d'une correspondence des d'Humières provenant du château de Monchy près Compiègne." *Bulletin de la société historique de Compiègne* 6 (1883): 78–140.

Prarond, Ernest, ed. *De Abbavilla et chronique du pays et comté de Ponthieu*. Paris, 1902.

Serres, Jean de. *Mémoires de la troisième guerre civile et des derniers troubles de France*. N.p., 1570.

Tournon, Cardinal François de. *Correspondence du cardinal François de Tournon, 1521–1562*. Ed. Michel François. Paris, 1946.

Secondary Works

Ariès, Philippe, and Georges Duby, eds. *Histoire de la vie privée*. Vol. 3, *De la Renaissance aux Lumières*. Ed. Roger Chartier. Paris, 1986.

Selected Bibliography

Arriaza, Armand. "Mousnier, Barber, and the Society of Orders." *Past and Present*, no. 89 (November 1980), pp. 39–57.

Aumale, Henri d'Orléans, duc d'. *Histoire des princes de Condé pendant les XVIe et XVIIe siècles.* 7 vols. Paris, 1863–96.

Bauman, Richard. *Let Your Words Be Few: The Symbolism of Speaking and Silence among Seventeenth-Century Quakers.* Cambridge, 1983.

———. and Joel Sherzer, eds. *Explorations in the Ethnography of Speaking.* Cambridge, 1974.

Beik, William. *Absolutism and Society in Seventeenth-Century France.* Cambridge, 1985.

Belleval, René de. *Trésor généalogique de la Picardie.* Vol. 1, *Notes d'un généalogiste du dix-huitième siècle.* Amiens, 1859.

———. *Les Fiefs et seigneuries du Ponthieu et du Vimeu.* Paris, 1870.

Benedict, Philip. *Rouen during the Wars of Religion.* Cambridge, 1981.

Bernstein, Basil, ed. *Class, Codes, and Control.* Vol. 1, *Theoretical Studies towards a Sociology of Language.* London, 1977.

Billacois, François. "La Crise de la noblesse européene (1550–1650): Une mise au point." *Revue d'historie moderne et contemporaine* 23 (1976): 258–77.

———. *Le Duel dans la société française des XVIe–XVIIe siècles.* Paris, 1986.

Bitton, Davis. *The French Nobility in Crisis, 1560–1640.* Stanford, 1969.

Bloch, Jean-Richard. *L'Anoblissement en France au temps de François I.* Paris, 1934.

Boissevain, Jeremy. *Friends of Friends.* New York, 1974.

Bossy, John. *Christianity in the West, 1400–1700.* Oxford, 1985.

Briggs, Robin. *Early Modern France.* Oxford, 1977.

Burguière, André. "The Fate of the History of *Mentalités* in the *Annales.*" *Comparative Studies in Society and History* 24 (1982): 424–37.

Burke, Peter. *Popular Culture in Early Modern Europe.* London, 1978.

———. "Languages and Anti-Languages in Early Modern Italy." *History Workshop*, no. 11 (1981), pp. 24–32.

Calonne, A. de. *Histoire de la ville d'Amiens.* 2 vols. Paris and Amiens, 1899–1900.

Chartier, Roger. "Histoire intellectuelle et histoire des mentalités. Trajectoires et questions." *Revue de synthèse*, 3d ser., nos. 111–112 (1983), pp. 277–307.

———, Marie-Madeleine Compère, and Dominique Julia. *L'Education en France du XVIe au XVIIIe siècle.* Paris, 1976.

Clanchy, M. T. *From Memory to Written Record: England, 1066–1307.* Cambridge, 1979.

Clarke, Stuart. "French Historians and Early Modern Popular Culture." *Past and Present*, no. 100 (1983), pp. 63–99.

Constant, Jean-Marie. "Gestion et revenus d'un grand domaine aux XVIe et XVIIe siècles d'après les comptes de la baronnie d'Auneau." *Revue d'histoire économique et sociale* 50 (1972): 165–202.

Selected Bibliography

———. *Nobles et paysans en Beauce aux XVIe et XVIIe siècles.* Lille, 1981.

Cressy, David. *Literacy and the Social Order: Reading and Writing in Tudor and Stuart England.* Cambridge, 1980.

Crouzet, Denis. "Recherches sur la crise de l'aristocratie en France au XVIe siècle: Les Dettes de la maison de Nevers." *Histoire, économie, société* 1 (1981): 7–50.

Davis, Natalie Zemon. *Society and Culture in Early Modern France.* Stanford, 1975.

———. "The Historian and Popular Culture." In *The Wolf and the Lamb: Popular Culture in France from the Old Regime to the Twentieth Century,* ed. J. Beauroy, M. Bertrand, and E. T. Gargan, pp. 9–16. Saratoga, Calif., 1976.

———. "Ghosts, Kin, and Progeny: Some Features of Family Life in Early Modern France." *Daedalus* 6 (Spring 1977): 87–114.

Decrue de Stoutz, F. *Anne, duc de Montmorency.* Paris, 1889.

Delaborde, Jules. *Eléonore de Roye, princesse de Condé.* Paris, 1876.

Devyver, André. *Le Sang épuré: Les Préjugés de race chez les gentilhommes français de l'ancien régime, 1560–1720.* Brussels, 1973.

Dewald, Jonathan. *The Formation of a Provincial Nobility: The Magistrates of the Parlement of Rouen, 1499–1610.* Princeton, 1980.

Deyon, Pierre. "A propos des rapports entre la noblesse française et la monarchie absolue pendant la première moitié du XVIIe siècle." *Revue historique* 231 (1964): 341–56.

Dontenwill, Serge. *Une Seigneurie sous l'Ancien Regime: "L'Etoile" en Brionnais du XVIe au XVIIIe siècle, 1578–1778.* Roanne, 1973.

Douen, O. "La Réforme en Picardie (depuis les premiers temps justqu'à nos jours)." *Bulletin de la société de l'histoire du protestantisme français* 7 (1859): 385–609.

Drouot, H. *Mayenne et la Bourgogne: Étude sur la Ligue, 1587–96.* 2 vols. Paris, 1937.

Duby, Georges. "The Diffusion of Cultural Patterns in Feudal Society." *Past and Present,* no. 39 (1968), pp. 3–10.

Dufour, Alain. "L'Origine des guerres de religion d'après quelques livres récents." *Bulletin de la société de l'histoire du protestantisme français* 106 (1960): 232–40.

Eisenstein, Elizabeth. *The Printing Press as an Agent of Change.* Cambridge, 1980.

Febvre, Lucien. *Philippe II et la Franche-Comté.* Paris, 1912, 1970.

———. *Le Problème de l'incroyance au XVIe siècle: La Religion de Rabelais.* Paris, 1947.

———. *Life in Renaissance France.* Ed. and trans. Marian Rothstein. Cambridge, Mass., 1977.

———, and Henri-Jean Martin. *L'Apparition du livre.* Paris, 1958.

Feuchère, Pierre. "La Noblesse du nord de la France." *Annales: E.S.C.* 6 (1951): 306–18.

———. "Dans le nord de la France: La Permanence des cadres territoriaux?" *Annales: E.S.C.* 9 (1954): 94–100.

Foisil, Madeleine. *Le Sire de Gouberville.* Paris, 1981.

Fossier, Robert. *La Terre et les hommes en Picardie.* 2 vols. Paris and Louvain, 1968.

———. *Histoire de la Picardie.* Toulouse, 1974.

Furet, François. "Quantitative History." In *Historical Studies Today,* ed. Felix Gilbert and Stephen Graubard, pp. 45–61. New York, 1972.

———, and Jacques Ozouf. *Reading and Writing: Literacy in France from Calvin to Jules Ferry.* Cambridge and Paris, 1982.

Geertz, Clifford. "The Javanese Kijaji: The Changing Role of a Cultural Broker." *Comparative Studies in Society and History* 2 (1961): 228–49.

Ginzburg, Carlo. *The Cheese and the Worms: The Cosmos of a Sixteenth-Century Miller.* New York, 1982.

Goffman, Erving. *The Presentation of Self in Everyday Life.* New York, 1959.

Gonin, F. "Essai sur la population protestante de l'Oise jusqu'en 1831." *Bulletin de la société de l'histoire du protestantism français* 109 (1963): 205–36.

Goody, Jack. *The Domestication of the Savage Mind.* Cambridge, 1977.

———, ed. *Literacy in Traditional Societies.* Cambridge, 1968.

Goubert, Pierre. *Beauvais et le Beauvaisie de 1600 à 1730.* Paris, 1960.

———. "L'Ancienne Société d'ordres: Verbiage ou réalité?" In *Clio parmi les hommes.* Paris and The Hague, 1976.

Graff, Harvey J. *The Legacies of Literacy: Continuities and Contradictions in Western Culture and Society.* Bloomington, Ind., 1987.

———, ed. *Literacy and Social Development in the West: A Reader.* Cambridge, 1981.

Greenblatt, Stephen. *Renaissance Self-Fashioning from More to Shakespeare.* Chicago, 1979.

Hale, J. R. "Sixteenth-Century Explanations of War and Violence." *Past and Present,* no. 51 (1971), pp. 3–26.

———. "Violence in the Late Middle Ages: A Background." In *Violence and Civil Disorder in Italian Cities,* ed. Lauro Martines. Berkeley, 1972.

Halkin, L. "Pour une histoire d'honneur." *Annales: E.S.C.* 4 (1949): 434–44.

Harding, Robert R. *Anatomy of a Power Elite: The Provincial Governors in Early Modern France.* New Haven and London, 1978.

Hautecoeur, L. *Histoire de l'architecture classique en France.* Paris, 1963.

Herlihy, David. "Some Psychological and Social Roots of Violence in the Tuscan Cities." In *Violence and Civil Disorder in Italian Cities,* ed. Lauro Martines. Berkeley, 1972.

Hexter, J. *Reappraisals in History.* Evanston, Ill., 1961.

Selected Bibliography

Holt, Mack P. "Patterns of *Clientèle* and Economic Opportunity at Court during the Wars of Religion: The Household of François, Duke of Anjou." *French Historical Studies* 13 (1984): 305–22.

———. *The Duke of Anjou and the Politique Struggle during the Wars of Religion.* Cambridge, 1986.

Hymes, Del. *Foundations in Sociolinguistics: An Ethnographic Approach.* Philadelphia, 1974.

Issac, Rhys. "Dramatizing the Ideology of Revolution: Popular Mobilization in Virginia, 1774 to 1776." *William and Mary Quarterly*, 3d ser., 33 (1976): 357–85.

———. "Books and the Social Authority of Learning: The Case of Mid-Eighteenth-Century Virginia." In *Printing and Society in Early America*, ed. William L. Joyce, David D. Hall, Richard D. Brown, and John B. Hench. Worcester, Mass., 1983.

Jackson, Richard A. "Peers of France and Princes of the Blood." *French Historical Studies* 7 (1971): 26–46.

James, Mervyn. *Family, Lineage, and Civil Society.* Oxford, 1974.

———. *Society, Politics, and Culture.* Cambridge, Eng., 1986.

Jouanna, A. "La Notion d'honneur au XVIe siècle." *Revue d'histoire moderne et contemporaine* 15 (1968): 597–623.

Kaplan, Steven L., ed. *Understanding Popular Culture: Europe from the Middle Ages to the Nineteenth Century.* Berlin, 1984.

Karabel, Jerome, and A. H. Halsey, eds. *Power and Ideology in Education.* New York, 1977.

Kettering, Sharon. *Patrons, Brokers, and Clients in Seventeenth-Century France.* Oxford, 1968.

———. "Forum: Fidelity and Clientage. Patronage and Politics during the Fronde." *French Historical Studies* 14 (1986): 409–41.

Kent, Dale. *The Rise of the Medici: Faction in Florence, 1426–35.* Oxford, 1978.

Kingdon, Robert M. *Geneva and the Coming of the Wars of Religion in France, 1555–1563.* Geneva, 1956.

———. *Geneva and the Consolidation of the French Protestant Movement, 1564–1672.* Madison, Wis., 1967.

Labatut, J.-P. *Les Ducs et pairs de France au XVIIe siècle.* Paris, 1972.

Lambert, E. "Les Limites de la Picardie." *Société archéologique, historique et scientifique du Noyon: Comptes rendus et mémoires* 34 (1972): 53–65.

Leguai, André. "Un Aspect de la formation des états princiers en France à la fin du moyen âge: Les Réformes administratives de Louis II, duc de Bourbon." *Moyen âge* 70 (1964): 49–72.

Le Roy Ladurie, Emmanuel. *Les Paysans de Languedoc.* Paris. 1966.

———. "Système de la coutume: Structures familiales et coutume d'héritage en France au XVIe siècle." *Annales: E.S.C.* 27 (1972): 825–47.

Lewis, P. S. "Decayed and Non-Feudalism in Later Medieval France." *Bulletin of the Institute of Historical Research* 37 (1964): 157–84.

——. *Later Medieval France: The Polity.* London, 1968.

——. *The Recovery of France in the Fifteenth Century.* New York, 1971.

Lytle, Guy Fitch, and Stephen Orgel, eds. *Patronage in the Renaissance.* Princeton, 1987.

Major, J. Russell. *Representative Institutions in Renaissance France.* Madison, Wis., 1960.

——. "The French Renaissance Monarchy as Seen through the Wars of Religion in France." *Studies in the Renaissance* 9 (1962): 113–25.

——. "Crown and Aristocracy in Renaissance France." *American Historical Review* 69 (1964): 631–45.

——. "Noble Income, Inflation, and the Wars of Religion in France." *American Historical Review* 86 (1981): 21–48.

——. "Forum: Fidelity and Clientage. The Revolt of 1620: A Study of Ties of Fidelity." *French Historical Studies* 14 (1986): 391–408.

Mann, Hans-Dieter. *Lucien Febvre: La Pensée vivante d'un historien.* Paris, 1971.

Mauss, Marcel. *The Gift.* Trans. Ian Cunnison. Glencoe, Ill., 1954.

Medick, Hans, and David Warren Sabean, eds. *Interest and Emotion: Essays on the Study of Family and Kinship.* Cambridge, 1984.

Meyer, Jean. "L'Histoire des provinces françaises et la rénovation des études régionales." *Revue historique* 246 (1971): 39–58.

——. *La Noblesse bretonne au XVIII siècle.* Paris, 1972.

Mours, Samuel. *Le Protestantisme en France.* Paris and Strasbourg, 1958.

Mousnier, Roland. *Les Hiérarchies sociales de 1450 à nos jours.* Paris, 1969.

——. "Les Concepts d'"ordres,' d''états,' de 'fidélité' et de 'monarchie absolue' en France de la fin du XVe siècle à fin du XVIIIe." *Revue historique* 247 (1972): 289–312.

——. *Les Institutions de la France sous la monarchie absolue.* 2 vols. Paris, 1974.

Muchembled, Robert. "Famille, amour et mariage: Mentalités et comportements des nobles artésiens à l'époque de Philippe II." *Revue d'histoire moderne et contemporaine* 22 (1975): 247–55.

——. *Culture populaire et culture des élites dans la France moderne.* Paris, 1978.

Nordhaus, John David. "*Arma et litterae*: The Education of the *Noblesse de Race* in Sixteenth-Century France." Ph.D. dissertation, Columbia University, 1974.

Ong, Walter J. *Orality and Literacy: The Technologizing of the Word.* London and New York, 1982.

Orléa, Manfred. *La Noblesse aux Etats généraux de 1576 et de 1588.* Paris, 1980.

Parker, David. "The Social Foundation of French Absolutism, 1610–1630." *Past and Present*, no. 53 (1971), pp. 67–89.

Selected Bibliography

Peristiany, J. G., ed. *Honor and Shame: The Values of Mediterranean Society.* London, 1965.

Perroy, E. "Feudalism or Principalities in Fifteenth-Century France." *Bulletin of the Institute of Historical Research* 20 (1945): 181–86.

———. "Social Mobility among the French Noblesse in the Later Middle Ages." *Past and Present* 21 (1962): 25–38.

Ranum, Orest. "Courtesy, Absolutism, and the Rise of the French State." *Journal of Modern History* 52 (1980): 426–51.

Richet, Denis. *La France moderne: L'Esprit des institutions.* Paris, 1973.

Roelker, Nancy L. *Queen of Navarre: Jeanne d'Albret.* Cambridge, Mass., 1968.

———. "The Appeal of Calvinism to French Noblewomen in the Sixteenth Century." *Journal of Interdisciplinary History* 2 (1972): 391–419.

———. "The Role of Noblewomen in the French Reformation." *Archiv für Reformationsgeschichte* 63 (1972): 168–95.

Romier, Lucien. *Les Origines politiques des guerres de religion.* 2 vols. Paris, 1913–14.

———. "Le Protestantisme français à la veille des guerres civiles." *Revue historique* 134 (1917): 1–51, 225–86.

———. *Catholiques et Huguenots à la court de Charles IX.* Paris, 1924.

———. *Le Royaume de Catherine de Médicis.* 2 vols. Paris, 1925.

Ruble, A. de. *Le Mariage de Jeanne d'Albret.* Paris, 1877.

———. *Antoine de Bourbon et Jeanne d'Albret.* 4 vols. Paris, 1881–86.

Sabean, David Warren. *Power in the Blood: Popular Culture and Village Discourse in Early Modern Germany.* Cambridge, 1984.

Sahlins, Marshall. *Islands of History.* Chicago, 1985.

Salmon, J. H. M. *Society in Crisis: France in the Sixteenth Century.* New York, 1975.

———. "Storm over the 'Noblesse.'" *Journal of Modern History* 53 (1981): 242–57.

Schalk, Ellery. "The Appearance and Reality of Nobility during the Wars of Religion: An Example of How Collective Attitudes Can Change." *Journal of Modern History* 48 (1976): 9–31.

———. "Forum: Fidelity and Clientage. Clientage, Elites, and Absolutism in Seventeenth-Century France." *French Historical Studies* 14 (1986): 442–46.

———. *From Valor to Pedigree: Ideas of Nobility in France in the Sixteenth and Seventeenth Centuries.* Princeton, 1986.

Schnapper, Bernard. *Les Rentes au XVIe siècle: L'Histoire d'un instrument de crédit.* Paris, 1957.

Scribner, Robert. "Oral Culture and the Diffusion of Reformation Ideas." *History of European Ideas* 5 (1984): 236–54.

Shimizu, June. *Conflict of Loyalties: Politics and Religion in the Career of Gaspard de Coligny, Admiral of France, 1519–72.* Geneva, 1970.

Sutherland, N. M. *The French Secretaries of State in the Age of Catherine de Medici.* London, 1962.

———. *The Huguenot Struggle for Recognition.* New Haven, 1980.

Wheaton, Robert, and Tamara K. Hareven, eds. *Family and Sexuality in French History.* Philadelphia, 1980.

Wood, James B. "Demographic Pressure and Social Mobility among the Nobility of Early Modern France." *Sixteenth Century Journal* 8 (1977): 3–16.

———. *The Nobility of the "Election" of Bayeux, 1463–1660.* Princeton, 1980.

Yates, Frances A. *The Art of Memory.* Chicago, 1966.

Zeller, Gaston. "Gouverneurs de province au XVIe siècle." *Revue historique* 185 (1939): 225–56.

Index

Albret, Jeanne d', queen of Navarre, 32n, 35, 58, 89, 138, 157–58
Amboise conspiracy, 34, 100–101, 124–27, 159, 199
Anjou, Henri de Valois, duc d', 50
Anjou, Nicolas d', marquis de Mezières, family and household of, 160–73

Bèze, Théodore de, 49
Billacois, François, 206–7
Bloch, Marc, 20
Bourbon, Antoine de, duc de Vendôme and king of Navarre, 86–87, 100–101, 115; as governor of Picardy, 36, 82, 91; household of, 25, 148–51, 160–62, 171, 173–79, 181–83; landholdings of, 35–36, 135, 137–39, 148–60; as Prince of the Blood, 34–35, 58, 200; royal ordinance company of, 173–79. *See also* Bourbon family
Bourbon, Charles, cardinal de, 35, 42, 74–75, 87, 145; career of, 83–84
Bourbon, Charles de, duc de Vendôme (d. 1537), 35–36, 79–81, 99–100, 137
Bourbon family, 25–26, 34–37, 42–44, 79–90, 173; landholdings of, 26–28, 80–81, 136–39. *See also entries for individual family members*

Clanchy, M. T., 112
Clientage: historiography of, 1–16, 23–25, 132–36, 186, 196–98; and patronage, 19, 21–22, 69, 72, 76, 102; in 17th century, 205–6
Coligny, Gaspard de Châtillon, amiral de, 5, 36, 52, 56–57, 91–92, 129; family of, 39

Condé, Eléonore de Roye, princesse de, 36, 71, 82, 89, 100, 141–47, 158–59
Condé, Henri de Bourbon, prince de (d. 1588), 45, 152–53
Condé, Louis de Bourbon, prince de (d. 1569), 4, 33–34, 115; death of, 33, 37; family of, 34–36, 53, 79–90 passim; as governor of Picardy, 36, 106–8; household of, 44, 118–20, 176–79; as Huguenot leader, 32–35, 38–39, 45–46, 48, 50–51, 54–58, 134–35; landholdings and estates of, 28, 36, 45, 81, 135, 139–47, 153–54; marriages of, 82, 139–47; as Prince of the Blood, 34–35, 95, 100, 126, 200; in rebellion against crown, 7, 16–17, 32–34, 38–39, 43–46, 58–59, 65–67, 100–102, 124–27, 133–34, 144, 199–201; royal ordinance company of, 176–79; self-defense of, 65–68; as young man, 5, 70–72, 81–82, 84–85, 95–96, 127–28. *See also* Bourbon family
Correspondence, 17–19, 26, 183; as evidence of noble relationships, 69–78 passim, 88, 90–93, 97–98, 127–31; and oral communication, 103, 105–8, 114, 117–18, 127–31. *See also* Literacy; Oral culture and communication
Courtesy and deference, 160, 184, 206–7; in correspondence, 72–78 passim, 96–98, 103, 127–31

Davis, Natalie Z., 11n, 22, 31n, 78n, 113n
De Thou, Jacques-Auguste, 40–41, 49n, 51–52, 61

Index

Dowries, 142–43; and movable goods, 167
Dueling, 125, 206–7

Eisenstein, Elizabeth, 187–88, 192–93
Elias, Norbert, 194–95

Family relationships, 77–93 passim, 99
Febvre, Lucien, 19–21, 196
Food: expenses and supplies of, 160–61, 163–66; ritual importance of, 161, 164, 166–68, 198
Foucault, Michel, 21n

Gendarmerie, 12, 29, 30, 41–42, 61–64, 148, 150–51; and household service, 174–79. *See also* Military commands and commanders
Genlis, François de Hangest, sire de, 41; in civil wars, 41–43, 48–51, 59–63, 92–93; family of, 167n
Gifts, 72–74, 76, 98, 129–30, 164, 167–68, 198
Ginzburg, Carlo, 22, 203
Gouberville, Gilles, sire de, 109, 203
Gouvernements and *gouverneurs*. *See* Governments; Governors, provincial
Governments, 26; of Picardy and Île-de-France, 26–28
Governors, provincial, 11–13, 26, 132, 135–36
Greenblatt, Stephen, 193–94
Guise, François de Lorraine, duc de, 36, 43, 83, 90, 95–96, 115, 125–28, 184, 199–201, 204; family of, 5, 34, 37, 87–89, 100, 115, 124–25; followers of, 6, 118; as rival to Montmorency, 5, 17, 19, 69–72, 90–91, 122–23

Harding, Robert R., 11–16, 132–33, 135–36, 196–98
Haton, Claude, 43–44, 52n, 123
Homage, 152, 155–56
Honor, 18, 65–68, 74, 76, 204–8; anthropological analyses of, 76–77; display of, in household, 160, 166–73, 184; and events, 18, 122–27; and hierarchy, 93–99; and shame 18, 99–102
Households, 12–13, 85–86, 134, 159–85 passim; accounts of, 26, 148, 160–61, 183; and landholdings, 178–79; service in, 17, 170–81 passim
Huguenot nobles, 31, 33, 38–68 passim. *See also* Condé, Louis de Bourbon, prince de

Huguenots, 31, 37, 53, 58–59; in towns, 40, 105–6; leadership of, 5, 32, 52n, 53–54, 57, 59. *See also* Protestantism; Reformed religion; Religious Wars
Humières, Jacques, sire d', 106–8, 117–18, 123
Humières, Jean, sire d', 69–70, 91–92, 129
Humières family, 30

Imperial Wars, 29–30, 34, 61, 73, 91–92

Kelly, Joan, 207–8

La Fère: château and seigneurie of 26, 137–38, 141, 145, 158, 178; dependencies of, 26–28, 136–38; religious wars and, 45, 59, 122
Language: and *mentalité,* 20; nobles' uses of, 21, 96, 103; of patronage, 21; of verbal self-defense, 65–68, 204. *See also* Courtesy and deference; Literacy; Oral culture and communication; Sociolinguistics
La Noue, François de, 202–3
La Rochefoucauld, François, comte de, 39, 94–99, 120–23, 143, 181, 198
Letters. *See* Correspondence
Literacy: measurement of, 108–9, 111; of nobles, 108–13, 203–4; and printing, 187–88; and self, 22, 192–95, 203–4; and writing, 26
Lorraine, Charles, cardinal de, 57, 74, 83, 87–89

Major, J. Russell, 2–3, 7–12, 39, 134
Médicis, Catherine de, 6–7, 46, 54–59, 93, 113, 125–27, 199–201
Mentalité, 19–21, 196
Mercenaries, 54–57
Mergey, Jean de, 94–99, 102, 120–23, 181, 184, 197–98
Military commands and commanders, 8, 11–13, 17, 29–30, 43, 61, 82, 90–92, 95–96, 99–100, 128. *See also* Clientage; Gendarmerie; Governors, provincial; Religious Wars; Violence; Warfare
Montmorency, Anne de, duc and connétable de, 36, 57–58, 99, 101, 158–59; as rival of Guise, 5, 17, 19, 70–72, 90–91, 122–23, 125
Morvilliers, Louis de Lannoy, sire de, 39–41, 90, 109–10, 117, 129; in civil wars, 39–43, 46–48, 50, 56, 59, 105–6, 134–35

Neuschel, Kristen Brooke, 1951–
Word of honor.

Bibliography: p.
Includes index.
1. France—Civilization—16th century.   2. France—Nobility—History—16th century.   3. Social structure—France—History—16th century.   4. Politics and culture—France—History—16th century.   I. Title.
DC33.3.N48   1989   944'.028   88-47916
ISBN 0-8014-2181-0 (alk. paper)